VINCENT O'BRIEN'S GREAT HORSES

Vincent and El Gran Senor, winner of the 2000 Guineas and Irish Sweeps Derby, 1984.

VINCENT O'BRIEN'S GREAT HORSES

IVOR HERBERT and JACQUELINE O'BRIEN

PELHAM BOOKS

ALSO BY IVOR HERBERT

BOOKS

The Filly, Red Rum, Arkle, Six At The Top, Spot The
Winner, Longacre, Come Riding, Over Our Dead
Bodies!, Scarlet Fever, Winter's Tale, The Winter Kings,
The Queen Mother's Horses, The Diamond Diggers,
The Way To The Top, Point-to-Point, Eastern
Windows.

TELEVISION

Odds Against?
The Queen's Horses
Derby 200
Classic Touch
Stewards' Enquiry

VIDEO

Tattersalls
Keeneland's Golden Year
Grand National Campaign
The Jockey Club

CINEMA

The Great St Trinian's Train Robbery

THEATRE

Night of the Blue Demands (with Frank Launder)

First published in Great Britain by
Pelham Books Ltd
44 Bedford Square
London WC1B 3DP
1984

Herbert, Ivor
    Vincent O'Brien's great horses.
    1. O'Brien, Vincent   2. Horse trainers—
    Ireland—Biography
    I. Title   II. O'Brien, Jacqueline

    ISBN 0 7207 1547 4

Printed by
Butler and Tanner Ltd
Frome and London

Contents

Acknowledgements

We would like to thank not only Vincent O'Brien for the time and care he has given to the making of this book, but also his brothers, Dermot and Phonsie and the staff present and past at Ballydoyle, particularly T.P. Burns (associated with Vincent O'Brien since 1942), Willie Fogarty, manager (joined 1950), John Brabston, headman (who joined the stables in 1967), Davy Walsh, blacksmith (joined 1950), Vincent Rossiter, senior work rider (joined 1961) and Gerry Gallagher, travelling headman (joined 1953) and Brian Molony. Pat Eddery has also given helpful contributions to the story of Golden Fleece.

In England our thanks are due to the research work of Patricia Smyly, and to the interpretation by Andrea Hessay of fifty thousand words of Ivor Herbert's handwriting.

Jacqueline O'Brien gratefully acknowledges the work of Michael O'Toole and John Derby 'without whose help,' she says, 'I could not have produced the photographs.'

We would also wish to thank John Beaton of Pelham Books, for his patience over unavoidable delays (an author's constant plea) and for his overall enthusiasm from start to finish.

T.P. Burns

Willie Fogarty

Brian Molony

Davy Walsh

Vincent Rossiter

Gerry Gallagher

John Brabston

BALLYDOYLE HOUSE,
CASHEL,
Co. TIPPERARY.
CASHEL 203/4.

I was very pleased when Ivor Herbert and
Jacqueline said they wanted to put together
a book about some of the great horses I've
been lucky enough to train.

I've helped them as much as I could and
certainly answered plenty of questions.
The men who have been with me over many
years have also contributed their ideas.

I've known Ivor for 25 years as a trainer
and writer and I was sure he and Jacqueline
would make a good job of the book. I feel
they have - and it certainly brings alive
for me many of our greatest days.

Photo credits

The authors and publishers are grateful to the following for permission to reproduce copyright black and white pictures: J.L. Arnaudet 187; Associated Press 69, 119 (bottom), 136 (top), 189; Baron 76 (bottom), 77; BBC Hulton Picture Library 54, 59, 60, 62, 63, 71; P. Bertrand 96, 97 (bottom); Michael Burns 129; J. Cashman 81, 87, 88, 136 (bottom), 137, 138, 175, 194; Lin Cawfield 112; Central Press 109, 116 (top), 119 (top), 140, 153; Cheltenham Newspaper Co. 26, 29; Cork Examiner 18; Daily Express 134, 193; Fotosport vi (top left); Leo Frutkoff 149; Liam Healey 201; Independant Newspapers 36 (top), 49, 66; Irish Press 57, 65 (bottom), 176, 177 (top); Irish Times 22, 30, 48; Charles O'Brien 196; Frank O'Brien 36 (bottom), 43, 45, 55, 61, 76 (top); Jacqueline O'Brien frontispiece, vi, 34, 84, 85, 99, 102, 114, 145, 147, 163, 165, 169, 181, 192, 202, 205, 209, 215, 217, 219, 221, 223, 225 (top); PC Photos 21; Press Association 106, 107, 117, 133, 168; Provincial Press Agency 90, 154, 185, 186; Ruth Rogers 177 (bottom), 183, 200, 225 (bottom); Selwyn Photos 178; Sport and General 28, 37, 39, 41 (top), 46 (bottom), 73, 75, 92, 93, 94, 105, 116 (bottom), 156, 158, 173, 212, 213; Sporting Life 174; Sun 125; Fiona Vigors 121, 143, 179; A. Well 97 (top). Every effort has been made to trace copyright owners but in some instances this has not been possible and it is hoped that any such omissions will be excused.

The colour photography is all by Jacqueline O'Brien with the exception of the following: Cottage Rake (between pages 56 and 57) photo Desmond Mackey; Sir Ivor and the O'Brien family (opposite page 112) photo Maymes Ansell; presentation at Ascot (opposite page 161) photo Wallis Photographers; Alleged (inset opposite page 168) photo P. Bertrand; Golden Fleece after the Derby win (opposite page 169) photo Paddock Studios. Paintings reproduced in the book are by Peter Biegel, Rosemary O'Callaghan-Westropp, and Richard Stone Reeves and are credited accordingly.

The authors and publishers are also grateful to Timeform for permission to quote from their 'Racehorses' Annuals.

Prologue

Bodyless, like seahorses, twenty-five tossing heads and necks seem to swim along behind the tall tawny barriers of baled straw.

The light is submarine, too. Pearl-grey, an Irish morning shafts down through panels in the humped roofs of these gigantic barns, vast as a columned cathedral. There are no hoof-beats. The fall of the million-dollar hooves is silent on the tan. The lads do not sing, whistle or shout out quips to one another. The air is dedicated, devout. The nodding lines of heads and necks weave up and down and round in a long chain worth perhaps twenty-five million dollars on these hundred pacing feet.

Only the chink of bits, the flutter of pink nostrils, snorts and quick flicks of exercise sheets as colts hoist themselves to give a kick of *joie de vivre*, disturb the strange, grey, granite enclosing silence.

In the centre stands a slim man, immaculate. His clothes – fawn cavalry twill trousers and neat waterproof jacket, a trilby hat and gloves – look not just made to measure but fresh that morning from the tailors. Even his knee-length brown leather boots gleam. Outside the barn's sliding door stands that small bath of fresh water, carefully maintained, so that the master's boots and shoes are unsullied when he has finished work.

He stands, head cocked a little to one side, eyes bold and quick, ears almost twitching to catch any sound of roughness in his horses' breathing as they canter past. Not like a robin, for there is nothing cocky in the man's stance. More like a wary finch, alert to dangers, poised to fly. But the glance is that of a hawk.

At a hundred paces he spots a quiver in a colt's eyelid, follows it round, calls softly across, 'Anything wrong with that horse's left eye?' The rider instantly starts forward in his saddle, looks, calls back, 'No, sor. T'is foine now, sor,' as the file of horses pass again behind a barrier.

Behind the slight, intense figure, silent as acolytes in a semi-circle, stand his assistants watching him and his horses.

He moves. They follow. He strides quickly across the silent tan, head jutting forward. The string of horses now in full view appears at one end of the barn, passing under the sharper shafts of light. Their trotting done, they walk proudly towards him, necks arched, eyes bold. They are all sizes, all colours. But they share the arrogant look of class.

Each pauses. Each lad leans forward and down to listen, to catch exactly what the Boss is saying in his murmuring quiet voice with so little Irish in it.

The instructions are brief and precise. 'You go with George, a nice pace now ... start from the boundary then pull up at the top of the first hill. ... Pat – not too strong a pace in the early stages ...'

The string pulls out of the wide mouth of the barn into the drifting morning drizzle. As their hooves touch the bright wet Irish turf, they begin to dance, spring, buck, snort. Outside, the lads' cajoling voices blow back, like the hosts of black rooks floating out of the bare tree-tops onto the soft west wind, as the horses pass beneath them.

They work in pairs from the bottom of the hill where the starting stalls stand this side of the lodge at the foot of the avenued drive. Up here in the old days ran the schooling fences where men like brother Phonsie, 'The Brab', Martin Molony and Bryan Marshall, would turn their tweed caps back to front and swing the Grand National horses up over the black birch fences for home.

There were no crash helmets then. There were no multi-million dollar yearlings. Ballydoyle, bought in 1950, was a working farm, cross-hatched with Irish banks, hedges, ditches and drains. They, like the jumpers, are all gone now.

The small figure climbs briskly up into his gazebo, fashioned in Georgian-style but busy with telephones and timing apparatus. Behind is the pad where his helicopter lands to whisk him away to catch 'planes to Britain, France and the United States, and to business meetings in Dublin, at the Phoenix Park or The Curragh. The great trainer is a man of affairs now. He has an honorary doctorate from the University. His advice is widely sought.

Beyond his grey house, gradually extended over the years, the newer gallops spread like a lovely racecourse. Mountains, velvet-green and tinged with purple, ring the place in a hazy half-circle. There to the south-west lie the Galtee mountains, and Churchtown in County Cork, where he was born and began and won those Cheltenham Gold Cups. To the south stand the Knockmealdowns and then, further round, the Comeragh mountains. He loves this place. He had thought briefly once of training on The Curragh, of training in England or America. He would have been unhappy anywhere else. This is his kingdom. From here, from the new landing strip where the chute of the gallops starts on the bottom, his raiders fly off to foreign fields.

East of Ballydoyle the highest mountain is Slievenamon, 'hill of the woman' in Irish. Here, on its peak in the old days, sat an Irish king picking his bride from the quickest and strongest of the local girls. The first to reach him from a level start he made his queen; an apt background to the thoroughbred empire now rooted, established and flourishing one thousand years later beneath the mountain.

The horses in detailed groups canter on up the far slope of the new gallops across tilting acres which, thirty-four years ago, were a patchwork of fields, hedgerows, trees and a copse. They pull up to walk down the left-handed slope slightly resembling Epsom's Tattenham Hill. They pass the stone grey Norman watch-tower before they canter quietly on again towards the single figure of the watching man. Towers with empty arrow slits like blind eyes, and gripped by ivy, once marched all across this countryside up from the rivers where the French-speaking conquerers landed. 'So that they could signal to one another,' murmurs the present landlord, a fervent patriot, 'when *they* were occupying this country!'

Work done, the horses circle him. He looks, listens, questions the riders. Then the horses, gently warm, walk away, back to the boxes padded waist-high in heavy rubber matting, and ankle-deep in shavings. Their heads look out through over the half doors. 'Horses like views,' he says, as he does. 'They like to see what is going on, to be part of the activity.' As he does ...

The house, flanking and commanding the yard, is quiet too. On its other side a trim garden graced with giant trees, clumped with shrubs and rosebeds, slopes away downhill towards the gallops, the swimming pool, an isolation yard, and the security patrol men in their cabin by the locked gates on to the winding road from Cashel.

The trainer places his boots in line with the rows of his polished shoes, beneath an orderly parade of coats and hats. Passages and rooms are lined with paintings and photographs of famous winners. The dining room glows with the silver and gold of trophies won.

He appears silently, as if by magic, in rooms, on the unexpectant rim of conversations, listens, adds a necessary comment and, as mysteriously, vanishes down spotless corridors on soundless feet. He does not tolerate untidiness. The trainer and part-owner of millions of pounds and dollars-worth of present racehorses, of stallions now at stud and of broodmares, yearlings and foals out in paddocks in Ireland and America, is engrossed in deep thought. His brain weaves plans.

So he dislikes crowds and shuns parties. He is both too busy and too diffident to need visitors. Occupied with his own empire, he is courteous to callers but fundamentally brief. 'Do I *need* to see them, dear?' he murmurs to his wife. 'Could you not ...?'

He fills his guests' glasses liberally with whatever they want from the bar in his glass-roofed sun-room, while sipping something non-alcoholic himself. He listens head tilted to the conversation, selecting only sometimes from un-important chat that single fragment of information which interests him. On this, like tycoons in other fields, he stoops like a hawk. A visitor from England may bring some news helpful to his cause: the favourite for the Guineas worked disappointingly and sweated up; there has been heavy rain at Epsom ... At these points his eyes brighten. He is quick with questions till he's satisfied.

Over lunch at the head of the long mahogany table he takes a little excellent wine. He eats sparingly, carefully, of the good food. He thaws. His recollections wing back to the loved horses and great victories of the old, first days. He is warm with pride for his family. He would not know what to do without his wife, he says. Affection shimmers. He is proud of the successes of his eldest son, David. He depends upon the shrewd counsel of his son-in-law, John Magnier, lord of the Coolmore kingdom of studs. His whole spare frame blossoms and his eyes glow when talking to any of his grandchildren.

Vincent O'Brien has founded a very rich, very famous dynasty. He has come a long, long way from Cottage Rake to El Gran Senor. This is that story, a slender thread of connections pursued from that small start, and a tale in which such threads so narrowly divide catastrophe from triumph.

1

'And we had this little gamble'

Horses have run through Vincent's life before he could even walk. 'At the age of three,' he recalls, 'I remember sitting on my father's knee singing out the breeding of horses he had at that time.' He can still rattle out those bloodlines sixty-four years later.

Dan O'Brien was an Irish farmer, and Vincent was the eldest son of his second family. The father kept good horses on his farm at Churchtown and raced them, but for himself and for fun and not as a professional. 'He wasn't,' says Vincent, 'particularly keen on the training of horses anyhow. The head-man in the yard had quite a bit to do with the working of the horses so it was easy for me to take an interest.'

Vincent was sent away to college but did not enjoy school. 'I never liked it. I couldn't settle down there. The confinement was more than I could stand. I wanted to be out and about doing things. I persuaded my father to allow me to leave college between fourteen and fifteen.' Vincent was adamant that he wished to learn about training and he convinced his father. 'He sent me to Fred Clarke, who was training at Leopardstown Racecourse, and I spent a year there and then came back to the farm.'

The next few years were the happiest of Vincent's young life. His father and he loved horses, and enjoyed working with them. Vincent took over the training gradually and unofficially. But he was working from the ranks up. 'I rode the horses, groomed them and mucked them out.'

Phonsie, his youngest brother, was at school still but he remembers, 'Oh Vincent was training the horses; doing everything. He was the big chief.'

Dan O'Brien bought young horses to break and make into hunters. 'It was the greatest fun,' says Vincent, 'to get four boys out of the yard and the five of us would ride these horses four or five miles across country four or five days a week, a different line every day. There was never a stop. It was action all the time!'

Vincent like many trainers started humbly with point-to-pointers. His father had a good grey point-to-point mare called White Squirrel. Her name is not mentioned in the heavy-weight record books, but White Squirrel was basically the springboard of Vincent's career. It started as things would go on, with a trial then a gamble.

He had prepared the grey mare for point-to-points in 1941, but foot and

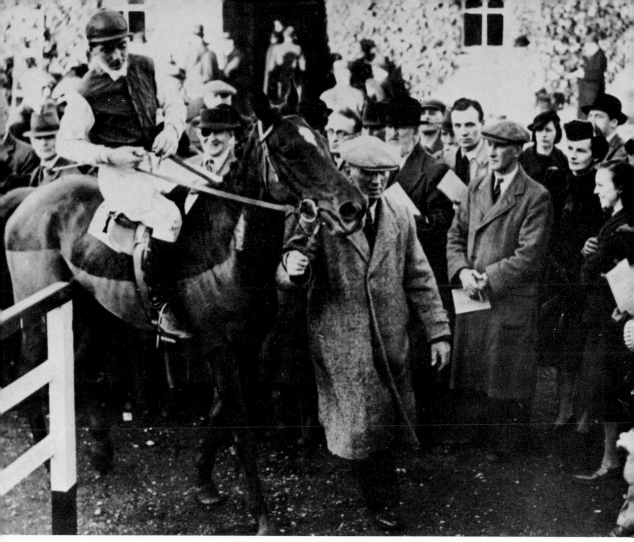

Vincent as an amateur rider coming in on Hallowment after winning at Limerick in the early years of the war. His father, Dan O'Brien, the owner and trainer leads him in. Although it was an amateur race, professional jockeys were allowed to ride and carried 5lb extra. Charlie Smirke came in second . . .

mouth disease stopped them. 'As far as I know,' says Vincent, 'we've only had foot and mouth twice in Ireland and that was during the two wars – a strange coincidence. Some said the Germans spread it!'

Without point-to-points the grey mare's season was finished. 'But one morning I was short of something to jump off in front of a couple of our flat race horses. So I rode the mare myself. I was very surprised how well she worked with them. A week later I worked her again with the same horses. She did even a little better. I thought to myself: 'This is rather good. We'll have a little gamble on this mare.'

'I didn't say anything to my father then, because he'd get quite excited and tell all his friends. If it worked out, I'd tell him at the right moment, which was as near the race as possible!'

Vincent took over the mare himself, grooming her and riding her daily until the day picked for the gamble at Clonmel. The humble point-to-pointer was going to contest a twenty-seven runner amateur flat race. And point-to-points in the war years were much inferior to the semi-official steeplechases they later became.

'I was pretty short of cash at that time. To earn a bit I had started breeding greyhounds from a bitch my father had given me and I was making a little money sending them as saplings to a man in England who sold them for me. It was working out quite satisfactorily until war broke out. Then there was no dog racing. The man said the dogs were now useless to him but he'd pay their fares back. It was just as difficult to sell them here but I finally managed to get rid of one for £4. This was all I had in the world.

'The day the grey mare was due to run I got a very good friend of mine to come to the races with us. I told my friend, "Just before the betting opens on the race, go to my father and tell him he ought to have a bet on this mare." My father never gambled, but he gave my friend a tenner and he got 20 to 1 for ten pounds. There was a scramble after that. The best they could do for my £4 was 10 to 1. But we won, and it was great. So that was my first little gamble and it was a good bit of money for me to win in those days.'

Vincent did quite a lot of race-riding but most of his father's horses ran on the flat and so were ridden by professional jockeys. The happy years of those first winners were soon threatened by his father's death in 1943. For a time it seemed as if Vincent would have to give up training and start another trade.

'Through a marriage settlement', says Vincent, 'the whole place had to go to a member of my father's first family. I found myself more or less without a home and with very little money. Farming was in a very bad way due to the war. There were four in my father's first family and four in the second and there was very little money for any of us when everything was divided. So I knocked about for several months wondering what to do. With the war the money had gone out of cattle. Top grade beasts were selling for as low as 30/- each.'

In England racehorses were making little or nothing as Vincent would discover. When his father died, Vincent's wish was to go on training. 'But nobody knew me. I'd no idea that I could even set up as a trainer. I was prepared to do anything to get started in life. I thought of opening a butcher's shop in Buttevant. Fortunately I was able to get horses to train and spend my life doing what I most wanted.

'I was also able to train on the farm which, on my father's death, passed to my eldest half-brother. Luckily, he had no interest in horses so I was able to rent the yard and the gallops from him.'

When Vincent set up training on his own, and was looking for owners who would send him horses, Jackie O'Brien, a wool-merchant from nearby Fermoy wanted to give him a helping hand. His client, Mr Frank Vickerman, a wealthy wool-broker, born in Stroud, Gloucestershire, had moved his Yorkshire business to Dublin. Vickerman was not then interested in racing himself but thought a few young horses might make a welcome coming-home present for his son who was serving with the British Army in North Africa. Sadly, his son fell ill out in that distant desert war and never returned. Jackie O'Brien bought five or six very cheap yearlings in Dublin, in 1941. Vincent comments, 'Horses were selling for nothing then.' In 1943, Jackie O'Brien suggested that a couple of them should be put into training with young Vincent. Vickerman agreed. 'He was my first owner,' says Vincent.

In 1944 Frank Vickerman won £5,000, the equivalent of £50,000 in the 1980s on the famous O'Brien gamble on the Irish Autumn double with Good Days and Drybob, two horses in Vincent's stable. Vincent, aged twenty-seven, and in his first year's training, had bought Drybob at Newmarket Sales in 1943 for 130 guineas as a re-submitted lot. The buyer's intended owner had failed to conclude that deal. By the merest chance Vincent overheard the trainer who had bought the horse reporting this to a friend. The horse was going to be put up again. This genuine reason for resale suggested to Vincent that he might acquire a real bargain, since other buyers would be suspicious that something was wrong with the horse. 'Actually he made more,' says Vincent, 'having been sold for 115 guineas on the first day!'

Sydney McGregor from Warwickshire, who had bred the 1932 Derby winner, April the Fifth, owned and trained by the West End light comedy actor, Tom Walls, met Vincent at the Sales. He found him a buyer for half of Drybob, and decided to send him a horse called Good Days. 'I am sending him,' Sydney said, 'with a view to the Cesarewitch next back-end.' This attitude pleased Vincent almost as much as the offer of the horse. 'I thought to myself, at least this is a man who is prepared to wait a year and take a pretty long view, which is always good.'

O'Brien prepared Drybob to dead-heat for the Irish Cambridgeshire and Good Days to win the Irish Cesarewitch. He had been desperately short of money. 'Luckily for me,' he recalls, 'Frank Vickerman asked me, "How about a bit on the double?" I very modestly said, "Have me £2 each way." Frank Vickerman had £10 each way and stood to win £10,000 and I £2,000 with odds of 800 to 1, but Drybob deadheating halved our bets. It was a wonderful beginning!'

2

'It was the luckiest thing that could have happened!'

Three slender threads kept Cottage Rake, the first of Vincent O'Brien's great horses, in the trainer's care. The horse who would make the young Irishman's name first known and then famous in Britain, failed two veterinary examinations, and was bought finally by accident out of misunderstanding.

Looking back in 1984 on the great chasers since World War II, Vincent O'Brien assesses his triple winner of the Cheltenham Gold Cup. 'I believe Cottage Rake ranks with Prince Regent and Arkle as the greatest winners of the Gold Cup. However, in my opinion, neither of the others had the speed of Cottage Rake who won the 1½-mile Naas November Handicap when he was a novice chaser, in addition to the Irish Cesarewitch. Arkle, on the other hand,' Vincent goes on, 'finished out of the money in a "bumper" at Leopardstown. And Prince Regent similarly finished unplaced in the Irish Cesarewitch.

'Cottage Rake,' says Vincent, 'was very well bred on his dam's side. She traced to Stella, one of the great foundation mares. There are very few chasers with the speed to win the Irish equivalent of the Manchester November Handicap, and he was capable of really quickening after jumping the last at Cheltenham. He proved that in the first Gold Cup he won. Happy Home came to the last – oh, I'd say a good length and a half in front, and on the run in, Cottage Rake undoubtedly proved he had superior speed. He ran him out of it. And the following year with Cool Customer, who was a very good horse, Cottage Rake's speed told after they jumped the last together. He won the Emblem Chase at Manchester beating Silver Fame. It was a tremendous finish. Aubrey Brabazon dropped his whip before the last, but he rode the race of his life, and Cottage Rake's speed won the day. He was truly a great chaser.'

But he was one which Vincent might not have trained for more than two races. If either intending purchaser had accepted their vets' qualifications about the horse's wind and paid a price of £3,500, Cottage Rake would have left the family farm at Churchtown where Vincent had started training.

Cottage Rake's first owner was his breeder, a popular bachelor Dr 'Otto' Vaughan, who was anxious to sell the horse which had been bred at his brother Dick's Hunting Hall Stud in Co. Cork. Dr Vaughan's surgery was in Mallow's main street and he kept the horse in a yard at the back. He sent Cottage Rake up to Goff's Sales at Ballsbridge as a five year old, but failed to sell him.

'During the summer months of 1945 when Cottage Rake was a six year old,'

Cottage Rake in the stable yard at Churchtown in the early days. From left to right *Vincent, Sidney Ryan (The Rake's lad), Maurice O'Callaghan (headman) and Vincent's brother Dermot, his assistant.*

Vincent recalls, 'The Doctor said to me "I've got a Cottage horse. Would you like to take him to train?" I said, "Right, I will. Where is he?" He said, "Not very far away from you." I discovered he was only a couple of miles from where I lived and running out on an actual bog! I mean for a thoroughbred horse to be out on a bog at that time of his life was incredible!'

Phonsie O'Brien, Vincent's youngest brother, set off in a pony and trap to collect the horse. The recollection of this humble start sets Phonsie off into damp-eyed laughter. For the horse who thus arrived at Churchtown would win over the next few seasons: the Naas November Handicap, as big an Irish punting medium as the English equivalent, (Cottage Rake, after two unplaced runs, significantly started 3 to 1 favourite); the Irish Cesarewitch over two miles at 5 to 1; the Leopardstown Chase; three Cheltenham Gold Cups in successive years; and the King George VI Chase at Kempton Park's Christmas meeting in 1948.

Vincent vividly remembers Cottage Rake's arrival in 1945. 'I thought: this horse is going to take time to build up. But, coming up to Christmas, the Doctor kept asking when the horse was going to run. So I felt I'd better run him at Limerick on Boxing Day in a maiden hurdle, because there was no doubt he was getting very impatient. So I put one of my boys on – actually it was Danny O'Sullivan, who later became my headman. The horse jumped off in front and won unextended at 10 to 1. For his next race, the bumper at Leopardstown, I got Pat Hogan to ride. He was nicknamed "P.P.". There was no better man to hounds and he excelled as an amateur rider.' Forty years later, Mr Pat Hogan is an important element in Robert Sangster's racing and breeding operation.

In Ireland, two mile amateur flat races, the 'bumpers', remain even today the shop window for potential Irish chasers and hurdlers. In February 1946, all runners in them were big types, bred to be jumpers and capable of humping 12 stone, and an amateur. The bumper at Leopardstown, one of Ireland's classier tracks, was the Corinthian Plate, and chosen for Cottage Rake's next outing. 'Cottage Rake won so well that he impressed a lot of people,' Vincent says. 'There were a number of them trying to buy the horse.' The first purchaser at £3,500 was Tony Riddle-Martin for that very sporting Yorkshireman, Major 'Cuddie' Stirling-Stuart. The horse would have left Churchtown and gone to be trained by Riddle-Martin. But the thread which bound twenty-seven year old Vincent O'Brien to 'The Rake' just held as Maxie Cosgrove, the expert vet who later looked after the supreme Arkle, turned the horse down for his wind. Not only did the Major reject the horse but within three years he had to watch his reject beat him for the prize he most highly cherished – the Cheltenham Gold Cup. Cottage Rake came with the latest of runs and endured his hardest race to catch Major Stirling-Stuart's beloved Cool Customer on the final hill and beat him by two lengths.

'The Rake's' jockey was that superb horseman with the delicate hands, Aubrey Brabazon, with whom the triple Gold Cup winner – the only one between Golden Miller and Arkle – will always be linked. But Aubrey had also been Cool Customer's regular jockey. To commemorate Aubrey's victories on Cool Customer, Major Stirling-Stuart had commissioned a special pair of cuff-links. He did not wish to post them. 'We'll meet at Cheltenham, of course, Aubrey,' said the Major. And in the sweat of the old unsaddling pen behind the wooden changing-room, the Major left his Cool Customer in second place, to cross over to congratulate Aubrey and to hand him the cuff-links.

The second purchaser appeared in the summer. It was a partnership between Mr 'Jock' Skeffington, later Viscount Massereene and Ferrard, and his mother-in-law, Mrs Lewis. Had they accepted Alan Baker's report that, though the horse 'made a noise', it was unlikely to affect him unless he caught a severe cold, the horse would have been destined to go to that crack English trainer, Captain Ryan Price, in Sussex. Price was then infinitely better known in England than was Vincent. He was already near the top of the British National Hunt racing. He, too, would later make the switch, like Vincent, but on a smaller scale, to train classic horses on the flat.

Thrice thwarted, Doctor Vaughan remained a definite seller. He liked hunting and point-to-pointing, and had only sent his horse to young Vincent down the road to try and market him. But Vincent was very keen not to lose such a potentially good horse out of his small yard. The Doctor would not be dissuaded from selling. 'It suddenly struck me,' Vincent says, 'I've got to wake up and move pretty quickly to try to find someone to buy Cottage Rake and keep him with me.' What really hustled O'Brien was hearing that the Doctor was making enquiries in England as to how much they'd charge to train the horse over there!

By skill and a brave wager Vincent, with his bet on Drybob and Good Days, had achieved his first large capital sum which would be the foundation of his fortune. More, he had made his first contact with an owner of means. That prime need of any trainer touched him forcibly when he realised that unless he could persuade Mr Vickerman to stump up for Cottage Rake, he was going to lose the best horse so far to fall into his hands.

Yet Frank Vickerman only bought the horse from Dr Vaughan through Vincent, and for Vincent to train, because the prosperous wool merchant had been too business-like in his first venture into the inexact science of private horse-dealing.

And something else had gone wrong with Cottage Rake since the vets had rejected him for making a noise. Vincent had already cleared with Mr Vickerman the possible risk with the horse's wind. He told the Englishman exactly what the two vets had said about Cottage Rake, giving Alan Baker's opinion that the noise was unlikely to affect his wind unless he caught a bad cold. The horse would be sold with this affliction for £3,500. 'The money would come,' remarks Vincent, 'out of what Frank Vickerman had won on the double on Good Days and Drybob. But then, just at that time,' Vincent recalls, 'the horse wasn't pulling out a hundred per cent sound in the mornings. So I thought I'd better have an opinion on it in fairness to the purchaser. I got a vet to have a look at him. He said, "I think he's suffering from slight rheumatism in his

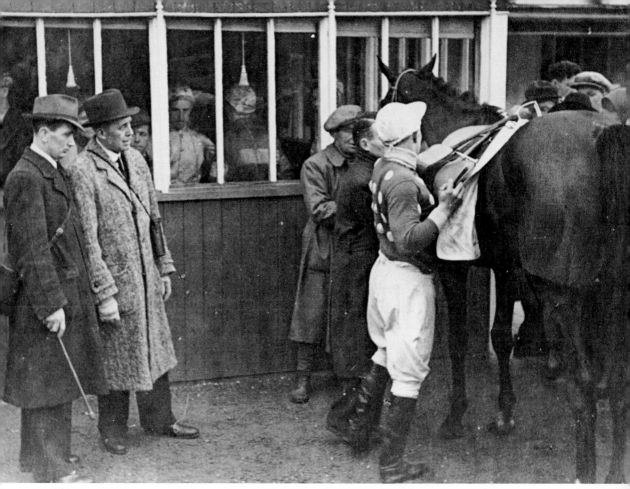

16 February 1946 Vincent and Dr 'Otto' Vaughan, Cottage Rake's breeder and then owner watching him being unsaddled after winning the Corinthian Maiden Plate at Leopardstown worth £96 10s. The winning rider is the famous Mr Pat ('P.P.') Hogan. After this many people tried to buy the horse.

shoulder," and I told Frank Vickerman. Vickerman asked me, "Well, what are we going to do about it?"'

So Vincent had to say to the man who had come to his rescue, 'Well, the vet says he's got rheumatism. It's hard for me to advise you to take him.'

'In that case, then,' said Mr Vickerman, 'we'd better leave it.'

Forty years later, a wide smile lightens Vincent's face at the recollection of another happy roll of the dice. For Frank Vickerman couldn't 'leave it'. He had already written out his cheque for £1,000 to Dr Vaughan in part-payment for the horse. He believed that was how horses were bought. When Vickerman went to cancel the deal, he found that Dr Vaughan had already put the cheque through and considered the payment sealed the deal. Mr Vickerman had no option but to take the horse. 'And, of course, it was *the* luckiest thing that could have happened,' declares Vincent, 'because, as I say, Cottage Rake went on to be proved one of the great chasers of all time.'

3

'The frightened bookies quake'

As it turned out, neither the wind infirmity nor the rheumatism would prove impediments to 'The Rake's' glorious career. Phonsie recalls, 'You could hear a little roughness at the start of the season, before the horse was fit,' then, with a delighted chuckle, 'but wasn't it a great thing the noise put off those other buyers?' As for rheumatism, Phonsie remembers, 'getting hold of some potheen to rub into Cottage Rake's shoulders to ease the rheumatism or arthritis or whatever it was. After you'd been in the stable, you'd come out with your head reeling, the smell was so strong! We didn't go on with it for long. We realised the potheen wasn't doing the horse any good either!'

Cottage Rake won the Naas November Handicap in November, 1946, and

In the season 1947–48 Cottage Rake won on the flat, over hurdles, the Cheltenham Gold Cup and was second in the Irish Grand National carrying 12 stone 7lb. Here he wins the Irish Cesarewitch at The Curragh on 8 November 1947 ridden by Georgie Wells.

the Irish Cesarewitch a year later. At the end of that season, in March, 1948, he won his first Cheltenham Gold Cup. 'The Rake' gave Vincent his first major English victory when beating Happy Home one and a half lengths after the latter had led him fully that distance over the last fence. Vincent was watching by the last fence with a big crowd around him, unable to see what happened after the horses had thundered past him up the hill. It was in the days before the public address system. 'I didn't know who had won, and it was no use asking anyone around because they knew no more than I. I made my way across the course and up the back of the stands to the old winner's enclosure, and it was not until I saw Aubrey on Cottage Rake putting his hand to his cap, acknowledging acclamations, that I thought "he must have won!"'

Three and a half weeks later, Cottage Rake ran second in the Irish National, carrying 12st 7lb trying to give three stone to the winner, Hamstar.

'At the time I had him,' comments Vincent, 'most chasers were pretty strong horses: Cottage Rake was unusual. He was rather lightly built and finer. He showed more quality than the average chaser, but then he always had much more speed than the average chaser.'

Tommy Burns, that good jockey whom racing people call 'T.P.', has known Vincent from his beginnings. 'I even rode an odd horse for his father.' T.P. was Vincent's assistant at Ballydoyle after he gave up riding until Christmas 1983, when he ended their thirty-five year long association to become assistant to Dermot Weld on The Curragh, where he could live with his family. Sitting in his office overlooking the main yard at Ballydoyle, Tommy said, 'Cottage Rake wasn't the most robustest horse. In handicaps he couldn't give the weight away. Not like Arkle. I think he never really liked the Irish Grand National course at Fairyhouse. It didn't suit his class, his speed. But how few horses win three Gold Cups! He had to be great!'

Even after that first Gold Cup when he beat Happy Home, Frank Vickerman was seriously considering selling his horse at a profit. Had he done so to a buyer outside the stable, Vincent's reputation in Britain would have been very much delayed. Mr Vickerman had prolonged discussions with Vincent over his horse's value and the question of buying out the share in the horse held by Mrs Lewis, the lady who had been an early contender to buy him with her son-in-law, Jock Skeffington.

Business-like, tough letters linger in Vincent's files. Frank Vickerman declares that his great horse must repeatedly campaign in England due to the lack of big prizes in Ireland yet this means the expense and uncertainty of overseas travel. 'However,' writes Mr Vickerman in a typed letter from his home in Dublin, 'I do not want anyone other than you to train "C.R.". So, could you find a purchaser for him at £15,000? What about 'Mrs L'?'

It was unheard of in those days for a chaser to sell for this sort of money, but in May, 1948, Mr Vickerman was suggesting to Vincent that his co-owner, Mrs Lewis, might be persuaded to sell with him at even more, £20,000 plus a contingency of 20% of his future winnings, 'as he is undoubtedly the best chaser in the world today', wrote Mr Vickerman. In July, he told Vincent that Mrs Lewis could dispose of her one third at £5,000, but he wanted £16,000 for the whole horse. 'Dorothy Paget is definitely interested,' he wrote.

This was an ominous threat to any young trainer in those times. The immensely rich and most eccentric daughter of Lord Queensborough – she was a cousin of American multi-millionaire Mr 'Jock' Whitney – not only would, but could buy any horse she liked. She dominated jumping with her vast string. She had already won five Gold Cups with Golden Miller, one more with Roman Hackle and would win yet another with Mont Tremblant in 1952.

Fortunately for Vincent and Mr Vickerman, the nocturnal Miss Paget, with her bevy of secretaries, her room full of back numbers of the *Sporting Life*, and her night chef to cook her great meals at 3 am, was kept at bay. But, in July, Vickerman made out another strong case for selling Cottage Rake. 'He has no future in Ireland,' he wrote. 'He must be raced in England, but there will be no racing in England if there is war with Russia. If not, there are the difficulties of travel with fog and frost and I will not race him unless he remains with you.' Vincent skilfully, finally, fortunately persuaded him again to keep his horse.

Cottage Rake's objective in 1949 was a second Gold Cup, and on the way he won two of the most important chases in England – the Emblem Chase at Manchester in November 1948 beating Silver Fame, and the King George VI Chase at Kempton in December 1948. Again in this race Roimond, one of Lord Bicester's chasers, landed over the last fence in front of him, but with his devastating burst of speed The Rake shot past him to win as he liked. After this Meyrick Good of the *Sporting Life*, wrote, 'Cottage Rake is probably the best horse that has come out of Ireland since Cloister and Jerry M.'*

So different are the racecourses of Kempton and Cheltenham that very few horses can win the two great classics of the steeplechasing season. The flat, easy, three miles round right-handed Kempton, cannot compare with the climbing, dipping and struggling uphill finish of three-and-a-quarter miles round

---

* The massive Cloister who could carry a 15 stone man foxhunting won the Grand National in 1893, and Jerry M – 'powerful enough to pull a brewer's dray' – won the race in 1912. They were exactly opposite types to Cottage Rake.

(opposite): *Four months after the Irish Cesarewitch The Rake won his first Gold Cup at Cheltenham. Here he is being led out by Vincent's future headman, Danny O'Sullivan, before the start of his second Gold Cup in 1949. The rider of course is Aubrey Brabazon.*

Cottage Rake has won his second Gold Cup (1949). Here he is led in by Mrs Vickerman and closely followed by Vincent (partially obscured by The Brab's right elbow) and Phonsie. Note the course blacksmith who will be standing in the same position a year later.

Cheltenham. Cottage Rake was one of the rare stars of the quality of Arkle, Silver Buck and Mandarin, who could win both great races.

But before Cottage Rake's second and hardest Gold Cup victory, he had a grave and worrying set-back. In February, his preparation was seriously held up by a cold with a dirty nose. Illness befell him at exactly the wrong time for a trainer preparing a horse for an attempt on steeplechasing's crown within four weeks. O'Brien recalls, 'I considered that the Gold Cup might come too soon for him but ...,' with a typical shrug and flick of his hand, conveying his sharp knowledge of the inexorable march of time.

Those were very anxious weeks. There had been those dire veterinary warnings about the dangers to his wind if he got a bad cold ... Cottage Rake needed time. And time, for once, was granted by a quirk of nature.

'Hatton's Grace and Castledermot were affected by this mild 'flu at the same time,' Vincent reflects. In those pre-vaccination days, a trainer could at least instantly tell when his horses were about to go down with colds and coughs or 'flu. Symptoms were not suppressed. Trainers, cursing, knew the worst. They had to stop working their horses. They were not then, as they are often now, misled into running a horse which appears well at home, only to disappoint on the racecourse when put under full pressure.

That spring of 1949, Hatton's Grace, who now enters our stage, was running in his first Champion Hurdle with Aubrey Brabazon riding. Castledermot, ridden by that much-loved leading amateur, Lord Mildmay, 'the last of the Corinthians,' as he was called, had been prepared for the four mile National Hunt Chase. This amateur 'Grand National' for novice horses in those days took an undulating rural ride round behind the stands. It was very often, in spite of these uncertainties, the scene for well-backed Irish gambles. Castledermot proved no exception and Quare Times would later follow in his hoof prints.

Hatton's Grace was a 100 to 7 shot and won his first Champion Hurdle. Castledermot was 6 to 4 favourite in a field of seventeen and won the National Hunt. Both had recovered from their bouts of 'flu in time. Would Cottage Rake, in view of the roughness of his wind and the warned risk against catching a bad cold, be fully fit?

Fortunately, he was not to be tested immediately. After the first two days of the meeting and the stable's double with Hatton's Grace and Castledermot, a severe frost gripped Cheltenham, the turf turned rock-hard and Gold Cup day was lost. 'The Rake' had an extra vital month in which to get fully fit for the toughest race of his life.

This time there was an even better horse than Happy Home to take him on. At the elbow before the last fence Cool Customer held three advantages: he was almost two lengths ahead; he had the inside; and 'The Brab' with the delicate hands had gone for his whip on 'The Rake'.

This pressure before the last seemed certain to drain Cottage Rake's final speed. To the joy of the Irish throng and to the grief of Yorkshire, Cool Customer's commanding lead over the last was first nibbled away, then gobbled up as 'The Rake' flew up that hill. He caught Cool Customer and went away. He won by two lengths. He was now proved a great horse, and in that toughest struggle of his life, Aubrey's strength, coolness and exquisite timing were magnificent. His defeat of Cool Customer made this one of the greatest Gold Cup battles ever, likened by oldtimers to the famous duel between Golden Miller and Thomond II.

A year later all was easier, though superstition shook Mrs Vickerman with pre-race doubts: Cottage Rake was number 13 for his third Gold Cup.

The Rake's battle song preceded him to Cheltenham, correctly enshrining his partnership with Brabazon:

'Aubrey's up, the money's down,
The frightened bookies quake,
Come on, me lads, and give a cheer;
Begod, 'tis Cottage Rake.'

On 9 March, 1950, he won his third successive Cheltenham Gold Cup, making mincemeat of Lord Bicester's top-class chaser, Finnure, who had been undefeated all season till that day, thrashing him by ten lengths. Only four other horses dared take on 'The Rake', for he was the Arkle of his era.

Hats were flung into Cheltenham's buzzing air to celebrate The Rake's hat-

The Brab smiles his way to victory on The Rake – Cheltenham Gold Cup 1950.

Here we are again, 1950; and the same leading characters.

trick. There was another nice bouquet of plaudits for Aubrey Brabazon for, in Vincent's words, 'he rode perhaps the brainiest race of his career.'

Aubrey Brabazon cunningly slipped his field on the descent for home, half a mile away. The Finnure camp had planned, by setting a doddling pace, to blunt that famous Cottage Rake final thrust which he could produce, when others could not, at the end of a hard run race. But their plot rebounded and Aubrey Brabazon's warm and gentle smile as he sails at ease over the last fence reflects his pleasure in his generalship and in the victorious feel of riding a comfortable winner. After the race, Meyrick Good, who wrote for the *Sporting Life* for fifty years, commented, 'Never in my life have I seen the Gold Cup won with greater ease' and the *Life*'s Tom Nickalls reported that, 'Cottage Rake would not have blown out the proverbial candle.'

O'Brien outwardly cool as always in the winning enclosure, said, 'Cottage Rake came back today as I expected. No,' he added to news-thirsty pressmen, 'No plans at the moment . . . we've lived only for this week.'

At the Cheltenham meeting of 'The Rake's' final triumph, Vincent's plain but brilliant little hurdler, Hatton's Grace, won his second Champion Hurdle,

Cottage Rake's connections; Mrs Con Vickerman, Vincent, Aubrey Brabazon and Mr Frank Vickerman, the Yorkshire wool merchant who moved to Dublin and became Vincent's first owner.

so the stable and 'The Brab' accomplished their second Gold Cup-Champion Hurdle double, and a new star was shining in O'Brien's remote yard by the white house at Churchtown.

Aubrey went on to Hurst Park on the Saturday after these three triumphant Cheltenham days a little fatigued by rides and celebrations. He dropped his hands on an odds-on favourite when winning easily and was marched before the Stewards to be fined. *Brabazon Caught Napping* bawled an evening paper headline. 'If so,' said Vincent O'Brien quietly, 'It was the only sleep poor Aubrey got all week.'

In the *Sporting Life* Meyrick Good opined 'many thousands of racegoers would rate Cottage Rake a greater Gold Cup winner than either Easter Hero or Golden Miller....' Strong words of the highest praise. 'The Rake' is not generally placed with Golden Miller or with Arkle. This lack of top esteem for an astonishing triple Gold Cup winner, who could additionally win famous races on the flat is due in large part to the long drawn-out decline of his final years. Men remember the last acts played by a hero.

After running fourth in the Irish Grand National of 1950, carrying 12st 7lb,

'The Rake' was off the course for more than a year. The leg trouble he developed was not caused in a race, not even in training, but at home at grass on holiday in the summer.

'Each season when he'd finished,' Vincent reports, 'I'd let him out every day at Churchtown on the Lawn Field with a donkey for a companion. Each night there were cattle put in the field to graze it. In the morning, the cattle were driven down the back of the farm to the fields by the river. This morning, the chap in charge of the cattle did not show up, and they were not taken out of the field. The horse was let out as usual and started to graze. The donkey meanwhile had wandered in amongst the cattle. When the horse put his head up he couldn't see the donkey. He was so upset at losing his friend that he went round the field at a hell of a rate, got too close to a corner and did some damage to a tendon. It was got right, but he was never the same horse again. It upset Vickerman very much, but,' clicking his tongue as horsemen philosophically do, 'it was just one of those things ... But when we patched him up, Vickerman took him away and sent him to England to be trained. He won nothing of any consequence over there.'

Mr Vickerman transferred his hero to the English stables of Vincent's great friend Gerald Balding (the popular polo-playing father of trainers Toby and Ian) where 'The Rake' used to stay for his triumphant raids on Cheltenham. Sadly his great career ended not with a glorious bang but in a whimper at unsalubrious Wolverhampton ridden by one R. Francis whose name, to the amazement of the racing world, would later appear on a string of best-sellers. He was third in a race valued at £204. He was finally retired and ended his days on a farm at Fermoy.

Vincent O'Brien had turned the thrice-rejected chaser into a horse the equal in his time of Golden Miller and Arkle in theirs. In return, 'The Rake' had launched his trainer. His first Gold Cup had brought enquiries from other owners, like the Keoghs with Hatton's Grace and Knock Hard. Cottage Rake's third Gold Cup made O'Brien's name feared by other trainers and famous in the islands. The trumpets sounded in the English press. Fame had touched O'Brien early. Approaches from other clients began.

Vincent O'Brien had set forth on the difficult and upward path which would lead him towards the classic winners on the flat. Every trainer needs one great horse to make his name. Cottage Rake was Vincent's.

Thirty years later, 'The Rake's' trainer looks back to compare the first great chaser he trained with the second, Knock Hard. 'Cottage Rake was a very good-legged horse with quality limbs; much more quality than you'd see in other chasers in the old days. He stood over a good deal of ground. He had a grand bold head on him. And, oh yes, I liked him very much.

'He stood over *much* more ground than Knock Hard. Knock Hard had a short back and, for me, with that short back, he could never be a really proficient jumper at speed.' Here Vincent O'Brien humps his right hand in a hopping motion. 'Cottage Rake was a shade long over his loins and could do that –' a long swoop, bending his wrist to show the bent back jumpers need – 'Royal Tan was the same and they were the best two jumpers I ever trained. I maintain that jumping at racing speed comes easier to horses who are not short over the loins.'

4

'If it had been me, I'd have warned you off!'

It was the thread of betting which led Vincent O'Brien to his treble Champion Hurdle winner, Hatton's Grace. The plain little gelding's victories at Cheltenham in 1949, 1950 and 1951, overlapped Cottage Rake's Gold Cup treble from 1948 to 1950. The same ownership connected O'Brien to Knock Hard, who won him his fourth Cheltenham Gold Cup in 1953. Both horses belonged to the Keogh family. Harry Keogh 'liked to have a bet,' says Vincent. In those days, O'Brien was a powerful gambler, as his betting books show. (See page 34). He needed capital. Without a rich and generous patron, successful betting is still the only way a young trainer can set himself up.

The thread lay through the man, visibly triumphant in winner's enclosure photographs of the time, who used to place commissions for both O'Brien and Harry Keogh. The man was Nat McNabb and he knew exactly how well O'Brien was doing. He knew how accurately O'Brien could assess form and prepare a horse, and he strongly urged Harry Keogh to move his horses to this outstanding young trainer in Co. Cork.

'Knock Hard,' says Vincent O'Brien, 'had a flat race pedigree.' He was a chestnut gelding, foaled in 1944, by Domaha out of Knocksouna by Beresford. 'He had a lot of speed, too, speed enough to win the Irish Lincoln, anyway.' He was sold as a yearling in the war's shattered markets for just seventy-five guineas.

The first attempt at a gamble on Knock Hard was in the Irish Cesarewitch. He had been tried at home with the Champion Hurdler, Hatton's Grace, and, in Vincent's words, 'smothered him for speed'. So he was specially prepared for the coup – which did not come off. Knock Hard was not the hero of the play. At The Curragh, matters were dramatically miscast. Jacqueline O'Brien recalls, 'Vincent and the owners had an enormous bet on him. Hatton's Grace was run in the race in order to get a better price. They went in first and backed Hatton's Grace which pushed out Knock Hard's price in the market, and then they backed Knock Hard.'

Phonsie O'Brien, Vincent's younger brother, ruefully remembers the day. 'I had £116 all saved up when I left Churchtown for The Curragh that day. I had £100 on Knock Hard at 10 to 1. He came down to 6 to 4 or something like that. Herbert Holmes rode Knock Hard and Martin Molony rode Hatton's Grace. Holmes' instructions were that he was not to go to the front till he was

157   *Self*

MEETING	DATE	HORSE	Amt. On	Price	Tax	WIN	LOSE	CREDIT
		Balance brought forward (Pg 112).						2418. 2. 10
Curragh	Nov. 3	Ashburn	393. 0. 0				393. 0. 0	2025. 2. 10
Clonmel	„ 8	Lucky Dome	116. 10. 0	2/1	8. 14. 9	224. 5. 3		2249. 8. 1
„	„ „	Playa Toro	193. 10. 0	2/1	14. 10. 3	372. 9. 9		2621. 17. 10
Leopardstown	„ 10	Cockatoo	92. 10. 0	6/4	5. 15. 7	132. 19. 4		2754. 17. 2
Thurles	„ 15	L. Dome	156. 10. 0	7/5	7. 0. 6	118. 1. 6		2872. 18. 8
Naas	„ 17	Illyric	20. 0. 0				20. 0. 0	2852. 18. 8
„	„ „	Silk Cottage	95. 10. 0				95. 10. 0	2757. 8. 8
Cheltenham	„ 14	Royal Tan	556. 10. 0	6/5		667. 16. 0		3425. 4. 8
„	„ „	L. By Blue	25. 0. 0				25. 0. 0	3400. 4. 8
Birmingham	„ 19	Knock Hard	175. 0. 0	4/7		100. 0. 0		3500. 4. 8
Navan	„ 24	L. Dome	100. 10. 0				100. 10. 0	3399. 14. 8
Gowran	„ 29	The Dipper	200. 0. 0	5/2	17. 10. 0	482. 10. 0		3882. 4. 8
„	„ „	„ „	7. 15. 0	2/1	11. 7	14. 13. 5		3897. 3. 1
Naas	Dec. 8	Knock Hard	193. 10. 0				193. 10. 0	3703. 13. 1
do	Feb. 2	L. Dome	143. 10. 0	6/1	25. 2. 3	835. 17. 9		4539. 10. 10
do	„ „	H. Grace	96. 5. 0				96. 5. 0	4443. 5. 10
Leopardstown	„ 9	Royal Tan	214. 0. 0				214. 0. 0	4229. 5. 10
Baldoyle	„ 16	Silk Cottage	100. 0. 0	4/1	12. 10. 0	387. 10. 0		4616. 15. 10
do	„ „	Hattons Grace	100. 0. 0	9/13	2. 4. 8	428. 11. 2		5045. 7. 0
Cheltenham	Mar. „	Wye Fly	46. 0. 0				46. 0. 0	4999. 7. 0
„	„ „	Cockatoo	57. 10. 0	5/1		257. 10. 0		5256. 17. 0
„	„ „	H. Grace	196. 0. 0				196. 0. 0	5060. 17. 0
„	„ 4. 5. 6	Treble	33. 10. 0				33. 10. 0	5027. 7. 0
„	„ 5	Royal Tan	464. 0. 0			1856. 0. 0		6883. 7. 0
„	„ 6	Ashburn	1452. 0. 0				1452. 0. 0	5431. 7. 0
„	„ „	Knock Hard	296. 0. 0				296. 0. 0	5135. 7. 0
„	„ „	Talk Palm	310. 0. 0				310. 0. 0	4825. 7. 0
Curragh	Apr. 3/51	Pan the Jack	57. 15. 0				57. 15. 0	4767. 12. 0
Cheltenham		H. Grace	+ 4. 0. 0				4. 0. 0	4763. 12. 0
Sandown	Mar. 15	H. Grace	202. 0. 0				202. 0. 0	4561. 12. 0

Some famous names here in Vincent's betting book, Knock Hard, Hatton's Grace, Royal Tan (a win of £1856) all appear. At the end of that Cheltenham, Vincent is £4561 12s ahead of the books.

inside the last furlong. After having my £100 on, I had £16 left, so I had £5 each way on Hatton's Grace ... Mr Holmes goes to the front going down the hill before he even got to the straight on The Curragh! He's sitting there as if he's got the race pretty well sewn up. Then along comes Martin Molony on Hatton's Grace and catches him in the last furlong and beats him.

'If he'd been ridden in any other way,' sighs Phonsie, 'twenty-seven out of twenty-eight times, he'd have beaten Hatton's Grace eight lengths. And Mr Holmes said afterwards he was going so easy, nothing in the world could catch him. He couldn't contain himself any longer.'

Phonsie groans, then laughs. 'The result of my bet was that I won £1, instead of the £1,000 I was supposed to win!'

The solo voice on the whole of The Curragh cheering for Hatton's Grace was that of his attractive owner, Moya Keogh.

Amazingly enough, the attempt to recoup the losses incurred in the long distance Cesarewitch was made the following spring in the Lincoln over just a mile and the most competitive, high-gambling race at the start of the Irish Flat Season.

'I ran him in a novice chase at Naas,' says O'Brien, 'only two weeks before the Lincoln, the object being to extend his price in the Lincoln. Few would believe that a horse that had just run over fences could win a Lincoln. He won the chase, incidentally.'

'I won the Irish Lincoln on him by six lengths,' says T.P., smiling, head tilted, in the office at Ballydoyle. 'In the Lincoln he was six lengths up after he'd gone three furlongs and stayed there. There was great talk of Arkle coming to The Curragh and winning that two mile race. But our fellow was winning over one mile! He was a fine big chestnut horse. A lovely horse. Classier even than Cottage Rake.' The recollection of those past triumphs make Tommy Burns smile. He adds, wryly, with that touch of poetry which crops up in the conversation of the Irish like stones in their sad, green fields, 'Ah, the glorious little hours of one's life ...

'Knock Hard,' he goes on, 'was more or less a flat horse that was turned to chasing. I rode him in a five furlong race myself and then, at the other end of the scale, over the longest distance. They always reckoned here,' Tommy Burns concludes, 'that Knock Hard was never really in love with jumping.'

Phonsie O'Brien, that laughing likeable character, came late into the racing game, and yet, in under two years, became Ireland's top amateur rider under National Hunt Rules, riding fistfuls of winners for his smaller, slighter brother. He was at school during the early days at Churchtown and only started riding in races in 1949. In 1950 he was Ireland's leading amateur. At O'Brien's famous Limerick Christmas meeting of 1950 the yard sent out eight winners from Churchtown; Phonsie rode seven of them.

Knock Hard in training at Ballydoyle before the grand new gallops were laid out. Note where the gaps have been broken in the existing farm fences and compare with the picture on page 84. And below Vincent's small string, and one sheep, prepare to work.

Phonsie rode Knock Hard in his first Gold Cup. He had been substantially backed and was only a length behind the winner, Mont Tremblant, when he fell two out. Phonsie states adamantly, 'I was hack-cantering at the time. He'd have won by fifteen lengths. Yes, he would, only he slipped going into the second last fence. Dave Dick on Mont Tremblant was with me, kicking and pushing beside me. There was I, just sitting. Knock Hard was cantering and whatever way it happened, he just slipped, taking off . . . There it was.'

Another coup was planned for the following autumn. Phonsie continues, 'There was a decision taken that Knock Hard should go for the Manchester November Handicap and to be eligible to run in England the horse had to run on the flat. So I was the jockey to get him handicapped. Several amateur flat races in England were selected and I rode him. At Lewes he coasted in at long odds on.' At Worcester they met a very good hurdler, Noholme, ridden by that charming, talented actor, Mr Teddy Underdown. 'Vincent, Harry Keogh, and Sydney McGregor,' Phonsie recalls, 'had a massive gamble on Knock Hard – something like £14,000 to 8. I was meant to hold him up, which I did. Then a gap suddenly appeared. I coasted up on the inside of Mr Underdown and sat there. He appeared to have the race won. I waited and waited, then gave my fellow one crack and we won by a neck. Oh, he was a class horse. A brilliant horse. The speed he had! Of course, at Worcester I'd had a bet myself. Amateurs are allowed to bet, aren't they?' says Phonsie, chuckling.

The gamble at Manchester only just failed. 'We were beaten a head by a high-class horse, Summer Rain, who had been third in the Derby,' says Vincent. 'Harry Keogh asked, "If you could run Knock Hard at Kempton in the King

Knock Hard wins the Southdown Welter Plate by 20 lengths, Lewes 1952.

George VI Chase, it'd be great". It would have given him a chance,' says Vincent calmly, 'to get his money back.' This astonishing statement is unlikely ever to have been made before, or contemplated again, by any trainer of racehorses. Here is a man who, having prepared a senior gelding for a gamble over one and a half miles on the flat in one of Britain's most competitive handicaps, coolly resolving that the just-lost thousands might be regained in a matter of six weeks over three miles of fences in Britain's semi-classic steeple-chase.

'To run at Manchester,' says Vincent, 'the horse had to find a fair bit of speed so we brought Knock Hard back here, and I took him easy, trying to get him to relax again. He went to Kempton and Tim Molony rode him. He went into that first fence taking a really strong hold – he took off boldly and jumped so strong that on landing his forelegs went straight out in front and his hindlegs shot straight out behind along the ground. Tim said if he'd tipped a little bit to right or left, he'd have gone, but he just went straight on, and got back on to his feet again. The horse got a bad fright. Tim said he was never the same through the race after that.' In spite of the mishap and nearly three miles of uncertain, unenthusiastic jumping, Knock Hard had the class and final speed to finish third to Halloween and Mont Tremblant. Vincent said, 'A month after the race Tim said to me that if he had really got at the horse he would have won, but he was easy on him because he had been frightened.'

John Hislop, then writing a racing column in the *Observer* noted that on Boxing Day 1952, 'The Prime Minister was there and had a winner.' (This was Britain's only keen racing Premier since the war, Sir Winston Churchill). Hislop commented significantly on Knock Hard, 'he carried a wonderful bloom in his coat'. This was symptomatic of a well-trained O'Brien horse, but hard to bring about in winter. Hislop added 'But he'll never make a top class chaser till he learns to jump better.' The comment was fair.

After Kempton Knock Hard ran at Leopardstown. His running there coupled with other races drew Vincent O'Brien under the suspicious examination of the Irish Stewards, which later led to his suspension for three months.

Vincent tells the story. 'Knock Hard was handicapped to give Lord Bicester's good horse Mariner's Log twenty-one pounds. That was quite something, though we didn't realise at the time what kind of a horse Mariner's Log would turn out to be. A jockey called P. J. Doyle rode Knock Hard – he was retained by the stable at the time – and I said to him, "I don't want this horse to get a hard race. He's got a lot of weight. But, you know, be there to win if you can". Doyle had the reputation of really getting at a horse and could have given him a very hard race. Right. Doyle went out and rode. Now the horse, after his fright at Kempton wasn't inclined to jump his fences as boldly as he used to. He was drawing back a bit. As a result, Mariner's Log beat him, and there was a good deal of chat that day that the horse wasn't trying. At that time old Judge Wylie was a Steward of the Turf Club. With his experience on the Bench he could run the Turf Club; a few well chosen words and he was in command. Later in the year I went into St Stephen's Green Club – the Judge was a member and I was, too. It was the year Paddy Prendergast was in trouble with the English Stewards over the running of his horse, Blue Sail, at Ascot. The Irish Stewards didn't agree with the English Stewards' findings. They held an enquiry themselves in Ireland, and found no discrepancy between Blue Sail's running in Ireland and his running at Ascot.

'When old Wylie walked into the Club, I knew he'd been at the Turf Club, so I asked him, "Any news on the Prendergast case?"

'"Oh yes," said the Judge, "we could find no discrepancy there." Then he said to me, "If it had been *me*, I'd have warned *you* off over Knock Hard last January at Leopardstown."

'Just like that. This was November. That shook me a bit. So I came home and thought about it and decided to ring him up and ask if I could meet him.

'I sat down and talked to him about what had happened in the King George VI at Kempton. But I don't think he believed me. . . . So anyway the horse went off to run in the Great Yorkshire Chase and Tim Molony was at him, at him all the way, pushing and niggling at him all the way. Then when he jumped

Knock Hard, the horse who 'didn't like jumping' and had a bad heart, winning the 1953 Cheltenham Gold Cup ridden by Tim Molony followed by (left) Dave Dick on Mont Tremblant, fourth, and Galloway Braes, Bert Morrow third. Halloween (Fred Winter) was second.

the last and saw a clear way ahead of him with no fences there he just sprinted home.

'After the race Tim said to me, "Don't have any doubt about it: he doesn't like jumping after the fright he got at Kempton. He doesn't like it."

'To be sure there wasn't any other problem, I decided to get a vet down from Dublin from the University to do a cardiograph on the horse. I'd a feeling there could be something wrong with his heart. ... I was in the box with the vet and the machine while he was testing the horse and saw the reading coming out on the machine. The vet was looking at it and shook his head at me. He didn't like it. So I brought him into the office and he said, "I'm sorry to have to tell you that the situation is that Knock Hard could drop dead at any time." '

The instant gravity of this unequivocal report burst like a bomb. 'Incidentally,' Vincent comments, 'I told Wylie this as well, but he just ...' and Vincent shrugs. Now it seemed that the life of this great chaser hung by a thread which could break at any moment. What should O'Brien do?

'Of course I told Harry Keogh and he thought about it. Harry said finally "Well he's got no value now. We can't sell him. The diagnosis could be wrong, we might as well go on with him." '

The risk of a severe injury to a jockey riding a horse whose heart suddenly stops is higher than from any other accident. The horse may collapse in mid-air over a jump. This is, indeed, the likeliest instance, when he has just used maximum energy to launch his half ton bulk into the air. If he does die in that second, he crumples to the ground.

O'Brien's first duty was to warn Tim Molony. 'I told him exactly the position and what the vet had said. But Tim's a very brave man. He just laughed and said he wasn't worried.' I too, after the Great Yorkshire, felt the vet could well be wrong!

Knock Hard therefore set off for Cheltenham to contest his second Gold Cup with some peculiar qualifications. He did not enjoy jumping, an activity rather necessary for any steeplechaser, let alone one attempting the classic. He was suffering from a bad heart, an affliction which could, and in his case finally did, make him drop dead during the far less arduous test of a day's foxhunting.

Knock Hard had run in Mont Tremblant's 1952 Gold Cup, starting second favourite to Freebooter. By now any horse trained by O'Brien running at Cheltenham was fancied by the public and feared by English owners and their trainers. The stables' domination of the Gold Cup from 1948 to 1950 and of the Champion Hurdle from 1949 to 1951 was matched all down the line to the novices' hurdle, then called the Gloucestershire Hurdle – and now more cumbersomely the Waterford Crystal Supreme Novices' Hurdle.

It used always to be run in two divisions because of the number of runners.

Tim Molony rides Knock Hard into the winners' enclosure at Cheltenham, led by Moya Keogh, giving Vincent his fourth Gold Cup. Nat McNabb waving his hat on the right has plainly landed another hefty commission.

Lady Lily Serena Lumley to whom Knock Hard was given on his retirement takes him hunting from her parents' home. The horse finally died when out hunting.

It was O'Brien's custom between 1952 and 1959 to win at least one of the divisions and often both, as in 1955, '56 and '58: ten Gloucester victories from 12 runners in eight years. 'The other two finished second,' Vincent adds. T.P. Burns rode seven of them and Phonsie O'Brien two.

Knock Hard's jockey for the 1953 Cheltenham Gold Cup, Tim Molony, that brave and sporting horseman with the face of a battered Roman centurion, got up on the horse knowing he did not like jumping and that he had a groggy heart. He took on stars like Halloween, Mont Tremblant again, Teal, the 1952 Grand National winner, Mariner's Log, Rose Park, Galloway Braes again, and E.S.B. who three years later won the Grand National in which the Queen Mother's Devon Loch mysteriously collapsed. The ground was fast and the weather foggy. Rose Park, Mont Tremblant and Galloway Braes loomed out of the mist together starting down the hill. They appeared to be the only three left in it. Knock Hard was a long way back and seemed to be struggling. It would have occurred to any jockey with a trace of caution that this horse with a bad heart might be feeling it; he might be on the point of finally collapsing. Not so the heroic Molony.

Vincent O'Brien remembers clearly, 'Tim was at him, driving him, kicking him, pushing him all the way. Then he jumped the last like that –' (making the gesture of a brilliant leap) 'and he was up the hill and away – when he saw there was no obstacle ahead of him.' That renowned final acceleration again burst like a rocket. Knock Hard at the post was an amazing five lengths ahead of Halloween who had run through beaten horses.

That race was the zenith of Knock Hard's erratic but dazzling career over fences. The brilliant flat racer who could win over distances between one mile and two miles on the flat 'ran well next year in that big 'chase in Hurst Park, the Queen Elizabeth Chase' says Vincent. 'But after that his form began to deteriorate.

'I'd sold him in the meanwhile to Frankie More O'Ferrell, and I said to Frankie, "Look here, we'd better not persevere with him". So there was a girl in the north of England who'd been over here a couple of times, Lord Scarbrough's daughter, Lady Lily Serena Lumley. I said to Frankie, "How about giving her the horse to hunt," for she's very keen on hunting. Frankie thought it an excellent idea. She had been fully acquainted with the vet's report on the heart. She hunted him for a season or two, and by God, didn't he drop dead under her one day!' The earl's daughter was shaken, but uninjured. If Knock Hard had collapsed in the mêlée of a race, it would have been a sadder story. That thread had finally broken, as predicted, but the start of a new one was spun. Lily Serena had come to stay with the O'Briens as the friend of the daughter of a Yorkshire solicitor, Hedley Nicholson. It would be this Mr Nicholson who led Vincent O'Brien to his first rich American owner on the flat.

5

'The ugly duckling of the parade ring'

Hatton's Grace arrived at Vincent O'Brien's with his stable companion, Knock Hard in the summer of 1948. The horse belonged to Harry and Moya Keogh and had been in training with Barney Nugent. T.P. Burns remembers the Keoghs having a number of horses with the Nugents, 'who were a horse-dealing, hunting and hireling sort of family who lived close to Tom Dreaper of Prince Regent and Arkle fame.'

The so-called 'ugly duckling of the parade ring' who doesn't look so plain in this photograph. After coming to Vincent he won three Champion Hurdles, an Irish Lincoln over 8 furlongs, the Cesarewitch over 2 miles and ended up winning a steeplechase. He was one of the most popular horses ever with the Irish crowds.

Hatton's Grace was bred by the Victor Stud of Co. Tipperary and sold at Goffs Sales to John Kirwan, a trainer from near Gowran, for 18 guineas. He was bought as a store. 'Dan Corry of the Irish Army jumping team bought him,' says Vincent, 'Dan used to do a bit of bumper riding and must have trained the horse himself for a time. Then Moya Keogh shared him with Dan and afterwards bought him out. Dan won a bumper on Hatton's Grace at Bellewstown, I think.' He did – it was worth £74.5s! Colonel Dan Corry was for many years a prominent member of Ireland's International Show Jumping Team which Irish Government policy then restricted to serving members of the Irish Armed Forces.

Dan Corry, a very popular character, had time amidst his military duties to ride in races. But Bellewstown is not quite Ascot or Leopardstown. Indeed you could not find much lower class form than this in all Ireland, and it cannot have occurred to any of the horse's connections then that he might ever even run in a minor race at Cheltenham.

After his bumper win however, and trained by Barney Nugent, Hatton's Grace ran with some distinction over hurdles and between 1946 and 1948 he won three races. He came to O'Brien in the summer of 1948. Vincent was not favourably impressed by the looks of the horse who would win him three Champion Hurdles. 'He wasn't an imposing individual at all. He was small, and his neck was rather light and a little short which took from his appearance. But he had good limbs, good depth of heart. Otherwise a light bodied horse.'

T. P. Burns remembers Hatton's Grace with loving enthusiasm, 'He was a marvellous little horse. In between his three Champion Hurdles, he won the Lincoln and two Cesarewitches.' Tommy Burns rode him often. 'He was narrow when you got up on him, and there was not much neck. He didn't need a lot of work, and he needed to be rested off between races. But he was as tough as nails. Sadly, I didn't ride him in his Champion Hurdles. Aubrey Brabazon won the first and second in 1949 and 1950, and Tim Molony the third in 1951. In my opinion he had more charisma with the public than any Irish horse with the exception of Arkle.'

Hatton's Grace won his first Champion Hurdle on only his third run for O'Brien, and at the age of nine when most hurdlers are losing their speed. Described by the *Irish Press* as 'Mrs Keogh's old horse', he beat National Spirit, hot favourite and a year younger, who had won two Champion Hurdles and who was the darling of the English crowds. Hatton's Grace won as he liked, jumping the last flight in front and accelerating on the flat to win by six lengths.

Moya Keogh, who had owned the horse for four years, led him in exclaiming 'He is only a little bit of a horse, but isn't he *splendid*?'

John Hislop described Hatton's Grace as 'A most unimposing horse, being

Supervised by Vincent, Hatton's Grace boxes up on his way home from another victorious raid on Cheltenham.

small, rather mean-looking, and a washy bay ... all the more credit to his trainer, O'Brien.'

The *Irish Field* wrote huffily, 'This was a dumbfounding result to serious students of racing, for Hatton's Grace had never before shown form up to this standard.' But that was the way it was with O'Brien in those days.

Then, in less than a month, the horse who had just won hurdling's highest prize round the two tough miles of Cheltenham in March, was being prepared for a cut at a hot flat race over a mile. 'The Irish Lincoln was on the first Saturday in April and Hatton's Grace won that easily with Morny Wing riding,' O'Brien remembers, 'and then he won the Cesarewitch for the first tim in November 1949.' Ridden by Martin Molony he beat his fancied stab companion, Knock Hard. As the *Sunday Independent* described it 'Wheelbarrows of late money made Knock Hard's price tumble from sixes and sevens to evens, and allowed Hatton's Grace to ease from three to eights in a market that provided as many late thrills as the race itself.' Martin Molony by sheer force of habit, on his first-ever Irish Cesarewitch mount produced an effort which provided the undoing of what was termed the 'right one' - Knock Hard.

The 'two Peter Pans' as Peter O'Sullevan dubbed them – National Spirit leading in blinkers from Hatton's Grace. Vincent's horse goes on to win his second Champion Hurdle ... and below *his third with National Spirit again making a last hurdle blunder.*

Next year at Cheltenham, Hatton's Grace came to the last hurdle pressing National Spirit who over-jumped. Aubrey seized the advantage and won.

Hatton's Grace was eleven years old when he ran in the Champion Hurdle in 1951. The course was waterlogged and the visibility only fair. The scene at the last hurdle looked like a photograph of Hatton's Grace and National Spirit the year previously. Except that in the year before you could see from the position of Denis Dillon's leg on National Spirit that the horse was just coming unbalanced as he came to the hurdle. In 1951 his horse, towering over Hatton's Grace, was even more unbalanced and he came down. It's an extraordinary thing that the two old horses should have come to the last flight in two Champion Hurdles in exactly the same way. Peter O'Sullevan called them the 'two Peter Pans', because they didn't grow any older. 'Quite remarkable ...'

Hatton's Grace coming in after winning in his homeland led in by his owner Mrs Moya Keogh. On our left is a famous Irish racing character of the times 'Buckets' and headman Maurice O'Callaghan. On the right, with race glasses, Vincent's original link with the Keoghs, Nat McNabb who used to put on the commissions for them.

Harry Keogh, 'a man who liked a bet', with his wife Moya and Vincent after another successful coup.

says Vincent. 'Hatton's Grace had an amazing heart the way he used to tackle that hill at Cheltenham.'

Hatton's Grace was the first horse to win three Champion Hurdles and the first eleven year old to win. It took nearly thirty years for the next one: Sea Pigeon.

In the eyes of the ignorant every winner seems handsome. But that good Irish commentator, Michael O'Hehir would not agree. He called Hatton's Grace 'the ugly duckling of the parade ring'. His insignificant looks actually boosted his popularity with his public as he started to win and win. David does not have to be Adonis to be supported against Goliath.

Phonsie O'Brien says of Hatton's Grace 'I found him a lovely ride at home and a precision jumper'. He rode him in his fourth Champion Hurdle. Hatton's Grace was then twelve years old and the horse who won was the brilliant five year old Sir Ken, then starting his own run of three successive victories. The second horse was Noholme, whom Phonsie and Knock Hard had beaten a neck to land the big gamble at Worcester. Of that last Champion Hurdle, Phonsie says 'At that stage of his career Hatton's Grace didn't quite have the speed to get with the leaders in the last half mile.' The going was too much on top for the old champion and he came very late on the scene. Vincent comments proudly, 'Yet he finished fifth, running on strongly.'

But Hatton's Grace was not yet done. This extraordinary little racehorse then ran in four steeplechases. He won the last in spite of being too old a hand to turn easily to fences, and Vincent O'Brien immediately retired him.

On his retirement, Michael O'Hehir added to his phrase 'the ugly duckling of the parade ring' – 'but he was a great-hearted and brilliantly versatile star in action on the racecourses of England and Ireland.' His six flat race and twelve National Hunt victories had earned the popular Keoghs the then princely sum of £2,885, or almost one thousand times more than he cost as a wartime yearling in neutral Dublin. He enjoyed a happily active retirement with Vincent at Ballydoyle. Three years after his last Champion Hurdle victory, Louis Gunning, the Irish racing journalist, described him at home: 'His fondness for racing and for showing how the hurdles should be jumped are still indulged by his trainer who allows the old fellow to lead younger horses in their work. What a capable schoolmaster for the novices!'

Hatton's Grace and Knock Hard had arrived at exactly the right time for a young trainer who had made money with some spectacular gambles, and who had made his name in the top league with one great horse, Cottage Rake. The two horses which so swiftly followed The Rake consolidated O'Brien's reputation.

Hatton's Grace's last Cheltenham was the meeting at which Knock Hard –

The two Keogh horses take each other on at Leopardstown 27 December 1949. Left Hatton's Grace (Aubrey Brabazon), the winner at 3 to 1 on, being led by Knock Hard (R.J. O'Ryan), second at 7 to 1.

'hack cantering' in Phonsie's recollection – had fallen two fences from home in the Gold Cup. Not all was disappointment though. The next of O'Brien's great horses first attracted English attention when Royal Tan won the National Hunt Handicap Chase, heavily backed down to 7 to 2 and ridden by Phonsie. A leading racing writer commented 'Many people left Cheltenham convinced they had seen the future Grand National winner ...'

6

'And I got talking to the girl'

By 1950 Vincent had resolved to find a training establishment of his own. He wanted not only to be independent, but he needed a place where he could train top-class horses. After months of meticulous searching he chose Ballydoyle in County Tipperary, an ordinary farm of 185 acres in rolling countryside with plenty of uphill ground on which to work horses.

He had moved forty miles north-east from Churchtown the other side of the Galtee and Ballyhoura mountains, after the end of Cheltenham week in 1951.

'At first we made gaps in the fences for the horses to work, and it took a year or so to be ready to train horses. The fields averaged 12 to 14 acres with substantial banks between them with stone wallfacings and hedges on top. Quite a job to start. I don't think I'd like to attempt to do it again!'

As families date things by major domestic events – marriages, funerals, births and christenings, so in the O'Brien household the two main sections of Vincent's steeplechasing life are divided, in Jacqueline's phrase to him, by, '*Your* Gold Cups and *our* Grand Nationals.'

The most influential thread in a man's life is the one which, for good or ill, binds him to a woman, and long were the coincidences by which Vincent O'Brien from Co. Cork met Jacqueline Wittenoom from Perth, Western Australia.

Vincent's journeys abroad had taken him no further than England. He crossed to buy horses at wartime Newmarket, carrying his khaki Travel Permit Card, marked 'Business Visitor' and stamped with a British visa. On it are marked where and when he drew cheques. He drew money out of Lloyds Bank, Cheltenham, on 7 April, 1949, four days before Cottage Rake's second victory in that postponed Gold Cup . . .

Ireland might seem an unusual country for a bright young girl – she was a graduate in economics – to visit in Europe but Jacqueline, whose father was an Australian Member of Parliament, had Irish ancestors. And Ireland, in the immediate post-war years, was a happy, well-fed party-going place to be. Dublin Horse Show week in early August was, in those days, invaded by British debs (forerunners of the Sloane Rangers) and their 'deb's delights'. They were intent on attending seven hunt balls in five nights and enjoying themselves in the beautiful Georgian houses which still flourished in a land which had, with difficulty, remained neutral.

Jacqueline's great-great grandfather, the Rev. J. B. Wittenoom, she explains, 'was the chaplain who founded the Western Australian colony which, unlike other parts of Australia, was not a convict settlement. He was a don at Brasenose College, Oxford and after his wife, to whom he was deeply attached, died suddenly he applied for the job of chaplain to the new colony. He took his sister and five sons, and they took five months to sail to Western Australia. His duties were to conduct church services, register births, deaths and marriages, and educate the colonial youth. He built the first church and school with his sister acting as bricklayer's mate. In Western Australia, he is well remembered and several places are named after him.'

Jacqueline's introduction to Vincent came through the hands of a notable Irish character, Waring Willis, who rode in races with success, bred a few, trained a few, and sold a few good jumping horses. He has the battered face of a jockey who has suffered his share of falls in action, and has very merry eyes. He was a good friend of Aubrey Brabazon who had ridden all those Cheltenham winners for Vincent.

Vincent recounts how he met Jacqueline by the merest chance. 'I left Ballydoyle one afternoon to go to Dublin, intending to go racing the following day at The Curragh. I dropped in at the Russell Hotel intending to have an early meal so as to get to bed early and do some work next morning, before going racing.' The thirty-four year old painstakingly dedicated trainer was certainly not intent upon an evening of frivolity in Dublin's fair city. He showed however impeccable taste, for the Russell, diagonally opposite the Shelbourne across St Stephen's Green, offered the best food in Dublin.

'But while I was having a drink in the Russell before my meal, Waring Willis, a great friend I'd known for many years, came in with Gerry Annesley, and they had this girl with them. They introduced me to the girl and asked me to have a drink.' Vincent was still planning on an early night. 'I said, "well, I'm just going to have a meal", but they persuaded me to have a drink. Then they persuaded me to have dinner with them. And during dinner I just started to look at this girl. ... After dinner we went across to the Shelbourne Hotel. Waring wasn't feeling too well – I think he'd had a succession of late nights! – and he went to bed rather early. So did Gerry Annesley, and I got talking to the girl. ...'

So far the threads of chance were running Vincent's way. He now took up the running himself.

'I asked her if she'd like to come racing next day at The Curragh, and I said I'd pick her up at the Shelbourne at a certain time. I came round but I found that Waring Willis was right back in the picture again. However, she came racing with me. After racing, we went across The Curragh and had drinks with Aubrey Brabazon. ... And it went on from there. That was May and she was going back to Australia on the fourth of July. I had to think pretty fast. I'd not much time.'

Jacqueline set off for England where she was going to take the boat to Australia from Southampton. Vincent hurried after her and proposed. The engagement was announced in August 1951 and they were married on the twenty-ninth of December in the University Church, Dublin, with the reception, suitably, in the Shelbourne Hotel.

Thirty-three years later Vincent recalls with a contented chuckle, 'That afternoon when I set off to Dublin and met Jacqueline for the first time, I had originally intended to turn right out of the gate and go south to Waterford. Something made me turn around and head north for Dublin!'

Jacqueline now plays an increasingly important rôle in the story. She watched – 'with hands trembling so much I couldn't hold my binoculars' – Knock Hard win the Great Yorkshire at Doncaster. Her first National Hunt Meeting at Cheltenham saw old Hatton's Grace's swan-song, the fall of Knock Hard in the Gold Cup and the rise of Royal Tan whose first Grand National loomed ahead. A trainer's wife at any level of the game can ease, speed, handicap or sabotage his prospects. Unlike most other jobs a trainer and his consort must work in complementary harmony to prosper. The surly wife loses owners and irritates the staff. The good one removes all the necessary social duties of a trainer's toil. Jacqueline before her marriage had had nothing to do with racing. Her relations and friends and contacts lay on the far side of the world.

What does she do to help Vincent?

'Well, just about everything,' Vincent declares. 'So far as my personal work's concerned, she's of the greatest help. I'm always glad to be able to consult her. It doesn't take her long to get to grips with whatever the trouble is and to help me out with it. She's been a tremendous influence in my life.'

7

'I was like 007'

Nine months before their marriage, the first of Vincent's three Grand National winners contested the 1951 race. Royal Tan, who was Vincent's first Grand National runner, was bred, coincidentally, less than two miles from Ballydoyle, as Phonsie O'Brien recalls. 'He was bred by the Tophams, an old hunting family from Tullamaine close to Ballydoyle, and the Carrolls stood his sire, Tartan, just down the road. Then Tim Hyde senior bought him and trained him for Ben Dunne – of Dunne Stores – together with a man called Darrar, who'd been his partner in the earliest Dunne's Store. Harry Keogh wanted a horse to follow in the footsteps of Castledermot, who'd won the National Hunt Chase at Cheltenham in 1949 with Lord Mildmay riding.'

There are some typically charming, modest letters in Vincent's scrapbook from that most admirable Corinthian, written naturally from Fairlawne, Peter Cazalet's magnificent house in Kent. Anthony Mildmay had come originally to stay a week-end with Peter, his close friend and companion-in-arms in the Welsh Guards. He stayed for thirteen years. In one letter the champion amateur apologises to Vincent for not riding Castledermot well enough. In another, after he had sought to buy the horse, he regrets that Castledermot had failed the vet.

The Keoghs bought Royal Tan for the four mile National Hunt Chase, which was nicknamed the 'amateur's Grand National'. In O'Brien's case this proved apt as Quare Times trained by Vincent and ridden by Bunny Cox won the National Hunt Chase and went on to win the Grand National but it was a very unlucky race for Phonsie O'Brien. He rode four favourites and never got past the fifth fence of the four mile journey. On Royal Tan he fell at the second fence, 'Right in front of the stands we went. He overjumped and that was it'.

Back in Ireland things went well and Royal Tan won his novice chases, progressed the next year to handicaps, 'and then,' says Phonsie 'he ran in the Irish National and the English National of 1951. I rode him in both races and was second in each. All in the space of ten days.'

(above) *Royal Tan in full suspension on the gallops at Ballydoyle. He is being ridden by Paddy Norris who married Frank Vickerman's daughter and became a trainer himself. Their son Robert is now resident vet at Ballydoyle.*

The horse that could not be told how to jump. Royal Tan blundered at the last in the 1951 Grand National, 'fell' at the last in 1952 and finally won in 1954.

The seven year old Royal Tan had been flown from Dublin to Liverpool for the race, a most unusual step then. It was the year of disasters. Thirty-four of the field of thirty-six failed to get round after a dreadfully ill-timed start which caught many of the riders off their guard and caused havoc at the first fence. The two survivors came to the second last together. As they landed, Phonsie called across to Johnny Bullock, 'What's that you're riding?'

Little Johnny shouted back, 'Nickel Coin.'

'Well, I think I've got you cooked,' cried Phonsie, and on they strode to the last fence. 'At the last,' he says 'Royal Tan was a stride in front. But he hit the top and he went down and down. Right down so that his nose got to one and a half inches off the ground.'

By balance and strength, Phonsie stuck to the horse. But his chance of winning was gone. He followed Nickel Coin home, beaten six lengths by the 40 to 1 mare, trained at Reigate by smiling Jack O'Donoghue. The O'Brien camp was sure that, bar for that last fence blunder, they would have won the

The blunder at the last in the 1951 Grand National when Royal Tan ridden by Phonsie O'Brien let in the mare Nickel Coin ridden by Johnny Bullock.

duel. Vincent recalls, 'Royal Tan was a brilliant jumper. My brother gave him a kick with his heels coming to the last, and the horse seemed to resent it. We didn't realise it at the time but later on I think it's true to say that he did not want to be told how and when to jump. He made a bungle of the fence and he was on the ground. Literally. But by some extraordinary effort he got back on his legs again and my brother was still on his back – a truly incredible performance on the part of man and horse.'

That last fence was going to prove disastrous to Royal Tan in the next Grand National. 'He came to the last again,' says Vincent, 'my brother again riding him, lying third. I don't know whether he gave the horse a kick or not. He was very close behind the leading pair. He made the same mistake, only perhaps a little worse, and that was that.'

Although Royal Tan was right on the ground he never toppled over, and he struggled back onto his feet again, but Phonsie came off, and the race was won by Teal.

Speaking of his instructions from Vincent, Phonsie jokingly says, 'When I used to ride for Vincent, I was like 007! He'd write down the instructions and

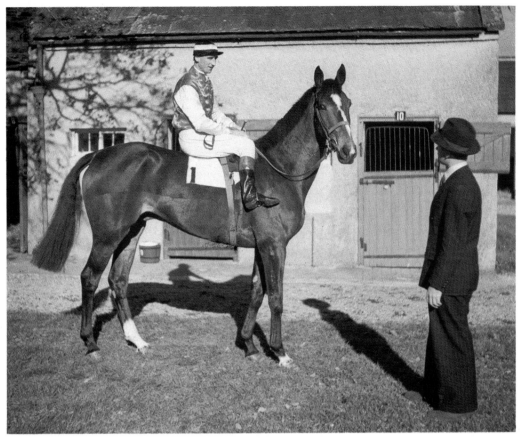

Vincent with 'The Rake', and 'The Brab' in the old racecourse yard at The Curragh – a wonderful partnership.

(Below) The companion painting of 'The Ugly Duckling', Hatton's Grace, who won three Champion Hurdles in a row.

These two paintings hang in the dining room at Ballydoyle. Above is Knock Hard painted at Churchtown where Vincent trained this fourth Gold Cup winner. The farmhouse where Vincent was born can just be seen on the right. The paintings are by Rosemary O'Callaghan-Westropp.

A unique photograph of Vincent's three Grand National winners – all trained here at Ballydoyle and taken outside the front door. Left to right: Early Mist, Royal Tan and Quare Times. John Stapleton, a wonderful handler of young horses, crouches down on the left. Vincent's head appears on the right.

These three pictures by Peter Biegel show (above) *Royal Tan at Valentine's 1954 in the lead from Tudor Line and* (below) *Sundew leading from Quare Times (hooped colours) and Steel Lock with M'as Tu Vu behind Sundew, Becher's Brook.*

(Opposite) *Early Mist leading from Mont Tremblant at the Canal Turn in the 1953 Grand National painted by Peter Biegel.*

Two more paintings from the Ballydoyle dining room. These, by the American artist Richard Stone Reeves, show Ballymoss (above) and (below) the great mare Gladness, both in McShain colours with Scobie Breasley and Lester Piggott. These were the artist's first paintings in Europe.

almost say, "when you've read this, swallow it" you know! Every occasion they read: under no circumstances jump the last fence in front.' Vincent felt that with the lengthy run-in the horse would be in front for too long, but Phonsie, with hindsight, maintains that if he had gone on the horse might not have made those two disasterous blunders at the last fence.

After Royal Tan's dramatic and expensive disappointment at Liverpool's last fence, he was, by an oversight in the Turf Club's conditions, still enabled to run in a two mile 'bumper' flat race at humble Listowel. Phonsie again rode Royal Tan. 'And I think Vincent had a sizeable bet, oh, a very sizeable bet in view of losing so much on the horse before. And I happened to scrape home on him by a neck. It was a lot more difficult than we thought it'd be, I can tell you,' Phonsie adds with a rueful smile, recalling the wagers lost before and the big one just recouping them at little Listowel.

An unusual view of the water jump at Liverpool. Royal Tan sails over it in the 1952 Grand National.

Royal Tan's bogey fence: the last at Liverpool in the 1952 Grand National again ridden by Phonsie. Note that one of his front feet is almost behind his tail. Amazingly the horse got back onto his feet again without tipping over but finally lost Phonsie and so is recorded officially as 'fell'.

Royal Tan went to Cheltenham that autumn to run in the three mile Cowley Novices Hurdle. He made the crossing from Waterford to Fishguard, but refused to get off the boat. Phonsie recalls 'It took the man in charge a hell of a time, at least an hour, to get him to step off the boat. No way did Royal Tan want to land in England after what had happened to him in the Grand National the previous year. And people say horses don't remember!'

Phonsie O'Brien had some horrible minutes on him during the Cheltenham race. 'The most terrifying race I've ever ridden in my life-time. About twenty-eight runners and there was a grey horse that fell early on. We met him coming towards us on the second circuit, really galloping at us! People were terrified. Bad enough meeting a hurdle at speed. But you meet another horse rushing towards you . . . Anyway, we avoided him and went on and won easy.'

It was Vincent's policy to run his National horses in hurdle races after Liverpool as he hoped this would make them forget about those fences. Royal

Vincent watches his string led by Royal Tan coming up the avenue at Ballydoyle.

Tan was a thinking horse. 'We always had lots of problems with him in the saddling stalls on racetracks,' says Phonsie. 'After his first National he would never walk out of a saddling stall once you'd put the saddle on. You had to get on his back in the stall and ride him out.'

He had other odd refusals too. In those days O'Brien's jumpers were schooled up the gentle slope which lies on the right hand side of the drive to Ballydoyle. Phonsie and the lads, without crash helmets, but with tweed caps turned back to front, would school the jumpers up the hill. Royal Tan would never go down unless he had a lead, and something else. 'All you had to do' Phonsie fondly remembers, 'was to tap him down the mane with a little stick. Just stroke him down the mane. That's all, and he'd go anywhere you'd want him to go. But if you put a guy on him who'd start kicking and driving him, he'd stand straight up on his hind legs and go nowhere.'

Vincent and Paddy Norris adjusting the saddle on Royal Tan on the gallops at Ballydoyle.

T.P. Burns who rode Royal Tan in hurdle races says of him, 'He was a typical Liverpool horse with a lovely kind and generous look. Not too heavily built, and a long-backed horse. He was a real character schooling at home; if you *asked him* to jump he'd bloody kill you.'

Leg trouble kept Royal Tan off the racecourse the next season and Bob Griffin the vet and Vincent had a struggle to repair the damaged tendon. Then in the summer of 1952 he developed splints, too, described by Vincent as 'more than usually troublesome'. Royal Tan was, therefore, off the course between the spring of 1952 until he ran in a hurdle race at Limerick more than one and a half years later in October 1953.

In addition, and at an advanced age, Royal Tan developed sore shins, an inflammation of the membrane between the skin and the cannon bone to which delicate two year olds are often subject. 'I should think,' jokes Dermot O'Brien, 'he should be in the *Guinness Book of Records* for getting sore shins as old as

Early Mist, the one of Vincent's three Grand National winners which he thought was most likely to win a Gold Cup. Bought by Vincent at the dispersal sale of the late J.V. Rank, the man who so dearly wished to win a Grand National, he won at Aintree nine months later for Joe Griffin.

Early Mist (Phonsie O'Brien) schooling over hurdles at home with Knock Hard (Danny O'Sullivan with his cap back to front, no crash helmets in those days . . .) These are now the gallops on the right-hand side of the drive.

he did.' The maddening complaint makes it extremely painful for a horse to stride out, let alone jump. It holds up training until the inflammation disperses and the membrane hardens.

So Royal Tan did not begin the unique sequence of the three different Grand National winners in a row all trained by one man. The record was remarkable and the horses' background even more so, for they were all of contrasting character and build. Their shared ability was to survive four and a half miles of Aintree quicker than any other horse on their day. Even odder, they were all so plagued with mishaps at various stages in training that it seemed unlikely that they would get to the post at Liverpool, let alone win that gruelling gamble.

It was Early Mist who won O'Brien his first Grand National. Before coming to Vincent O'Brien, he was owned by Mr Jimmy Rank, and trained by Tom Dreaper, already famous for training Prince Regent. Poor Mr Rank, the millionaire miller, had three sporting dreams; to win the Epsom Derby, the Grand National and the Waterloo Cup. He won none of them. He died in 1952 and all his horses were sold that summer. Early Mist, bought by a newcomer called Joe Griffin, won the National, trained by Vincent, the very next spring.

Early Mist and stable companions having a pick of grass after work with Phonsie 'rugging up'.

Early Mist, who was by Brumeux out of Southern Dawn, had originally cost 625 guineas as a yearling and had won six of his races when J. V. Rank's executors held a total dispersal at The Curragh on the day of the Irish Derby in June 1952. Wing-Commander Tim Vigors, who would make his name as a bloodstock agent by selling the Aga Khan's Derby winner, Tulyar, to America for a then record price, was writing a column in an Irish newspaper. He described Early Mist as 'a washy chestnut, but a fine, big, raking gelding'. At the Rank dispersal sale Vincent O'Brien bought him for 5,300 guineas on behalf of Mr Joe Griffin who had built a substantial fortune after the war.

'Early Mist wasn't altogether an easy horse to train', Vincent reflects with his quiet under-emphasis. 'After coming to me he gave trouble with a splint, which was so bad that it went right through his cannon bone, as it were, affecting both the inside and the outside of his foreleg. So he had to be fired for it on both sides, which was most unusual. A splint is usually one-sided. It appears as a bony enlargement either on the outside of the cannon bone or on the inside, but not on both. This peg splint did. Any rate, Bob Griffin fired him and did a first rate job on him, and I was able to train him for the 1953 National.'

His struggle back to fitness just fitted Vincent's tight time-table but it did not impress observers. On 7 February, Early Mist reappeared in a handicap hurdle at Leopardstown. He blew up and finished tailed off. After running in the Baldoyle Handicap Chase he went to Naas. He was so tired that, though he won, he staggered across Southern Coup and was disqualified. Tim Vigors wrote, 'For eighteen months I opposed Vincent's confidence in his ability to

Bryan Marshall comfortably wins the 1953 Grand National on Early Mist at 20 to 1.

A rapturous reception from Maurice O'Callaghan who appears to be knocking a police officer aside. Joe Griffin leading Early Mist in followed by his brother. Vincent with a very rare show of emotion on the right. Only jockey Bryan Marshall appears cool.

Early Mist escorted by John Stapleton and his proud owner Joe Griffin is welcomed by the Lord Mayor of Dublin at his civic reception after parading down O'Connell Street.

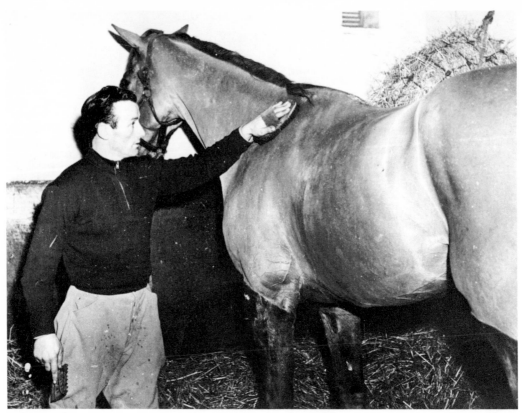

John Stapleton, in Vincent's words 'a great rider of a young horse' did Early Mist. Sadly he died young and was sorely missed at Ballydoyle.

win the Gold Cup with Knock Hard, so it is with some hesitation that I decry the chances of his two Grand National candidates.'

As it turned out, Vigors was again proved wrong and was again man enough to admit it. He became a friend and an associate of the O'Brien clan in that he sold his fine place, Coolmore, to Vincent who was later joined by Robert Sangster and his son-in-law John Magnier who developed it into one of the largest stud complexes in Europe.

Vincent did not consider Early Mist a natural jumper. Bryan Marshall, the jockey chosen to ride him in the National was 'the ideal rider' because says Vincent 'he gathered the horse at each fence and asked him to jump, and Early Mist did it for him. At Valentines he took off a bit far back. But he made it all right. And he brushed the last but he still went on and won by twenty lengths. Early Mist made several blunders during the race because,' says Vincent, tapping his forehead, 'he didn't have it up there. But he had a bit of speed. He wasn't a jumper as such.' This is a remarkable statement to make about a very easy winner of Britain's most difficult steeplechase. But Vincent is firm. 'He had a bit of class and of any of our three National horses, if one was to win a Gold Cup, it would have been him.'

Early Mist did indeed run in the Gold Cup at Cheltenham two years later. Ridden again by Bryan Marshall and strongly fancied by the Irish, he started at 5 to 1, and finished fourth. After snow first, then frost, the ground grew glutinous and the race went to Gay Donald, the 33 to 1 shot, who won at the longest price ever then recorded for jumping's classic steeplechase. But Early Mist's training had suffered further interruptions. After his grim peg splint which might have left him crippled, he then had trouble with his feet.

In 1953, Vincent topped the National Hunt list in England and the year yielded an astonishing treble; after the Gold Cup with Knock Hard, then the Grand National with Early Mist and then the Irish Derby with Chamier. The classic colt belonged to the Vickermans who had launched Vincent into steeplechasing. He bought Chamier's dam carrying the colt. Chamier won on an objection against Premonition, trained by Boyd-Rochfort, who was so incensed at losing the race that he hired a cinema in Newmarket to show his friends the newsreel. 'But this was not the same film,' Jacqueline explains, 'which the stewards saw.'

8

'Up came his neck and smashes me in the nose'

With Early Mist side-lined for the 1954 Grand National, Joe Griffin acquired Royal Tan from the Keoghs to make another attempt at the race. Bryan Marshall had won on Early Mist and so it followed that he took the ride on Royal Tan the following season. 'Bryan had been riding him in his prep races for the National,' says Vincent, 'but somehow he wasn't getting along with the horse.' He then adds one of his masterly understatements: 'We were getting quite concerned about it.' This meant that O'Brien was in a state of acute, but completely disguised, anxiety. He shows almost no emotion in either victory or defeat – 'I don't believe it's right.' This is a principle of behaviour more associated with the archetypal stiff-upper-lipped Englishman than the response expected from a mercurial Celt from one of Ireland's oldest and largest families. 'Quite concerned,' repeats O'Brien. 'In Royal Tan's final race before the National, the Thyestes Chase at Gowran Park, Bryan rode him. Going into the open ditch second time round, Bryan picked him up approaching it and gave him a couple of kicks. Well, the horse simply left Bryan sitting on his backside on the landing side of the fence. Bryan was big enough to say when he came in, "Well, he got rid of me..."

'We were more worried than ever.' Indeed time was fast expiring. The horse's timetable had been planned. There was no time for another prep race. Surely, it was also too late for a change of jockey. Yet the horse had been proved to be a jumper who would blunder if you tried to master him and Bryan Marshall after years of forceful riding was unlikely to change his style. 'Then,' says Vincent, 'my brother Phonsie who had been riding the horse and knew so much about him, said "Why not just tell Bryan to sit still on the horse and leave him be?" So I got permission from Gowran Park to take Royal Tan to school after racing between that meeting and the National. I got Bryan Marshall to come over and told him to leave the horse alone.'

With Royal Tan went his stable companion Churchtown. Bryan Marshall recalls that day's schooling. Carried away with excitement as he passed the stands where some of his mother's friends were watching, Bryan gave Royal Tan a show-off kick as the horse thundered down on the third fence. 'He nearly came down,' Marshall grimaces 'then up came his neck again and smashes me in the nose!'

To O'Brien's firm instructions were now added the horse's own painful strictures. For the rest of the schooling session, big powerful Bryan Marshall sat still as a mouse. Royal Tan jumped perfectly. Vincent remembers happily, 'Bryan came back with a grin from ear to ear and said "Now I've got it".'

In view of Royal Tan's unhappy memories of the track Vincent O'Brien had separated the horse from his four other runners at the 1954 Grand National meeting and sent him to be stabled twenty miles away from the scene, in the peace of the deserted racecourse stables at Haydock Park. Royal Tan's psychological as well as his physical disabilities had to be overcome.

Bryan Marshall started Royal Tan on the wide outside and held him up until he was nearly last. This was directly opposed to contemporary tactics

Everything finally comes good; Royal Tan (far side) wins the 1954 National in a desperate finish with Tudor Line. Note the jockeys' whips and the horses' leading legs ... below as they reach the post with Royal Tan in front, the horses under severe pressure have changed legs and the positions of their feet are identical.

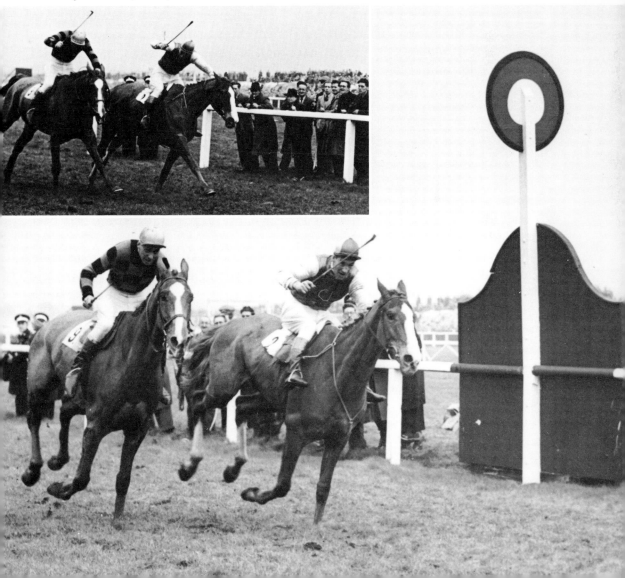

which held that, due to the risk of fallers, you should jump the first four fences as close to the front as possible. On the second circuit, in poor visibility Royal Tan could be glimpsed steadily picking his way through the fallers (twenty starters failed to finish) and making his way to the vanguard jumping magnificently. He was in front between the last two fences – 'Bryan did go on,' says Phonsie, 'in spite of the instructions.'

He jumped his bogey fence perfectly. It was his challenger Tudor Line, carrying a stone less, who screwed at the last fence. Royal Tan fought off Tudor Line's long, strong challenge all the way up the run-in to hold on by a neck. Irish Lizard who started favourite at 15 to 2 was third. Royal Tan's stable companion, Churchtown, ridden by Toss Taaffe, finished fourth. 'He burst a blood vessel,' says Vincent, 'between the last two fences.' Only five of the twenty-nine runners completed the course.

One of the most exciting Nationals ever was described by one journalist: 'The titanic struggle between the two chestnut horses over the last quarter of a mile was racing drama unsurpassed.' Another wrote 'Not since Battleship and Royal Danieli had such a grim tussle had there been such a finish.'

Joe Griffin enjoyed two ecstatic days at Liverpool; his Stroller, one of Royal Tan's stable companions, won the day before, and his Galatian won on National day. 'The Irish,' Jacqueline O'Brien remembers laughing, 'went just delirious.'

One paper commented later, 'Vincent dispelled the belief that had persisted so long in the world of racing, that Ireland is the only place to breed racehorses and that England is the place to train them.' Ireland continued to produce the jockeys to ride them. Bryan Marshall was the first man this century to ride two Liverpool Grand National winners in successive years. (Ernie Piggott, Lester's grandfather, had two victories on Poethlyn in 1918 and 1919, but the first wartime National was run at Gatwick.)

When Joe Griffin went bankrupt, Vincent sold Royal Tan to Prince Aly Khan and it was in the colours of this dashing gentleman that Toss Taaffe rode the old horse, then twelve, to be third to E.S.B.

Royal Tan was then retired and given by Prince Aly Khan to the Duchess of Devonshire, at whose family property, Lismore Castle on the river Blackwater, she would occasionally hack out the famous old horse. The Grand National hero who always insisted that things were done his way enjoyed his retirement, the property of the beautiful Mitford girl who, as portrayed in her sister Nancy's books, had always insisted she would marry a Duke.

Comparing his first two Grand National winners, Vincent says, 'Royal Tan was a brilliant natural jumper, so clever. He was like a cat and all his jockey had to do was sit on him. Early Mist was exactly the opposite and needed assistance from his jockey. He was the classier of the two.'

New jockeys for Royal Tan – Liz and Sue on board. Jacqueline holds future trainer David in the window.

Between Royal Tan's victory in 1954 and his third in 1956, Vincent produced his third successive winner of the National in Quare Times in 1955.

'The English,' says Vincent drily 'used to think that the name was Latin and pronounced it "Quaray Timees", but in fact Quare Times was called after a famous greyhound owned by Bill Quinn of Killenaule near the horse's birth-place.'

Quare Times was bred by Phil Sweeney, a great Irish breeder, living near Thurles in Co. Tipperary. In the early 1980s Sweeney was selling a number of top class horses like the Champion Hurdler Gaye Brief, and Gaye Chance to Fred and Mercy Rimell. 'Not the easiest man to buy from,' says Mercy 'but beautiful horses when you can get them.'

When Quare Times was a yearling in 1947 Sweeney sent him to the Balls-bridge Sales. He was beautifully bred for jumping (by Artist's Son out of the

The race which Vincent said Quare Times would win more than a year before: ridden by Mr 'Bunny' Cox, Quare Times lands a gamble in the four mile National Hunt Chase at Cheltenham, 3 March 1954.

Flamenco mare Lavenco) and was an obvious store type. As such he was bought by Mrs Cecily Welman for 300 guineas. 'A goodish price for a yearling at that time' comments Vincent, 'She gelded him and let him run out.' Mrs Welman allowed the youngster to grow and develop at her home near Mullingar in County Westmeath. She had the horse broken at home and only sent him to Vincent when he was five. Quare Times was six years old before he first ran and in that year he was unplaced in all his five races: on the flat, in an amateur maiden hurdle, and then in a novice chase at Gowran Park. He then ran into training difficulties and failed to win between November 1952 and January 1954. It was an inauspicious start.

'He had trouble with his knees, and various other bits in between,' Vincent says, 'which didn't make him the easiest horse in the world to train.' When he returned to Gowran Park to win a novice chase, Vincent O'Brien had been correct when, looking at the big horse who stood nearly seventeen hands, he shook his head and murmured to Mrs Welman, 'He will take a long, long time.'

The Grand National 1955 run on appalling ground. Quare Times ridden by Pat Taaffe (no. 10) landing over Becher's first time round. Note how deeply the horse's legs go into the mud.

Quare Times sails over the Canal Turn on his way to victory, Aintree 1955. Pat Taaffe is riding exceptionally short for a jockey in those days though his father had advised him to let his leathers down.

By the winter of 1953/54 the horse's strength had grown to match his size, and Vincent told Mrs Welman ten months ahead of the race, 'This horse is the right type for Cheltenham's "Amateur Grand National" – the four mile National Hunt Chase for novices. He will win the race,' he said. He won so impressively that racegoers that day, felt they had seen yet another Grand National winner for O'Brien.

But Quare Times suffered another set-back before the National. This time it was a bruised foot.

When the entries came out Quare Times was only one of four of Vincent's entries: he had included Early Mist and Royal Tan, the last two National winners now belonging respectively to Mr John Dunlop and Prince Aly Khan.

The ground was so wet that the Grand National was in doubt. Near the water jump the ground was actually flooded and the jump was dolled off. At noon there were still fears that the race might be cancelled. Vincent had said after Cheltenham that he had hopes for Quare Times in the National provided the going was not heavy. The rain sluiced down from clouds so low that one Irish wit exclaimed, 'There's hardly a falling space for the rain.'

Optimism about Quare Times' chance steadily ebbed away. Early Mist (Bryan Marshall) at 9 to 1 started second favourite to Copp (7 to 1). Royal Tan, ridden by Dave Dick, carried 12st 4lb on his eleven-year-old back. The going was so wretchedly wet, that even many spectators considered the race should be abandoned. The horses stood fetlock-deep in mud and water. The jockeys, delayed at the start for six minutes by an unruly outsider, crouched miserably in the rain.

'But in Pat Taaffe,' says Vincent, 'we had the ideal combination for the horse. Quare Times was a free galloping horse. He simply jumped over the top of all those fences. Pat rode very short for somebody as tall as he is. He sat up his neck and they got along beautifully together.'

It was a Taaffe family affair. In the stands were Pat's mother and father and his brand new fiancée, Molly Lyon. In the race, too, was Pat's brother, 'Toss', riding his father's first runner in the Grand National, Carey's Cottage. Mr Tom Taaffe used to disapprove of Pat's riding style. 'Once I had the notion of breaking him out of it, but he stuck to his own way and he was right.' The O'Brien's believe that Mr Taaffe told Pat to let down his leathers at least for the National. 'Instead,' says Jacqueline, 'I think Pat pulled them up a hole!'

Tudor Line, beaten by Royal Tan the previous year, headed Quare Times over the third last fence. 'But George Slack knew,' Jacqueline remembers, 'from the smile on Pat's face that he could beat him whenever he liked.' And

Mrs Welman with Quare Times in the winner's enclosure at Liverpool. She was an amazingly lucky owner for this was her first racehorse and first runner in the National. Perhaps she was lucky not to lose something out of her open handbag!

The winning combination at home. Left to right *Dermot, Major Bill Welman, Vincent, Cecily Welman and Pat Taaffe.*

'The feat of all time': three different Grand National winners in consecutive years mixed up in a family snapshot. Vincent carries Liz and holds Early Mist (left) and Royal Tan, Jacqueline holds Sue and Quare Times.

so he did, by twelve lengths. Vincent says proudly, 'The horse never put a foot wrong and Pat won easily on him.' Third, four lengths behind Tudor Line, came 'Toss' Taaffe on Carey's Cottage.

It was an all-Irish victory: for Quare Times was bred, owned, trained and ridden by them. And five of the first six horses home were Irish-bred.

Quare Times returned to Dublin by boat. He was paraded through Mrs Welman's local town, Mullingar, led by two bands and rapturously escorted by seven thousand local celebrants. 'He had two more receptions,' says Jacqueline, 'one in Thurles and one here in Cashel before Vincent finally got him back in his box . . .'

In the history of the Grand National, no other trainer has ever saddled three different winners in three successive years. Vincent's three were so very different horses, all of whom were beset by serious training problems.

No one knew more about the Grand National winners' ailments than Vincent O'Brien's vet, the redoubtable Bob Griffin, bluff-faced and bluff in character and a key figure still in Vincent O'Brien's operation. It is Bob who now

Quare Times in the main yard at Ballydoyle with Liz and Sue.

Vincent's three Grand National winners parading somewhat excitedly at the Royal Dublin Horse Show ridden by their jockeys. Bryan Marshall on Early Mist leads Phonsie on Royal Tan and Pat Taaffe on Quare Times.

examines the multi-million yearlings in Keeneland and the cheaper half-million dollar ones too.

Bob Griffin's connection with the O'Brien family stretches back to the days of Vincent's father Dan, who used to bring his horses up to race at The Curragh where Bob Griffin lives. 'Dan had two very good horses, Astrologer and Astrometer and I think Vincent learned an awful lot from his father.'

His praise for Vincent's training of the three Grand National winners is resounding. 'During their periods of preparation all three gave serious trouble necessitating severe treatment. And the treatment necessitated certain periods of convalescence. I used to say to Vincent, "If we do this he'll have to have so much rest." In each case Vincent would say "Well, now, I want to gallop them on a certain date and give them their first race on a certain date to have them in peak condition for the National. Can you do it?" I'd say, "If you can give me that period, I think I can." The decision was made immediately. What had to be done was done. And they all won the National.

'The dates when the horses came out and walked, the dates they trotted and cantered, the dates they galloped were practically to the hour, the dates which had been already arranged. The training programme was different for each horse. And I always thought how amazing it was that Vincent was able to say how one horse would have a different preparation to another, to have him in peak condition for the National. When I would suggest to Vincent, "this would be a good idea for the horses," if he agreed, expense never mattered. Nothing ever stood in the way of what was best for the horses.'

Bob Griffin adds a revealing light on the trainer's philosophy, which may surprise those who believe O'Brien only bothers with the crème. 'All through the years I've felt that Vincent always liked to think that there was good in every horse. He never discarded the horse and said "You're no damn good." His attention to the least important horse in the stable always appeared to me just the same as it was to the best.'

No one knows better this aspect of a trainer's troubled life than the veterinary surgeon frequently called to come down from The Curragh or to advise on the telephone, as in the case of those alarming incidents which developed at Epsom with two of O'Brien's Derby winners on the eve of their classics.

9

'I have this American and he wants to buy yearlings'

After the Grand National victories Vincent moved towards higher class flat horses. He now had his own training establishment which he was making one of the best in the world. It is difficult for a trainer to run a top class stable with both flat and national hunt horses so it was inevitable that Vincent, intent on providing the best conditions for training horses decided to concentrate on the flat where the really big money flows not only on the race-course but from the stud farms.

He needed to find new owners. Vincent says: 'I found out early in life that you had to move out and meet people, they don't come to you. With that in mind, with no orders, and no-one in particular to buy for, I set out in 1955 for Tattersalls' September Sales, then held at Doncaster during the St Leger meetings. If you're in the business, you'd better be around where things are happening.' The thread which drew Vincent O'Brien to those particular Doncaster Sales was extremely fortuitous.

O'Brien's contact in Doncaster was the Yorkshire solicitor Hedley Nicholson, with whom he had sometimes stayed when running horses in the north of England. Nicholson was not a patron of the Turf in that he did not own racehorses, but he was one of that sporting band who enthusiastically follow racing, know the form, and enjoy the occasional bet. His bets on the O'Brien raiders at Cheltenham had proved resoundingly profitable, and a warm friendship developed between the English lawyer and the Tipperary trainer. Hedley Nicholson was also a close friend of the then head of the National Farmers' Union in Britain, James Turner, afterwards elevated to the peerage for his services to agriculture as Lord Netherthorpe. In 1964, Nicholson's daughter, Belinda, married Lord Netherthorpe's heir.

On a visit to America with a group of farmers, Turner, who was not a racing man, had stayed in the Barclay Hotel in Philadelphia, which was owned by an extremely rich American. 'This was John McShain,' Vincent explains, 'whose father had emigrated from Ireland and raised a family in Philadelphia. There John worked his way up in the building contracting business to become one of the biggest men in the United States. He built the Pentagon and restored the White House, brick by numbered brick, also putting in a floor underneath it.'

The American gave James Turner and his group a typically good time in

The move to the flat, Vincent racing in Ireland with the very elegant Lord Dunraven, one of his early owners.

Philadelphia. So Turner, when thanking him, asked McShain to let him know the next time he came to England. When McShain later told Turner he would be over in September, Turner regretfully had to be away in Italy. So he asked Hedley Nicholson to look after McShain at Doncaster.

'When I met him at the races,' Vincent continues, 'Hedley was quite excited. He said to me "Look here, I have this American and he wants to buy yearlings!" I thought to myself: "Well, I've heard that one before. But however, maybe something will come out of it this time . . ."'

'I was a little slow to jump at it,' Vincent now reflects, 'for I'd heard all about rich Americans and yearlings, and I took it with a pinch of salt. But, any rate, Hedley Nicholson introduced me to John McShain at the sales on the first evening after racing. McShain was quite definite that he wanted to buy some yearlings, and that I should buy them for him. But his idea was that he would take the yearlings immediately to America.' McShain intended they should be trained in the United States, which was not at all what Vincent wanted. He bought the yearlings as if for racing in America, but he set about trying to convince his new patron that this would be a mistake. 'During the sales over the next few days I introduced him to various people, breeders mostly, and when they heard he was going to take the horses immediately to America they all said "For heaven's sake, don't do that! Keep them here for at least a year or two and you'll give them a much better chance." So he listened to what all these people had to say.'

The rich man made a cautious reappraisal. He would at least let Vincent take the five yearlings back to Ireland to be broken in and made. He would consider how well it went and decide later when to take them back to the United States. John McShain was careful, an outstanding businessman. He critically examined the economics of racing and Vincent learned from him. He told Vincent that as a boy he always kept his pocket money to lend to his brothers when they had run out of theirs. He lent it with interest.

Vincent now established his own close connection with the distant millionaire. He used the Irish postal service and the U.S. mail. He had discovered that John McShain liked nothing better than to receive detailed reports on his horses from the green fields of remote Tipperary to his busy city office. 'So I took a great deal of trouble from then on,' Vincent smiles, 'in corresponding with him! He enjoyed getting the reports and he promptly replied to every one. He banged them back! He told me he would read my letters first in his office, then he'd take them home with him and read them all over again with his wife, Mary.' O'Brien points a moral to anyone aspiring to a career in which private clients must be satisfied. 'I've no doubt at all that our association would never have reached the heights it did, if I hadn't taken the trouble to correspond with him.'

The letters worked. The yearlings stayed and became two year olds. They ran. O'Brien produced his first winner for McShain with the two year old, York Fair, at a racecourse in the little town of Mallow of which the American had never heard and which he could probably have bought for breakfast that August Bank Holiday. But the day was doubly happy for Vincent. 'I motored straight to Dublin from the races and in the nursing home I found my first son, David, just born and in his cot. Rather a coincidence . . .'

York Fair was 'quite a useful horse and won some nice races, including the Goucestershire Hurdle at Cheltenham,' but the star of the party, Ballymoss, did not immediately show his quality. The great horse who would win the Irish Derby, the St Leger, the King George VI and Queen Elizabeth Stakes at Ascot, and the Prix de l'Arc de Triomphe, started his career by getting beaten in a maiden race on The Curragh in July and then finishing only second at humble Mallow in September, 1956. 'He was beaten by Bell Bird,' Vincent adds, 'the great grandam of Ardross.' No one that day can have imagined that they had seen a horse capable of even running in one classic, let alone winning two. And a further disappointment lay ahead before that first season's end. Having won a race at Leopardstown in September, Ballymoss was sent to The Curragh a month later to run in a two year old stayers' plate. The ground had turned very heavy, Ballymoss was beaten into second place and Vincent was very disappointed. 'I hadn't realised then how unsuited he was to heavy ground.'

Following his win at Leopardstown in September Vincent wrote to John McShain on 1 October 1956:

'It was great to be able to send you a cable last night saying that Ballymoss had won for you. He put up a very nice performance indeed and the prospects for next season look bright ... I think Ballymoss' future depends on the improvement that we hope he will continue to make. We know that he stays and he has definite possibilities as a classic horse, although I would not say this in more than a whisper at the moment. I wondered what you and Mary would think of a try at the English Derby at the end of May before taking the colt to America? If he won it of course he would be a very valuable horse; his stud value could be in the region of $500,000. I suggest this as he is progressing so well here, and he has a long future ahead of him at three, four and five. If he went to America, and by any chance did not prove a success in different racing conditions there, we probably would be regretting not having let him achieve something worth while here. I hate to be too optimistic at this stage – however, think it over, and if you like the idea you had better make some holiday plans!'

A horse who loved soft ground and whose career was entwined with Ballymoss now makes a somewhat muted entrance on the stage. There was no great optimism at Ballydoyle about the arrival in 1954 of a 'biggish filly with a lot of scope' by Sayajirao out of Bright Lady. But this filly would turn out to be the wonderful mare, Gladness. And there was a connecting thread in the filly's breeding: Bright Lady, 'a top staying filly' in Vincent's words, was own sister to Good Days who had landed half of that original autumn double.

Gladness was a year older than Ballymoss but, being big and backward and having a patient owner as well as a patient trainer, she ran only once as a two year old and that not until November, 1955, when, unfancied, she ran unplaced in a maiden plate on The Curragh. Not only was Gladness' family slow-maturing but she had over-round joints. The summer of her two year old season was dry. The combination of firm ground and round joints made her hard to train before the autumn and, to make things more difficult, she got loose one day at exercise, galloped back to the yard and slipped up in it, injuring herself. She did not run at all through her three year old summer either. 'The ground had been very hard and her fetlock joints would not have stood on the firm going.'

At last she was dispatched to Manchester to contest a maiden plate. 'There was nothing left in Ireland at that late stage in which she could run,' Vincent comments. The season was ending and it was 16 November, 1956, when she ran in the 1½ mile Broughton Plate at Manchester, ridden by T.P. Burns. Vincent and the stable had a great deal of money on her, and Dermot travelled with her to get the wager on. Vincent is given to understatement. In the case of Gladness' first appearance that year on a racecourse, he refers to his wager as 'a substantial gamble'. The maiden filly trotted up, having been backed down by an avalanche of money to 8 to 11 on. It had been put about that the filly was crossing to England only to return to her breeder's stud in Warwickshire. 'Gladness was the medium of a very big betting gamble,' T.P. Burns reflects. 'It was a hush-hush sort of a job. She left here as if she was going back to Sydney McGregor's place, d'you see!'

There had naturally been a searching trial first for this maiden three year old who arrived, in T.P.'s words, 'a big scrawny t'ing'. Burns remembers, 'We took her to Gowran Park racecourse to gallop with a good batch of horses. And she did it well. As for the race, it was just a question of how much money they could get on. A field of about thirty maidens. And she trots up.'

(pp. 84–85): *The growth of Ballydoyle. An aerial photograph in 1959 shows the covered ride on the right and the main yard and also the long gallops in the distance. Below by 1983 two additional yards have been added and also the huge barns which are used for exercise in bad weather.*

(opposite): *Ballymoss and T.P. Burns going out for the first race of his three-year old career at The Curragh. His connections were sharply disappointed by his running.*

10

'It's a pity I didn't have you shot years ago!'

Gladness loved soft ground. Ballymoss at the start of the following season once again demonstrated that he did not act on it. The colt's and the filly's careers drew close together, for as each rose to the top of their profession, the colt would run when it was good to firm and the filly when it was good to soft. This would lead to bitterness, outrage and the loss of an owner. But, as Jacqueline O'Brien emphasises, 'Vincent always puts the horse first.'

Two-and-a-half months later at The Curragh again. Ballymoss easily wins the Irish Derby having been second three weeks earlier in the Epsom Derby.

Ballymoss 'ran deplorably' in his first three year old race, the Madrid Free Handicap. 'He finished right out the back door,' Vincent remembers. T. P. Burns, who rode him, says, 'The horse was hating it.' The ground was heavy. T. P. adds, 'We were all a little worried that he was always looking at mares. We wondered whether the bugger should be gelded.'

Ballymoss was by Mossborough, whose stock were not achieving great successes. Furthermore, their honesty and courage were in doubt. After Ballymoss' marked displeasure in the Madrids, Judge Frank Tuthill, a great expert, came to Vincent and asked ominously, 'Do you know that over in England they are now gelding all the Mossboroughs?'

To these psychological doubts was now added physical injury. Ballymoss bruised a foot. His training was impeded. It was without hope of any sort that he was allowed to accompany Gladness to the post for the Trigo Stakes in May. The filly was red hot favourite at even money. The unconsidered Ballymoss started the rank outsider but he was entered for the Epsom Derby and this was the last opportunity of giving him an outing to see if he was up to running in the great race.

The ground was fast, 'which was all against Gladness,' says Vincent. 'Also they went no pace. And up comes Ballymoss to win at 20 to 1.'

After this a decision had to be made whether to send Ballymoss across to

Epsom to run in the English Derby. 'There'd been discussion,' says T. P. Burns 'between the Boss, Dermot and me whether Ballymoss should take his chance, for the Trigo had, at least, put him in the picture.'

The decision to run was based on a mixed gallop which took place on The Curragh. 'I rode Ballymoss,' says T. P. 'I'd been associated with him from day one. In the gallop there were three or four of Paddy Prendergast's horses, and two of the McGraths' and we galloped one mile and three furlongs on the inside of the course. Ballymoss didn't just beat them ... he *trotted* over them! We were all amazed. It was then confirmed that he would take his chance at Epsom and he ran a very, very good race, just to be beaten by Crepello.'

To this Vincent adds quietly, 'he had a very short preparation for the Derby, due to that stone bruise in his foot. And I'm sure that he was a much better horse three or four weeks later on the day of the Irish Derby which he won very easily.' His price for the Epsom Derby had been 33 to 1. For the Irish classic he started 4 to 9 on ...

Ballymoss was beaten by the going again when he went to York for the Voltigeur Stakes and was defeated by Brioche. 'Heavy ground – typical York ground after rain,' said Vincent, and aimed the horse for his next classic, the St Leger.

Come Leger day it was raining again, and the O'Brien camp's spirits declined in the drizzle. But Doncaster's Town Moor lies on sandy soil, quite unlike the heavy going at York. The ground was wet for the St Leger, but not holding. Ballymoss went through it without difficulty and won with T. P. Burns riding, at 8 to 1.

T. P. recalls that the first question the American millionaire asked him at Doncaster after winning the St Leger was, 'How much money am I going to win?' T. P. comments philosophically, 'That's sad when you have just won a second classic out of your very first crop of runners.'

Vincent tells how after the Leger, he told John McShain that a full sister to Ballymoss was coming up at the Doncaster Sales that evening. He recommended McShain to buy her. The American declined, 'I don't believe lightning strikes twice in the same place,' he said. The filly, Minehaha, was second in the Irish Oaks. It was resolved to keep Ballymoss in training as a four year old and Gladness continued as a five year old. The two made 1958 a year of complete triumph for Ballydoyle. They swept all before them, winning in one glorious summer the Coronation Cup at Epsom, the Ascot Gold Cup, the Eclipse, the King George VI and Queen Elizabeth Stakes, the Goodwood Cup, the Ebor at York and, finally, the Prix de l'Arc de Triomphe.

Two new jockeys took the stage for the pair – Scobie Breasley for Ballymoss and Lester Piggott for the mare, Gladness. John McShain had been anxious to find English jockeys for his good horses. He wasn't familiar with the European

Royal Ascot 1958. Gladness and Lester Piggott in the McShain colours come in after winning the Gold Cup.

system of retained jockeys. He couldn't see why your Irish jockey should ride in England where – he thought – he had to be at a disadvantage. In America all jockeys have agents who approach the trainers and owners to book the best available horse for the jockeys they work for.

Scobie Breasley proved a great success. Jacqueline remarks to Vincent, 'You had great affinity with him.' Vincent nods. 'For me he was marvellous. He would wait and wait. Your horse had the easiest possible race. He'd just put him in front on the post. He was so gentle with horses.'

With Lester began the association that was to be so outstandingly successful between trainer and jockey. Lester Piggott always remembers the long and explicit instructions given him by Vincent before his first ride for his stable on Gladness, in the Ascot Gold Cup. He makes an amusing story of it.

'Well, I was very concerned,' says Vincent, who sees nothing funny about it at all, 'and I told him so. I felt I was entitled to tell him how she should be ridden, especially as he had not ridden her before. And I did so.'

Both Ballymoss and Gladness were sent across to Ascot for the King George

John McShain's wife Mary leads in Ballymoss after his St Leger win. T.P. Burns in the saddle again.

Ballymoss is led in after winning the King George VI and Queen Elizabeth Stakes at Ascot 1958.

VI and Queen Elizabeth. 'Ballymoss to run if it was firm; Gladness if it was soft,' says Vincent. 'It was firm: So I ran Ballymoss.'

Jacqueline relates how Gladness was bought by John McShain in the middle of her career to run in the Ballymoss colours. 'Her original owner was told she'd run at Ascot in the Gold Vase. So the owner's wife went and bought all her Ascot outfit. We made all the arrangements for them, and the travelling

John McShain being congratulated by Queen Elizabeth the Queen Mother after Ballymoss' easy victory in the £23,000 King George VI and Queen Elizabeth Stakes.

'The most impressive winner of a handicap I've ever seen' said bookmaker William Hill. Gladness carrying 9 stone 7lb including a youthful Lester Piggott canters away with the £10,000 Ebor Handicap at York, 20 August 1958.

In York's attractive unsaddling enclosure Vincent holds his great mare while John Rickman of the Daily Mail tries anxiously to obtain a quote. Maurice O'Callaghan the headman stands on the right.

arrangements for the mare. Then Vincent said suddenly, "The ground is too hard. I'm not going to run her." '

'So the owner was quite upset. He said "That doesn't suit me at all. We've asked friends to come. We've got the box tickets. We've done everything." But Vincent said, "It doesn't matter. The mare must not run." '

Vincent was now in danger of losing Gladness. Fortunate timing again, and his gentle persuasion averted the threat. He explains: 'The Irish Derby was ten days later and John McShain came over to see Ballymoss win it. Next day I told him "If Gladness can be bought, I would advise you to have her." The deal was completed in a day or so.'

After the troublesome Ascot decision both horses were sent to York for the

Vincent's favourite photograph of his favourite mare, Gladness, ridden by Lester Piggott.

Ebor. 'This time the ground came up soft so Ballymoss was not started. The crowd at York complained because Ballymoss was not running and so I paraded him for them. Gladness ran under 9st 7lb and won by six lengths in a canter,' says Vincent with satisfaction. Then he proudly adds 'I remember William Hill, the big bookie, saying to me at York the following year that the performance Gladness put up that day was the greatest he had seen in a handicap in his lifetime.'

Vincent then gives a small smile. William Hill, a powerful man who inspired awe among those who opposed him in the shadowy world of big betting, had said something else of a quite different nature to Vincent during that York

In spite of Vincent's fears that heavy rain would prove Ballymoss' undoing, the horse wins the 1958 Prix de L'Arc de Triomphe ridden by Scobie Breasley.

meeting. Hill, together with tough men of all sorts, including released prisoners had joined the hated 'Black and Tans', that paramilitary force raised in Britain to try to crush the Irish after World War I. Against this background the massive Hill saw fit at that York meeting to make his idea of a joke to Vincent O'Brien. He made it in front of two pillars of the English training profession, Noel Murless and Cecil Boyd-Rochfort. Hill, the ex-Black and Tan, remarked to O'Brien, 'It's a pity I didn't have you shot years ago.' Vincent tolerantly explains that this was not only for the bets he had personally won from Hill. 'There were a lot of other people who had won money from him on my horses from the days of Cheltenham onwards.'

Ballymoss' preparation for 'The Arc' was going well. The horse prospered, the ground was dry. 'He had a good trip to France, and I was very confident of his chance. There was ante-post betting on the race and I had quite a substantial bet on him. I'd asked Peter O'Sullevan, in fact, to place the bet for me. Then, just about noon on the day of the race, it started to rain. It poured. It never let up. I went and found Peter O'Sullevan and I asked him, "Is there any hope of laying off my bet?" So Peter said he would have a try. Then Scobie rode something for Alec Head in the second race and it finished last. Scobie came in looking depressed. He shook his head at me, attributing the poor performance to the state of the ground. And I thought, "Oh, my God!"

'Then I met Peter O'Sullevan again just before the "Arc" and he said, "I'm

Scobie Breasley unsaddling Ballymoss after winning the Arc. Vincent's hat is soaked by the deluge ... and the smiling winning jockey is escorted by a stern official to be presented to the President of France.

sorry, but I'm afraid I couldn't do anything about that – it's too late. It's impossible here anyhow" – so I thought, well, that's that, and I forgot about my bet.'

Then Scobie comforted Vincent. 'Don't worry,' he said, 'the horse handled soft ground in the Leger and if I find he can't handle the going, you know I won't knock him about.' Vincent adds, 'How true this was.' Then he says simply, 'the horse ran and he won.' He explains why. 'A year or two later I discovered that well over a century ago the French Jockey Club had reclaimed some of the land which is now Longchamp from what had been a backwash of the river Seine. That would be the first two furlongs (before they meet the rising ground) and then the last three furlongs of the 1½ mile course. This ground consists of silt washed up over the years. It makes for very light ground conditions which horses can get through without being held by it. The soil is flying, you think the ground is terrible. But it's not holding them at all, so Ballymoss got through it without any problem.'

After the Arc victory, Ballymoss was sent to America to run for the Washington International, John Shapiro's brainchild, at Laurel Park. John McShain was naturally especially keen to watch his great horse win on American soil. Hopes were buoyant and Scobie Breasley was superbly over-optimistic. 'He was so very relaxed about it,' says Vincent, 'that he said to me "The horse will win this swimming up a river!" And he rode a very relaxed race, too, I'm afraid. It was the only race Scobie ever rode for me where I could say he might have done better.'

His relaxed tactics were quite unsuited to the sharp seven furlongs circuit of Laurel Park. Down the back straight he was still back in mid-field. Eddie Arcaro shouted across to Scobie, 'How you goin'?'

'O.K.,' said Scobie.

'You want to be kickin' on then,' urged Arcaro. But it was too late.

'Scobie might have done better,' Vincent repeats, and then immediately puts his jockey's side. 'On the other hand, it may not have been his fault. The sun was low in the sky as they rounded the bend past the stands. Scobie was tracking Lester who was suddenly so blinded by the sun that his horse galloped into the privet hedge on the inside which then took the place of a running rail on the turf course. Both horses became unbalanced and crashed into the horses outside them. Of course, they both lost much valuable ground. Lester's horse cried enough. As for Ballymoss, by the time Scobie got him balanced and running again, the field was halfway down that short back stretch. There's no doubt Ballymoss suffered a shock from the incident. Probably from then on he didn't give his true running. But John McShain,' Vincent finishes sadly, 'was terribly disappointed.'

Gladness remained in training as a six year old but one of her tendons had

Vincent with Ballymoss. Early in his three-year-old career Vincent was gloomily advised 'Over in England they are gelding all the Mossboroughs'.

started to go. Bob Griffin had already fired her fetlocks to strengthen them. The courageous mare never forgave Griffin for so doing and immediately showed her dislike of him every time he ventured into her box.

Vincent, in spite of these physical disabilities, began to prepare the mare for an attempt on the King George VI and Queen Elizabeth Stakes at Ascot in July 1959. Up till then he felt that she had been considered only a stayer. He wished to prove to the world that she could lie up with and beat the best colts over the Derby distance.

She got through her prep race at Phoenix Park in April, and won it. But when Bob Griffin came to examine her, he wagged his head gloomily over her tendon. 'She'll stand only one more race,' he warned Vincent. So it proved. She finished second to Alcide in the 'King George VI' at Ascot, 'which,' says Vincent, 'was a tremendous performance considering the poor preparation I could give her.'

It would be pleasant to record that in their retirements, the two great running mates, Ballymoss and Gladness, whose careers had flowered together like climbing roses, overlapping as the weather changed and directions altered, would mate together and produce a festoon of great winners. They were indeed mated several times. They produced an able horse in Ballyjoy, 'But,' says Vincent, 'he was not over-enthusiastic.' The two also produced the 1966 Irish Oaks winner, Merrymate, but she was their only classic winning offspring.

Vincent O'Brien now wishes that Gladness had been sent to a stallion with more quality than Ballymoss. He cites the example of Meld, winner of the fillies' Triple Crown, the 1,000 Guineas, the Oaks and the St Leger, who, when mated with Charlottesville, produced the 1966 Derby winner, Charlottown. 'Charlottesville was an effeminate horse and suited the strong and rugged Meld. But Gladness was a big, rather plain, masculine mare,' says Vincent, 'and Mossborough got big, strong and rather plain horses.'

In addition to the manifold successes of Ballymoss and Gladness, John McShain established for Vincent one of the most important threads in the O'Brien story. For he introduced Vincent to Keeneland Sales on the edge of Lexington in Kentucky's Bluegrass by saying, 'Come to Keeneland and help me buy some yearlings.'

'In fact,' says Vincent regretfully, 'the yearlings I bought for him at Keeneland remained in America. It was only the horses I bought for him in Ireland and England that I was to train. But it was my introduction, that visit to Keeneland in 1958, to the American sales and to more American owners. And one of these was Raymond Guest, whom Tim Vigors had introduced me to at Laurel Park.'

It was for Raymond Guest, American Ambassador to Dublin, that Vincent O'Brien would buy and train his first winner of the Epsom Derby, Larkspur.

11

'They asked me a lot of questions and they stole my hat!'

Raymond Guest, a member of the American Establishment, had already met Vincent O'Brien at the Keeneland Sales on a steaming hot July day. He was an Anglophile, would become American ambassador to Ireland, and was very much a steeplechasing man. This love never left him. He possessed the first steeplechaser since the great Golden Miller to win both the Cheltenham Gold Cup and the Liverpool Grand National. Red Rum's million fans worldwide will not forget L'Escargot in the pale blue hood which represented part of the Guest colours, creeping up on and defeating their adored hero at Aintree in 1975.

It was as a steeplechasing man that Raymond Guest first approached O'Brien. The four Gold Cups and the three Grand Nationals convinced the vastly rich American that O'Brien was the greatest jumping trainer in Europe. Here was a man in Co. Tipperary who might accomplish one of Guest's British aims – victory at the top at Cheltenham or Liverpool. He sent Vincent an American chaser called Virginus, 'with the idea that we might win a Grand National,' says O'Brien, 'but he was awfully slow and I think we won just one race with him.'

However, the notion now came to Raymond Guest that it would be pleasant to win the Epsom Derby. He mentioned this to Tom Cooper, one of the world's top bloodstock judges, who directs the BBA (Ireland) and to Tim Vigors who had achieved sudden *éclat* by getting for 'Bull' Hancock the Aga Khan's Derby winner, Tulyar, for the then colossal amount of £250,000. Vincent had already established his close friendship with 'Bull' Hancock, the master of Claiborne, near Paris, Kentucky. Both Cooper and Vigors were friends of the O'Briens.

Guest's approach was originally to Tom Cooper – would he look out for a yearling with the pedigree and class to be a possible Derby winner?

'Tom Cooper talked to me about it,' says Vincent, 'and I was asked if I would train the purchase.'

Three threads drew O'Brien towards his first Epsom Derby winner: Guest's passion for steeplechasing and thus his admiration for O'Brien; O'Brien's friendship with the two Irish bloodstock agents; and John McShain's insistence that Vincent should make his first visit in 1958 to what Keeneland's senatorial

president 'Ted' Bassett, calls 'the Mecca of the thoroughbred world.' Such were the connections. But the colt was found in Ireland.

Tom Cooper took Vincent to look at a yearling of Phillip Love's, bred by him on his small, select stud in Co. Dublin. 'His stock,' Vincent reports, 'usually made the top prices at the Ballsbridge Sales.' The yearling they went to examine was by Never Say Die, who had won the 1954 Derby for another sporting American, Robert Sterling Clark a scion of the Singer Sewing Machine plutocracy, and whose brother Ambrose had been a keen supporter of British and American steeplechasing, winning the 1933 Aintree Grand National with Kellsboro' Jack. (The horse ran in the name of his wife Florence to whom Ambrose sold the horse for luck and for one pound.)

In 1960, when Vincent and Tom Cooper were looking at Mr Love's distinctly small, but well-made yearling, the wretched record of Derby winners in failing to sire Derby winners was not a public talking point. At that point not one Derby winner had been sired by a Derby winner since Mahmoud won in 1936.

'Larkspur as a colt was well-made,' says Vincent. 'He was a nice horse, but there was definitely a question as to whether he was going to grow big enough.' He goes further: 'His height was the one thing against him.'

With Tom Cooper, the quiet man whom Vincent would be asking twenty years later to make the preliminary inspections of the Kentucky yearlings, the other offerings at Ballsbridge were examined. 'But we decided that this was the horse we should buy. And we bought him. He made the highest price of the sale, somewhere between 12,000 or 13,000 guineas.' Twenty-four years later Vincent's memory scores again: the Never Say Die yearling made 12,200 guineas. The price was a record for a Ballsbridge yearling and created some excitement.

Vincent smiles. 'One famous English trainer was at the sales that day, and gave his opinion that the yearling was too small!'

Vincent does not greatly enthuse over Larkspur's first season. 'He was quite a useful two-year-old.' He makes one notable exception. 'He finished the season by running a good race in the Timeform Gold Cup and Tommy Gosling, who rode him, was very adamant that had he had a clearer run, he would have been close. Tommy was very positive about him and Tommy was a good judge.' Such perspicacity was not shared by the grandstand experts of the English Press. The colt finished seventh to Miralgo, owned by the British-born Geneva-based banker, Gerry Oldham, whose Citadel Stud has produced a host of winners, latterly all French-trained.

Timeform, the new sponsors of the race, dismissed his running in their valuable two year old race. 'He made little show in the Timeform Gold Cup,'

The late Maurice O'Callaghan, headman for over thirty years, doing the feeds at Ballydoyle.

they state in their piece on the little chestnut colt a year later. They rated him indeed 2 lb inferior to the little known French filly La Sega whose summary, by alphabetical accident, follows the Larkspur one. Raymond Guest and the O'Briens took a happier view. They returned to London by train and a good deal of champagne was drunk during the journey. 'By the time we got to London', says Vincent, 'we had next year's Derby winner!' They did not seriously suppose so, but the joys of racing lie in travelling hopefully.

Gerry Oldham, however, is a quiet character whose life is a private thing. He too was travelling back on the same train. 'He sat huddled in his corner, reading his paper,' Vincent remembers, 'and Raymond couldn't get over that. "The man who had just won the Timeform, sitting huddled in a corner and not celebrating!" Raymond exclaimed.'

On Larkspur's second outing the following year, he won the Wills Gold Flake Stakes at Leopardstown over 1½ miles. *Timeform Annual* stated 'But the bare result of that race was not informative ... he was not everybody's idea of a classic winner ...' But a professional handler of horses, the top class trainer Paddy Prendergast took an entirely different view. 'Prendergast went to Chester next day', Vincent remembers, 'and spread the news that this was a definite Derby candidate and all his people backed him.'

The stable's retained jockey Pat Glennon did not agree with the boss. He chose to ride the stable's other runner Sebring who was working more impressively at home. 'But then,' Vincent says, 'Larkspur always took things easy.'

They engaged an Australian jockey Neville Sellwood 'a top class rider', Vincent recalls, 'who was later that year very sadly killed in a riding accident in France.' On the Monday of the week before the Derby, just nine days before the race, Sellwood came over to Ballydoyle to ride work on Larkspur. Raymond Guest had come down the night before to stay to watch the gallop and Neville Sellwood had flown over from France. Then disaster struck.

They were sitting over breakfast in the long dining room which now glows with pictures of great horses and some of the trophies they won. The window at the end looks over the main yard. Vincent from his seat at the head of the table, saw down it and through the window into the yard. To his unease, he saw his head lad, then Maurice O'Callaghan, coming quickly across to the house. He got up and went out to meet him. Was everything all right?

It was definitely not. A swelling had come up overnight on the outside of Larkspur's near-hind leg below the hock. There was no question of working the horse. The gallop was cancelled. Raymond Guest feared the worst. Jacqueline O'Brien, left with a dispirited clump round her dining room table, suggested to Neville Sellwood: 'Why don't you at least get up and sit on the horse while he's walking round the covered ride.' Sellwood happily agreed, and this was the only time he sat on him before Epsom.

Larkspur wins the 1962 Derby. Note the riderless Crossen, one of the seven who fell.

Bob Griffin, the loyal vet, was immediately summoned to drive down from The Curragh. He examined the horse, was by no means discouraging, but prescribed fomentations and two days' complete rest. The Derby runner would thus be laid off work and box-bound seven days before the classic. 'I'll come down again on Friday,' said Bob, 'and see if the horse can work.' When he did so, he said cheerfully, 'I think you'll run him in the Derby.'

When Larkspur was first found to have the swelling below his hock and was laid off work, Vincent decided that he should inform the press of this hold-up in the horse's preparation. He said truthfully that there was a possibility that the horse would not run in the race. As a substantial betting man himself at that time he did not want the public to lose their money and enrich the bookmakers by backing a non-runner ante-post. The aftermath of this

After the 'disaster Derby' of 1962; three of the horses which fell include on the right Heathersett the favourite, in the foreground, back to camera Romulus and on the left against the rails Changing Times. Three jockeys were rushed to hospital and one horse broke a leg and had to be destroyed.

announcement has without doubt coloured O'Brien's views about giving the press detailed reports on his horses' progress. A good deal of his reluctance on this subject stems from the behaviour of the Epsom stewards in the minutes immediately following the Irishman's first English classic victory.

Having examined the leg and said Larkspur could work for the first time for six days, Bob Griffin checked the horse again. The swelling was no worse. 'You can send him to Epsom,' Bob told Vincent, and the horse travelled over.

On receipt of this good news, Raymond Guest promptly started to bet on Larkspur. It was this flurry of informed wagering in the same week in which Vincent had publicly pronounced his doubts which led to the Epsom stewards' suspicious summoning of the winning trainer. Why had Raymond Guest so soon backed his horse? Vincent shrugs. Raymond liked betting, as he would show again in the case of Sir Ivor. Jacqueline O'Brien suggests that, 'He really didn't want to face the fact that things had gone wrong. He'd been very depressed by the setback that morning at breakfast.'

One thing is certain. Nobody working in the yard at that time, when asked to rate Larkspur, fourteen years and five more Epsom Derby winners later, puts him anywhere but at the bottom of the golden six. Rejected by the stable jockey and box-bound seven days before the Derby, Larkspur was little fancied, except by his optimistic owner. He had drifted out in the ante-post market even before Vincent had made his announcement. On the day, he started at a longer price than he opened.

And then, of course, it was the Derby when 'They all fell down'. To be precise, seven fell, and of the field of twenty-six at least nine more were impeded, some seriously. King Canute II was too greatly injured to survive and was put down. Hethersett was one of the fallers and he went on to beat Larkspur in the St Leger. Larkspur had been just behind Hethersett in the middle of the field when the leaders, disrupted by the crash of the beaten Romulus into Crossen, started to go down like bowling pins. Hethersett was sliding on the ground as Larkspur neatly jumped him. A bigger clumsier colt would probably have tripped over him.

A pack of distraught loose horses pursued the leaders into Tattenham Corner, making Epsom's ridiculously steep and twisting descent look more than ever like the setting of a bucolic point-to-point rather than of the world's most famous classic race.

Larkspur, just behind the leaders, moved to the front with the greatest of ease and sailed home comfortably. Arcor was second and Le Cantilien just overcame the loose and blinkered Crossen in their disadvantaged race to the post. Well behind came Miralgo, Larkspur's conqueror in the Timeform, and then a horse who would make his name in quite another field, the future National Hunt sire, Spartan General. Larkspur's more fancied stable com-

On a happier note American owner Raymond Guest, that great Anglophile, leads in Larkspur and Neville Sellwood.

panion Sebring did not prove Glennon entirely wrong, for he finished fifth.

Plainly Larkspur's swollen leg, still 'up' only five days before the race, had not affected his performance. The press referred to it as a 'thoroughpin' 'but', Vincent says 'this was not the case'.

The Epsom stewards included Lord Derby and Sir Humphrey de Trafford. They would be busy that day trying to determine why seven horses fell in a flat race. But they first – and even before the jockeys had weighed in – summoned the victorious Vincent before them. They wanted him to explain the money bet on the winner after he had been announced a doubtful runner. Vincent reported the facts. The stewards promptly accepted his account. But Vincent was very angry. On top of being deprived of those first glorious minutes after he had won the Derby, Vincent's top hat had mysteriously disappeared while he stood in the Stewards' Room. He said afterwards very crossly to Jacqueline, 'They asked me a lot of questions and they stole my hat!'

Looking back on that first Epsom Derby Vincent says 'But I do believe that

Larkspur on that day was a good horse. He didn't have the soundest of limbs – I think that came through Never Say Die. But he was never quite the same horse again. His action was never as good. Racing all the way down the hill at Epsom had its effects. But they did not show up until the Irish Derby.

'He ran quite differently when Scobie Breasley rode him at The Curragh. Scobie shook his head when he came in and said, "He didn't like the ground. It was too firm. He felt it".'

Indeed he did. He was off the course for two months thereafter with sore shins. Vincent comments sagely 'The Never Say Dies had soft bone.' Poor Larkspur feeling the jar in his shins hung to one side up the straight. He struggled on up to second place, but finished fourth to Tambourine II. In the opinion of T.P. Burns, 'On Epsom Derby Day he was better than on any other day. Lucky? Sellwood said he'd have won anyway, no matter how many fell. Oh, he did the job that day all right!'

Larkspur was even more disappointing in the St Leger than he'd been in the Irish Derby. Then the ground had been far too firm. Now it was too heavy. He was labouring along at the back of the field, battled his way forward, got into a barging match with Spartan General and came off the worst from it. He finally finished sixth and Raymond Guest decided to retire him to stud and he stood for many years in Japan. But Vincent O'Brien had won his first classic outside Ireland, and just as important, his new American connections had been established.

12

'You could gallop him around the yard'

The fortunate Raymond Guest had to wait a mere six years before he got his second Epsom Derby winner. Sir Ivor was conceived in America only the year after Larkspur started work as a stallion.

Sir Ivor, about whom no one at Ballydoyle ever utters a syllable of criticism, ran in his classic year from April to November. He began by winning Ascot's 2,000 Guineas Trial Stakes in ground so appalling they could not move the starting stalls, took the 2,000 Guineas at Newmarket, and the Derby, was second in the Irish Derby, third in the Eclipse, and concluded his *annus mirabilis* in Europe by winning Newmarket's Champion Stakes. Finally in his owner's homeland, he carried off the Washington International in sparkling fashion. He was tough, honest, possessed of brilliant speed, yet also of a beautiful calm character. Few would exclude this paragon from a short list of the very best Derby winners. Vincent O'Brien and Lester Piggott find it extremely difficult to select the better between him and Nijinsky. The staff at Ballydoyle concur, including Golden Fleece to make the top three of O'Brien's six English Derby victors between 1962 and 1982.

The colt, foaled in 1965 by Sir Gaylord, out of a good American mare called Attica, was bred by an attractive lady who romantically descends from one of the very first white explorers to penetrate what is now the Commonwealth of Kentucky – that mighty hunter, Daniel Boone. Boone struggled westwards from Virginia over the Cumberland Mountains to find one of the Indians' best hunting areas. 'Kentucke' derives from the Indian description meaning 'dark and bloody ground'. A replica of the fort Boone founded against the Indians can be visited in South Eastern Kentucky. Daniel Boone's descendent is Mrs Alice Chandler, whose family were also involved in the founding of the Keeneland Association which uniquely runs a non-profit-taking racecourse (one of the prettiest in the States) and the largest bloodstock sales company in the world.

Sir Ivor's dam was a present. Attica won five races at three and four years old and was placed in two American Stakes races. She was by the great Mahmoud's son Mr Trouble, and was wittily named for students of classical Greek for she was out of Athenia and Athens was the capital of often troublesome Attica. Sir Ivor's granddam was a top-class race mare. She won ten races and was second in the Kentucky Oaks.

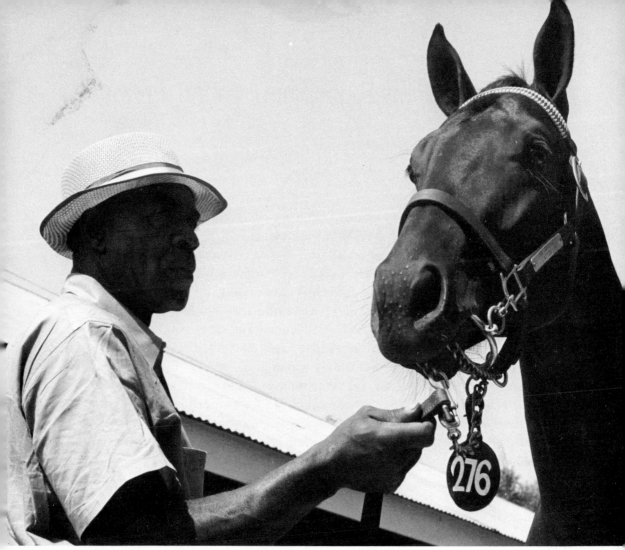

Sir Ivor as a yearling at Keeneland Sales sent up by his breeder Mrs Alice Chandler. Described by her as 'Tall, lanky, lopsided … but with a super set of legs', he was bought by Bull Hancock, Vincent's great friend, for Raymond Guest.

Mrs Alice Chandler stands cheerfully in a thunderstorm at Keeneland chatting about Sir Ivor. 'My father gave me Attica and said "Someday I think, Al, she may throw you a racehorse." She had produced three winners, none of them top-class, before Sir Ivor appeared.

'I sent her to Sir Gaylord,' says Alice Chandler, 'and got a nice big colt. But he was the *despair* of me! Because he grew tall and he grew lanky and he grew lopsided, and there was no way I could get him to the Summer Sales here looking good.' However Sir Ivor would turn out, Alice Chandler always admired his brains and loved his kindness. 'He was always very intelligent. Some people say horses have no sense, but that's not true. We have some terrible storms here. Well, one night when he was a yearling I could hear him nickering

Sir Ivor with the O'Brien family, used for their 1968 Christmas card. Left to right: Liz, Jane, Vincent, Sue, David (Secreto's future trainer), Jacqueline with Charles.

Vincent visiting Sir Ivor at Claiborne, near Paris, Kentucky in 1981 – and exchanging reminiscences.

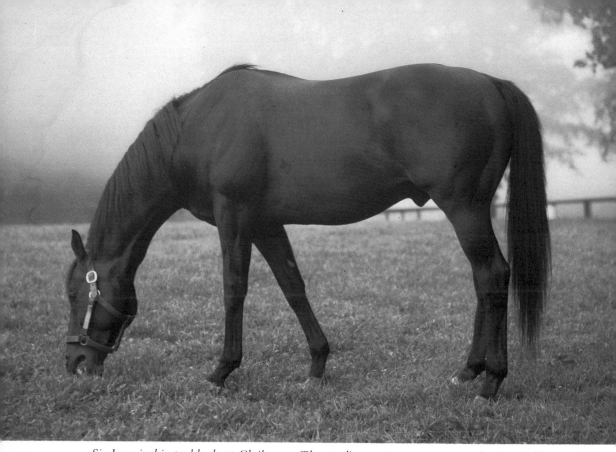

Sir Ivor in his paddock at Claiborne. The stud's previous owner was the late Bull Hancock, the famous Kentucky breeder, who bought the colt down the road at Keeneland Sales.

Dawn at Claiborne. The stallions – nearly 30 of them – are out all night in the heat of summer, and brought in to be washed down. This is Nijinsky.

over the top of the lightning and the thunder, so I went out to him with my raincoat flapping and with no shank, no lead rope. I called him. He flew up to me and slid the brakes on and I just reached up and grabbed him and took him into the barn.

'He never had a temperament problem. I think he flew water twenty times including the trip to Italy and then over here for the Washington DC International. Vincent did a marvellous job training him. But he had a super temperament to train.'

Raymond Guest had not sent Vincent anything else to train after the Larkspur triumph. Indeed it was to the renowned 'Bull' Hancock, master of Claiborne Farm, near Paris, Kentucky, that Mr Guest went. He wanted Bull, a famous judge of a horse, and the owner of one of the greatest stud farms in the world, to pick him out a yearling at Keeneland, down the road, that hot July of 1966. He gave Bull Hancock a limit of 60,000 dollars. Bull first selected for Raymond Guest an attractive colt by the English 2,000 Guineas winner of 1948, My Babu. The yearling went well over the limit, and was sold to Charles Engelhard the millionaire for whom Vincent would shortly come to train that most brilliant of all Derby winners, Nijinsky.

Vincent O'Brien had no connection with Mr Engelhard then, nor was he even at the Sales. It was left to Bull Hancock to go for a second best after the My Babu colt. He came to the colt by Sir Gaylord, described by his breeder as 'tall, lanky and lopsided'. In spite of lacking sales condition, Alice Chandler had sent him to the Sales hoping for the best – 'just as he was with a super set of legs'.

Mr Hancock was a true judge of a horse in that he could size one up undandified, underconditioned and with all the aesthetic disadvantages of having grown too quick, too early. From such acumen bargains sprout. Well under Raymond Guest's top limit of 60,000 dollars came Bull Hancock's winning bid of 42,000 dollars for Alice's colt. Bull Hancock rang Vincent asking him to take the horse to train for Raymond Guest. Vincent happily agreed. He also agreed to Hancock's suggestion that because of the yearling's apparent immaturity, he should stay over in Kentucky until the late autumn to be broken.

Sir Ivor did not arrive in Ireland until November. Even then, 'for an American sales-produced yearling,' Vincent remembers, 'he looked a rather backward type, as if he'd take some time. And even the following March when Raymond Guest was staying here at Ballydoyle I remember showing him the horse and saying "We wouldn't want to expect too much of him, you know, until the Autumn at the earliest."'

The lads in the yard at the time of Sir Ivor's arrival recall 'he was so big and backward – he was bigger than Golden Fleece – that you'd never think he would run as a two year old.' T. P. Burns adds, 'as a two year old you'd fear

Vincent and Bull Hancock shooting grouse in the north of England.

he'd grow into a monster ... but he grew sideways. When he did his first canters on the all-weather gallop, he was most unimpressive.' And Johnny Brabston chips in with, 'You'd think he was worth nothing and I remember the boss telling Mr Guest that he probably would not run at least until the autumn.'

Horses from time to time make fools of most of us. Even the best trainers can misjudge a horse's progress and the big ones frankly admit it. Looking back on Sir Ivor's two year old career culminating in his victory in the Grand Criterium at Longchamp, Vincent O'Brien still says with surprise, 'Thinking back to that March there's no way you could believe that he could have come on and done that! That he could have matured sufficiently to be trained for races like that! He came on suddenly in the early summer.' The lads remember Liam Ward driving down to ride Sir Ivor a bit of work in May and 'being impressed with him'.

'Come the month of May,' says Vincent, 'he had changed a lot and he came up to his first race on Irish Derby Day, the last Saturday in June at The Curragh. He was the sort of horse who needed a run, but I thought he'd win, and when he finished fourth I was quite disappointed. But Liam said to me afterwards, "The three that finished in front of him today will never do so again."' And Sir Ivor won next time out at The Curragh at the end of July, returned in September for a brilliant victory in the National Stakes there, and then flew to France to beat the best of their two year olds in the Grand Criterium.

As soon as Sir Ivor won his first race back in July Raymond Guest boldly struck an enormous Derby wager on his colt. T. P. Burns remembers 'That was a sparkling performance. He was waited with. He was always waited with. I remember his action was still poor going down. He'd no great action at the canter. But when he came to gallop! And Liam Ward always won a bit clever!'

His owner, too, was deeply impressed. 'Raymond had a friend staying with him,' Vincent recalls 'called Abe Hewitt, an American by way of being an expert on thoroughbred pedigrees, and so forth ...' Presumably Mr Hewitt encouraged Mr Guest, for Vincent goes on, 'Raymond was always somebody who loved to have a bet, and he and Hewitt decided they'd get some money on the horse at long odds for the Derby. They managed to find a well-known bookmaker who was on his yacht at Deauville, and they got a bet of £500 each way at 100 to 1'. The bet stood at £62,500. The anxiety of the bookmaker waxed grimly as he noted Sir Ivor's victories in Ireland's and France's top two year old races. At Longchamp Sir Ivor was ridden by Lester Piggott. 'He had him 5 to 6 lengths behind at the 2 furlong marker.' Lester said after the race: 'He quickened so fast he nearly ran out from under me!'

This news shook the bookie. He had already made vain approaches to Raymond Guest to get the wager reduced before O'Brien took a startling new step that winter, which nearly ended in a disaster for Sir Ivor.

Vincent O'Brien decided to send eight of the best of his horses, which naturally included Sir Ivor, to winter in the Mediterranean climate of Pisa. The pretty little racecourse and the winter training grounds are enclosed on three sides by woods in a quiet, level park on sandy soil not far from the sea and almost within sight of the Leaning Tower. It is, however, some way from the excellent stables which stand red-tiled and solid outside the parkland, and directly at the side of a straight and busy road, noisy with lorries, bordered by a deep dyke.

Johnny Brabston went out from Ballydoyle to Pisa on New Year's Day. 'The horse got an abscess in the foot which lasted three weeks fully, for sand had got in and he had a terrible leg. The old Italian blacksmith wasn't very clever and the leg swelled up like a balloon.

'Then Bob Griffin came out. He opened the foot up and his advice was to keep him walking and to keep bathing the foot. But, of course, having been idle, Sir Ivor got terribly fresh when we started to exercise him again. You could meet flocks of sheep coming at you with bells on them – on the road to

Sir Ivor and Lester Piggott going down to the post at Newmarket for the 1968 Two Thousand Guineas which he won at 11 to 8 and being led in by Raymond Guest after winning the race.

(opposite): On the morning of the Derby Vincent and Lester Piggott discuss plans, while Vincent Rossiter rides out on Sir Ivor.

the training grounds. Once I had to slip off him as the saddle went up his neck!'

Vincent continues calmly, 'The Italians have been sending their horses to Pisa for generations. You get mild weather and none of the cold winds you get in Ireland and England. I must say Sir Ivor did tremendously well out there, so much so that one morning he gave a jump and a kick going down the pathway by the side of that main road and he got Johnny off.

'I was behind him in a car with my head man. We nearly died of fright! We jumped out of the car and we got our hands wide out round him. But there was that long dyke with water in it. If he'd got away from us, he'd have toppled over into that dyke. But the three of us – because Johnny had landed on his legs and kept hold of the reins – luckily managed to stop him from getting away.

'It was a tremendous relief, I can tell you, when he didn't get loose. If he had, he could have gone to Rome or anywhere!' But even the remembrance of that scramble on the brink of disaster makes Vincent O'Brien give a shudder seventeen years later.

Spring came, and the horses returned to Ireland on 1 March. Sir Ivor was due to have his first race in the Gladness Stakes, but he was too backward to run. The lads remember, 'At home he'd pull himself up at the same spot on the gallops where he used to pull up as a two year old. It looked as if he wasn't genuine, and so it was very worrying. But the boss simply started his work further back. And all was fine.' Sir Ivor's prep race for the 2,000 Guineas was Ascot's 2,000 Guineas Trial, run in desperately heavy ground. He only just won, and was nearly caught. Piggott reported, 'The *horse* heard them coming – not me!'

Not everyone appreciated Sir Ivor's achievement in Ascot's mud. And Dermot O'Brien remembers that 'He'd been working a bit in-and-out at home, so two weeks before the Guineas we took him and two other horses over to Newmarket. We stayed in the Links Stables and worked there on the gallops.'

The lads say, 'The boss came over to watch his work. Special? The only thing special was the way he worked! The night before the race Lester Piggott said "Nothing will beat this horse".' But on Guineas Day at Newmarket many preferred Petingo, the impressive winner of both the Gimcrack and the Middle Park.

Sir Ivor, ridden with supreme confidence by Lester Piggott, caught Petingo in The Dip and won going away by 1½ lengths. He was instantly hot favourite for the Derby.

The only doubt surrounding Sir Ivor's chances in the Derby lay in his stamina. As would happen again with Golden Fleece, the stable had to wonder whether a horse possessed of such brilliant speed could in addition stay 1½ miles. But the combination of his calm temperament, his relaxed manner of racing and the configuration of Epsom strongly suggested he would. His speed at home was such that the Ballydoyle staff declare, 'Both Sir Ivor and Nijinsky would easily have won top class sprints.'

Raymond Guest could not keep his date at Epsom. On Derby Day he had to go to the opening of the Kennedy Park Arboretum in Co. Wexford to plant a tree to commemorate President John F. Kennedy's birthday. Even the richest

The end of the stupendous burst of speed which won the Derby for Sir Ivor and Lester Piggott at 4 to 5 on. Connaught, Sandy Barclay, right was second. Third was Mount Athos ridden by the now well-known TV commentator Jimmy Lindley.

Raymond Guest's wife, Caroline, leads in Sir Ivor after the Derby. Raymond, American Ambassador to Ireland had duties there which prevented him coming.

ambassadors must sometimes take on inconvenient duties, but Raymond's absence from Epsom on that day was the greatest disappointment of his racing life. His wife, Caroline, a descendent of Prince Murat, one of Napoleon's marshals, the innkeeper's son who became King of Naples, led the winner in.

Alice Chandler and Bull Hancock, breeder and buyer, came over from Kentucky. Both nearly had heart failure watching Piggott's tactics. Both were used to American race-riding where the pressure is strong all the way, and fancied runners almost always lie up in the leading cluster. Piggott waited. And waited. Just over a furlong from home, Bull Hancock put down his race-glasses miserably, 'There's no way the horse can win from there,' he said.

Alice Chandler, still excited, reviews the scene: 'The horse was tucked in solid on the rails. A hundred yards out and he had no shot of winning. Then you've never seen a horse run so fast in your life. We didn't believe he'd won. I've seen that film many, many times and I'll still give you 6 to 5 he got beat.' Hearing this, Vincent murmurs, 'Started to run? That's after Lester eased him outside Connaught.' One of the lads recalls, 'Poor Sandy Barclay on Connaught looked round and thought he could never be caught, never be beat. He came in crying!'

Connaught was beaten 1½ lengths at 100 to 9. Mount Athos (45 to 1) was third a further 2½ lengths behind. The winner, about whose chances his owner had obtained those delicious odds of 100 to 1, eleven months before, started odds on at 4 to 5, and the bookmaker had to pay out and try to look happy.

Even the carefully unemotional O'Brien declares 'Lester rode a spectacular race ... and I often wonder what the time was for that final furlong.' In America it would have been clocked and illuminated in the centre of their tracks.

There seems little doubt, in the light of Sir Ivor's subsequent career, that Piggott's brilliance that day was in conserving the pounce of what was really a great one and quarter miler in a 1½ mile race. The English Derby, due to its steep downhill, sharp bend, and its generally fast ground, can be won by horses who do not truly stay 1½ miles on a galloping track; and it often is. Something that helped Sir Ivor at Epsom was, according to the lads, 'That he was so handy, you could gallop him around the yard.'

It is significant that the only other 1½ mile race won by Sir Ivor was the Washington International, and Laurel Park, by English standards, is a very sharp and easy 1½ miles.

After the Epsom Derby, Sir Ivor was beaten on the wide and galloping expanse of The Curragh. Liam Ward struck the front 2 furlongs out, which was a very different tactic to Piggott's last 100 metre sprint at Epsom. He was outstayed by Ribero. Ward's comment on Sir Ivor was firm: 'He died on me.'

Only a week later he was back in England again for the Eclipse and was

Sir Ivor as a three-year-old in the summer of 1968 at Ballydoyle with Maurice O'Callaghan.

beaten by two older horses, the winner being the previous year's Derby victor Royal Palace. Piggott was criticised from the grandstand for riding Sir Ivor too confidently, but the ground was very firm and the colt came back to Ireland in Vincent's phrase, 'jarred of his knees'. He also came back 'looking fine', says T. P. Burns, 'he'd three races in six weeks, and he *still* looked a big burly horse.'

On the Sunday before the Prix de l'Arc de Triomphe the much travelled colt went to France for his prep. race at Longchamp. 'He was second,' says T. P., 'and he blew like a pig. We took him down to Lamorlaye and he stayed in a little block of three stables out in the forest. On the Thursday or Friday the boss came out and Sir Ivor did a good bit of work. And in the Arc he ran a hell of a race. He was only beaten by a very good horse indeed, Vaguely Noble, who got all the breaks in the race.'

'Vaguely Noble,' says Vincent, 'truly stayed a mile and a half. Also the soft ground was much in his favour.' Sir Ivor then very easily won the Champion Stakes and then he flew back to America for the Washington International.

Sir Ivor ends his triumphant career by winning the Washington DC International at Laurel Park. He won in Ireland, France, England and America.

The Laurel Race came at the end of one of the toughest three year old campaigns through which a classic horse could go. The ground was bottomless. It was covered with snow on the Sunday and it just melted out in time. The lads say that 'Lester was the only jockey who could have won on him'. The American press was critical of Lester Piggott's riding for he rode Sir Ivor in his usual style. He was lying only third or fourth swinging round the last bend into the short home stretch. Then the horse, for the last time, flaunted that astonishing acceleration for which he had become famous and won easily by three-quarters of a length.

Vincent goes out to Claiborne to see Sir Ivor and Nijinsky whenever he is at Keeneland Sales. One afternoon there, he is stroking Sir Ivor and murmuring to him, 'You look marvellous, old boy ... Doesn't he look great? What a wonderful sire of fillies he is. I only hope he gets a colt as good as himself.

'He always had the most wonderful temperament ... he was no trouble whatever. When he came to racing he was as tough as they come, never got upset and when he had to get down and really run, he always pulled out all he had to give.' There could be few finer tributes from a trainer to his horse, and it is odious to have to ask O'Brien to compare Sir Ivor and Nijinsky.

'Well, of course, they're two brilliant horses, but different in their characters in all respects. Sir Ivor was so self-contained. ... I think Lester, wholly for that reason, would probably lean toward Sir Ivor. Nijinsky was quite highly strung.

He wasn't as easy a horse to train as Sir Ivor. He was always on his toes so that he needed much less work than Sir Ivor. You had to be careful you didn't overwork him.

'Whereas with Sir Ivor,' and here Vincent in the Kentucky sunlight gives the horse the warmest of fond smiles, 'you were completely unconcerned about anything to do with him. So, of the two, he was the tougher horse...'

He weighs one against the other horse in his reflective mind and gives a small shrug. 'Two great horses,' he repeats. 'I'd hate to say which was the better.'

13

'If this goes on much longer, it'll turn to wine'

Lester Piggott, in the O'Briens' sunlit bar at Ballydoyle, was also weighing up Sir Ivor and Nijinsky. It was his last year riding for the stable. His practice was to come over about four times a year and he had flown over to ride work on a fresh May morning. He and Vincent were discussing how the morning had gone, their plans, and the opposition in races. The *Racing Calendar*, the *Sporting Life*, lists of the horse's engagements and diaries lay open on a low table. Jacqueline O'Brien came through from the back of the house bringing them coffee.

Asked to name the three best horses trained by O'Brien and ridden by him, Piggott said instantly 'Well, obviously Nijinsky, Sir Ivor and The Minstrel.' If you believe that the subconscious grades preferences, you have the great jockey's immediate response. Pressed to select them in order, Piggott hesitated. 'Very different, very hard ... I've always thought Sir Ivor my favourite. But Alleged was a great horse ... only beaten once ... won the Arc de Triomphe twice. But Sir Ivor – he was a great horse. Had a terrific turn of speed you know, and was a very *sensible* horse.'

And Nijinsky?

'I think Nijinsky probably on his day was the most brilliant horse I've ever ridden. On a few days in the summertime as a three year old ...'

Then, at a tangent, talking of his riding arrangements then with Vincent... 'no retainer... it's a gentlemen's agreement. We've been good friends all the time.... That's how it goes on...' He added, 'We've had a lot of great days and a lot of bloody awful days! Some of the best days we had were at Epsom obviously, and at Longchamp. I think the great days were with Sir Ivor, The Minstrel and Alleged. And the worst times, I suppose, were when Nijinsky got beaten in the Arc, and at Newmarket when he got beaten again in the Champion Stakes. Because he had had such a public build-up, and when he did get beaten, it was such a let-down. Hard to believe really...'

Several other things about Nijinsky are still hard to believe. He was bought by a happy accident and he was so difficult to train that, at one stage, his owner, Charlie Engelhard, new to the stable, was warned that he might prove

Nijinsky the champion with the heart-shaped blaze, probably the most brilliant of Vincent's horses so far ...

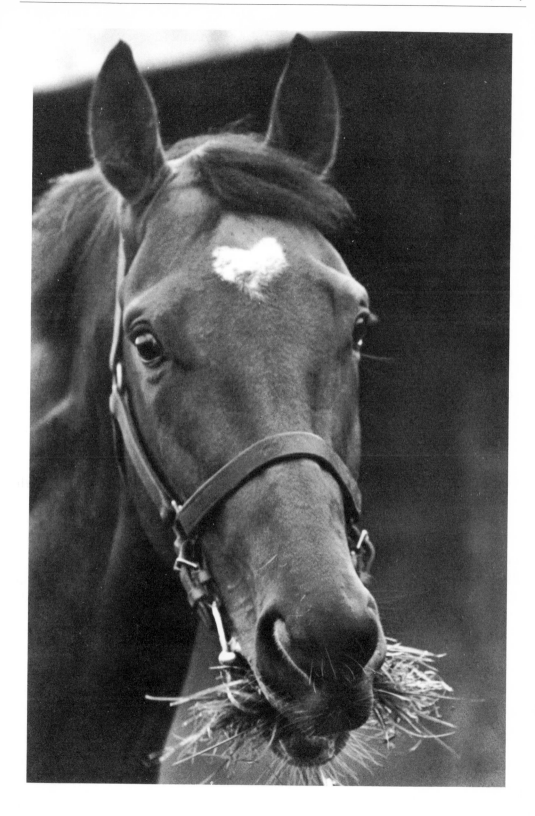

too intractable to run. 'If I hadn't first-class horsemen to ride him,' O'Brien says fourteen years later, 'I don't believe we would ever have succeeded with him. He could easily have gone the wrong way.'

With this the staff firmly concur. Finally, there was not only the serious matter of his temperament. Nijinsky, at the peak of his career, had to overcome an ailment which would render him almost entirely bald over his body and thus unrideable at a critical moment in his training.

Mr Engelhard, an immensely rich and portly American, was a very great friend of Vincent's, and it was tragic that he died so soon. Not all O'Brien's patrons have remained so close, and no one has ever suggested that Vincent O'Brien would be an easy man with whom to train. As the years have progressed and his successes have multiplied, it has been absolutely the case of what he says goes. Even from the small beginnings his maxim has been rigid: the interests of the horse come first. This does not always suit an owner. It particularly does not suit the owner to whom a racehorse is a trapping like a mink coat, Rolls-Royce or a yacht to be used and shed at will. And Jacqueline O'Brien adds that 'It sometimes doesn't even suit his wife and family!'

Charles Engelhard of New Jersey was born two months earlier than Vincent in 1917. He was chairman of the Engelhard Minerals and Chemical Corporation and Engelhard Enterprises Inc. He was an upper-class American, schooled at St Paul's and Princeton and a member of that exclusive, rather stuffy and awe-inspiring establishment, the Brook Club in Manhattan. In London he belonged to the much jollier Buck's and was an honorary member of the Jockey Club. He had four trainers in England, one each in France, USA and South Africa (where he was heavily into platinum) and in Ireland.

His bloodstock manager in Europe was the astute but charming David McCall, who had early evidence of Mr Engelhard's power and thoughtfulness. His employer told him once on the telephone that he'd like a chat and suggested rather to McCall's surprise, a meeting at London Airport. Arriving at London Heathrow, McCall was whisked through the VIP lounge and onto Engelhard's private jet. To David McCall's consternation this immediately took off.

'Where are we going?' he asked anxiously.

'Switzerland.'

'But I've no passport with me and how do I get back?'

'I'll send the plane back with you.'

It was Charlie Engelhard who had outbid Bull Hancock for the My Babu colt, which had been Bull's first choice for Raymond Guest ahead of Sir Ivor. As Alice Chandler says with pride, 'Sir Ivor really established Vincent's American connection.' Mr Engelhard with horses all round the world had no difficulty in assessing O'Brien's prowess. He wished to have a horse in training with him and he asked O'Brien to go up to Canada to look at a possible yearling. In the United States businessmen fly a couple of thousand miles for a meeting. So Canada to an American, particularly one based at Newark, New Jersey, just across the river from Manhattan, seems like Epsom from London. But to an Irishman it was a long way from Tipperary. Vincent says 'I thought, my God, it's a long way to have to go to see just one horse. But I had better do it.'

The circles of the rich are small and closely linked. The yearling Charlie Engelhard had heard about belonged to a man of comparable wealth, the Canadian tycoon E. P. Taylor, whose empire was based in Toronto. 'The yearling to be visited was by Ribot,' Vincent notes, 'and Charlie had enjoyed a lot of successes with Ribot horses around that time.'

Vincent set off for Canada. 'And when I saw the horse by Ribot, I saw that I could not recommend him. He had a crooked foreleg. But I thought as I had gone all the way there, I should look at the other yearlings and see what they'd got. I saw this Northern Dancer and he really filled my eye. He struck me as having the *makings* of a fine horse.'

The colt for whom Vincent O'Brien fell came from only the second crop of Northern Dancer. The sire, who would become such a dominant force in racing, was then scarcely known. As O'Brien comments, 'There was nothing at the time to suppose that Northern Dancer was going to be a really top sire.' As it has turned out, Northern Dancer became, by the early 1980s, the most influential sire of the decade, and so far as Europe is concerned it was Vincent who made him so.

Vincent flew to Canada at the end of July. The month of racing and the days of the sales and parties and polo in the beautiful spa town of Saratoga Springs in upstate New York was just about to start. 'So I went to Saratoga from Canada and met Charlie. I was staying with Jimmy Brady – James Cox Brady, who was Chairman of the New York Racing Association. He had a number of horses in training with me, including Long Look who won the Oaks. Jimmy was one of the nicest men I ever knew. He was a friend of Bull Hancock and Charlie Engelhard, and I really must say that I owe to him all my introductions to the leading people of American racing. He was so respected that once he had horses in training with you, you were really "in".

'I said to Charlie Engelhard that I couldn't advise him to buy the Ribot horse I'd seen in Canada but I had seen a horse there, by Northern Dancer out of Flaming Page, that I thought he should buy.'

The sales in Canada where the colt would be auctioned took place the following month. Charlie Engelhard accepted Vincent's recommendation and said nonchalantly, 'I'll put one of my men up in Canada in there to bid for him.'

Thus began the first of Vincent O'Brien's series of anxieties over the brilliant

Nijinsky. 'This man of Charlie's was entirely inexperienced where the buying of horses was concerned. And so I was worried what he might do. That he'd make some slip up ... and that I'd lose the horse.'

Another threat then roared over the horizon like a jet bomber. O'Brien got word that another Canadian tycoon, Garfield Weston, owner of Fortnum & Mason, who was additionally a friend of the vendor's since their schooldays, had been invited by E. P. Taylor to look at the Northern Dancer colt. He had gone. More ominously still he had taken with him Stuart Murless, a leading Irish trainer and brother of Noel, together with a partner of Bob Griffin's, to give the horse a veterinary examination. The mission looked serious. Vincent had to sweat it out till the day of the sales.

Fortunately for him, the Garfield Weston expedition decided that the big colt would take rather too long to come to hand. Charlie Engelhard's man needed, however, to overcome brisk competition for the colt which continued until, at 84,000 dollars, the sale price was a Canadian record. 'A hefty price,' comments Vincent, 'especially up in Canada.' It was double the price Sir Ivor had cost two years earlier.

Further troubles began as soon as the colt arrived at Ballydoyle. He refused to eat one oat. Several days passed. But this had nothing to do with temperament, nor with jet-lag. He did not eat oats because, as Vincent learned to his surprise from a telephone call to Windfields Farm in Maryland, the colt had never been offered oats before. 'At Windfields,' said E. P. Taylor's stud farm manager over the transatlantic telephone, 'we feed nuts.'

O'Brien was surprised as nuts were used mostly for feeding cattle at that time. 'I'd never fed nuts to horses myself ... It never even struck me at the time that a horse might have been used to eating nuts instead of oats. But I said to the manager, "Well fly me some nuts over straight away." But before the nuts reached Shannon airport, the horse had begun to eat oats so all was well.' Johnny Brabston adds 'He'd only been eating hay ... Then the day the special recipe nuts the boss had sent for from Canada arrived, he started eating oats.' And Johnny wags his head, as one does when speaking of a particularly contrary, perverse, cussed or, as Americans have it, an 'ornery character'. The great Nijinsky, who would win every race he ran in, bar the last two, and who became the first Triple Crown winner since Bahram, was all those things.

He was regarded, not only without admiration by the staff, 'he certainly wasn't the star of the yearlings' but with actual dislike. 'Some mornings it would take ages to get him out of his box' they now exclaim with a sort of glee. Good horses who are difficult are remembered with pride whatever offences they commit at home. 'He got straight up on his hindlegs,' they go on, adding with admiration for any animal that rears right up, yet does not fall over. 'Oh, but he had great balance.'

The 'most brilliant' Nijinsky, winner of the Triple Crown, cantering in his paddock in the dawn mist at Claiborne.

Nijinsky, taken at Claiborne in 1981 (the year before his son Golden Fleece won the Derby) with his groom Clay Arnold who collected both Nijinsky and Sir Ivor off the plane from Ireland and has looked after them ever since.

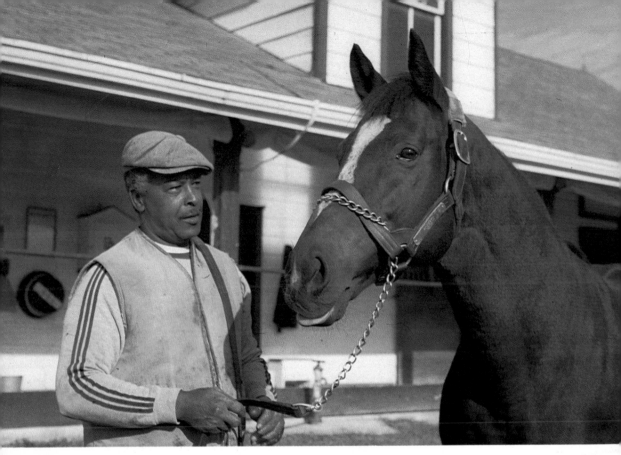

Roberto, Vincent's next Derby winner, back at Darby Dan near Lexington where he was bred by John Galbreath. This picture was taken in 1983. His groom is Floyd Wilson who has always looked after this successful stallion.

Northern Dancer, Nijinsky's sire, and considered by Vincent to be 'the greatest', pictured here aged 23 taken at Windfields Farm, Maryland, owned by his breeder, E.P. Taylor.

E.P. Taylor the great Canadian industrialist and breeder of Northern Dancer and Nijinsky. Here he is with his wife Winnie and Vincent at Saratoga.

Even when he got down to the gallops, Nijinsky often did not want to canter. The staff at Ballydoyle then chime in, 'Yet once he was galloping he went always as sweetly as a hunter!' Small chorus of agreement. ... Then 'he used to sweat. Early in his two year old year he'd rear up. If you stopped him, even for a second, he'd rear up. Frightened? No, it looked as if he had a temper.'

Another chorus of agreement. Then, almost with a cheer 'He was the best we ever had. ... Better than Sir Ivor. ... He was the best of all.'

Yet in the first months of winter work Vincent O'Brien had to sit down to compose a difficult letter to Mr Engelhard. This, after all, was the yearling Vincent had picked in preference to the one which Mr Engelhard, a new and valued patron, had asked him to examine. He had cost the most at the sales. Vincent wrote to Charlie Engelhard 'I am somewhat concerned about Nijinsky's temperament and that he is inclined to resent getting on with his work. My best boys are riding him and we can only hope he will go the right way.'

And after that, as is the way of life, things began to improve. Nijinsky was no trouble entering the starting stalls. He went to The Curragh to gallop and worked out of the stalls there, and everything went right. 'I was only following the other horses,' says Johnny Brabston, 'but I knew he was *some* horse.' When Liam Ward came down to ride work, he confirmed Johnny's words about Nijinsky: 'Between February and May we all thought here that if he goes the right way he'll be a good horse.'

Things went brilliantly. 'If it were not for two very capable work riders, Johnny Brabston and Danny O'Sullivan,' says O'Brien fairly, 'Nijinsky could easily have been spoiled. They had the strength to handle him and the patience not to knock him about.'

Once he was on the gallops there were no difficulties, provided he was allowed to get on his way. He still sweated freely. 'For a horse of his size,' Vincent says still with a trace of amazement, 'he came up to a race' – a regular O'Brien phrase – 'surprisingly quickly.'

He won the Erne Stakes at The Curragh at the start of July so easily that, as the lads recall, 'after that first race all Ireland was talking of him.' Word had flown about even before; he started odds-on. He never started odds against until he contested the Epsom Derby halfway through his three year old career.

Between 12 July and 27 September, he won four successive races on Ireland's Curragh, including the top two year old events, the Railway, the Anglesey, and the Beresford Stakes. 'In his races he never sweated,' say the lads, 'he'd pull up dry.' And Vincent says with less hyperbole, 'Well, as he progressed, he sweated less.'

With these four Irish victories behind him, Nijinsky crossed to Newmarket for the Dewhurst Stakes. This, too, he won in such style that he was made favourite for next year's classics, and was rated top of the Free Handicap. The difficult high-mettled horse of whom O'Brien had so nearly despaired nine months earlier, had won all his five starts in the space of a mere thirteen weeks.

He was a very hot property. His domination of the British and Irish two year old scene focussed attention on his sire, who now had another crop to run for him. Britons who, until O'Brien, had taken scant notice of the richness of American racing, began to tell one another that Northern Dancer had after all won two parts of America's Triple Crown. He won the Kentucky Derby, the 'Run for the Roses' round flat and urban Churchill Downs, Louisville, and also the Preakness. He had failed to stay the $1\frac{1}{2}$ miles of the Belmont Stakes in New York's greener suburbs on Long Island. They checked on Nijinsky's Canadian mother, Flaming Page. She had won Canada's top race for home-breds, the $1\frac{1}{4}$ mile Queen's Plate, and she had also won the 10 furlong Canadian Oaks.

This horse Nijinsky was now worth a fortune. The $84,000 paid for him was a bargain. And no-one yet knew how enormously Northern Dancer was going to influence the Turf.

Grey-haired Davy Walsh, who has shod all O'Brien's six Epsom Derby winners, remembers Nijinsky having only one physical setback that winter. 'He gave his hock a twist and was off work for two weeks.'

The spring came and the hot winter favourite for the Guineas was in tremendous form. Johnny Brabston rode him in all his home work. 'He looked great in the spring and his early work was terrific.'

His prep race for the Two Thousand Guineas was the race named after another famous graduate of Ballydoyle. Nijinsky won his sixth race from six starts by taking the Gladness Stakes on The Curragh. Runner-up to him was a future champion National Hunt sire, Deep Run. Nijinsky went to Newmarket protected with great security. O'Brien hired his own private detective to aid the official guards on The Links stables. He was a prime target for nobbling. Estimates on raceday were that he would cost bookmakers £500,000 if he won (William Hill would lose £75,000 and Ladbrokes about £110,000 alone). To keep their further liabilities down, the colt, 3 to 1 at the season's start, was pushed by the bookmakers to prohibitive odds on. He started 7 to 4 *on* favourite for the Guineas. *Timeform* Annual recognised something quite exceptional: 'In the paddock he outclassed his rivals as seldom a classic field can have been outclassed before.'

On Guineas morning, 29 April 1970, the *Sporting Life* headline below its one shilling cover price read in black capitals ¾″ high, 'WHO'S GOING TO BE SECOND TO NIJINSKY?'

'He will start the hottest favourite,' wrote Man on the Spot, 'since Colombo landed the odds of 7 to 2 on back in 1934.' Piggott was quoted by Our Man in Paris: 'The colt is at least 8 lb better than Sir Ivor when he won in 1968.'

Nijinsky won the Two Thousand Guineas by 2½ lengths from David Robinson's Yellow God. The example of David Robinson, the self-made radio and TV millionaire philanthropist, would later influence Robert Sangster towards his Ballydoyle connection.

Nijinsky's final preparation for the Derby took place neither at Ballydoyle nor Epsom, but at Sandown Park, a sister course to Epsom within the United Racecourses group managed by businesslike Tim Neligan. The Sandown arrangement had been prepared for O'Brien before. The quiet of the place, its remoteness from would-be dopers, press and photographers, and yet its short drive to Epsom were its combined attractions. Hot favourites have been nobbled too often before the Derby. No chances were taken.

But, at the eleventh hour, and in spite of all these carefully laid plans, something nearly went terribly wrong with the unbeaten colt who was a racing certainty to add the Derby to his Guineas.

Nijinsky flew over from Shannon and arrived at Sandown on the Friday night, five days before the race. On the Saturday, he trotted on the course. On Sunday he worked at half-speed (meaning a good swinging gallop), the reverse way along the backstretch back to the stables. On Monday, he did the same but a bit quicker and that afternoon he was moved over to Epsom. On Tuesday morning, his training was in accordance with O'Brien's established pre-Derby pattern: working uphill for four furlongs from the 1½-mile Derby start. After this, Nijinsky walked down Tattenham Hill with his working partner, Ribot Prince, and then they both hacked along – 'just lobbing' – along the straight, under the grandstands, towards the winning post and the racecourse stables.

So far so good. And so soon a fearful fright. Nijinsky, back in the racecourse stables, was rubbed down. 'The boss,' say the lads, 'was there watching. Then we noticed the horse starting to paw. He went on pawing and got down in his box and started to sweat.'

The symptoms seemed to be that of colic. The sweating increased but it was, the boys remember, a very hot day. Gerry rang the Epsom trainer, Irishman 'Boggy' Whelan, to ask him for the name of a local vet. Vincent comments, 'Boggy Whelan has been so helpful to the Ballydoyle horses over many years, and he saddles for me, if I can't be there for some reason.' Vincent telephoned the faithful Bob Griffin over in Ireland, asking him to fly over with all speed. Bob heard Vincent's concise report of the symptoms and said it sounded as if the horse had at least got 'a slight twinge of colic'. He said to Vincent, 'Even if I came over, I couldn't *treat* the horse. We couldn't give him any medication the day before a race.'

The normal veterinary treatment for colitis is the injection of a drug which relaxes the muscles and the intestines which are in spasm. The painful gas can then escape. But Nijinsky was within twenty-nine hours of the race. The local vet confirmed Bob's telephoned diagnosis. All they could do was hope and wait and pray that it passed.

The crisis lasted about 1½ hours which, for the O'Brien camp, seemed infinitely longer. Then the horse became easier. The lads walked across the course to the wood behind the start to gather some grass for Nijinsky. They mixed this with a little soda bicarbonate and some bran, and anxiously preferred it. Tensely, they waited to see if the horse was still feeling queasy and would reject it. Nijinsky ate the little meal. 'He was restful. We stayed watching. The boss was there all day. And, by the evening, the horse was as fresh as ever.'

The crisis had passed. The horse never again travelled without Demi O'Byrne, the young vet from Tipperary who cared for him so faithfully. Few people knew of the threat to Nijinsky. Even the bookmakers' notorious spy service failed. If word of Nijinsky's attack had leaked out, panic would have struck not just the betting market. The news would have touched those five or

Having won seven races in succession, including the Two Thousand Guineas, Nijinsky works on Epsom racecourse ridden by Johnny Brabston before the Derby of 1970.

six million citizens who bet only twice a year: on the Grand National and on the Derby. 'DERBY FAVOURITE STRUCK DOWN' would have made the evening papers and the O'Briens would have been besieged by reporters. O'Brien had no obligation to report the attack of colic which had so swiftly come and so blessedly gone. After his interrogation when Larkspur won the Derby, O'Brien

The O'Briens' three daughters from left Sue, Jane and Liz got off school to watch the race. It was said that their convent's building fund was faithfully placed on the winner!

had little inclination to issue further public bulletins about his horses' health, which might in the end only turn out to be misleading.

Nijinsky started favourite for the Derby at 11 to 8, the first time in his career he had started at odds against. Gyr, stoutly bred in the USA and strongly fancied at 100 to 30, set sail for home on the fast ground two furlongs out. Piggott had merely to shake up Nijinsky and show him the whip. The colt moved into top gear, went past Gyr and won comfortably by 2½ lengths. Gerry Oldham's Stintino was a further 3 lengths away third. The time of the race nearly equalled Mahmoud's record, clocked by handheld watches and so regarded in some quarters as suspect. The next time the record was going to be so nearly broken was twelve years later, when Nijinsky's son, Golden Fleece, took home the sixth Epsom Derby to Ballydoyle. Coincidentally, Golden Fleece would also prove only the sixth winner of the Derby to be sired by a previous Derby winner. Mahmoud by Derby winner Blenheim was hand-timed in 1936 at 2 min 33.8 sec. Golden Fleece's electronically timed figure was 2 min 34.27 sec. Nijinsky clocked 2 min 34.68 sec. After Nijinsky's victory, the Engelhards and the O'Briens were taken, as is customary, up to the Royal Box. But in the excitement of the race, the very stout Mr Engelhard's braces had broken.

He was thus presented to the Queen Mother clutching his grey top hat and his stick, while keeping his trousers up as best he could with his elbows.

'Oh, Mr Engelhard,' said the Queen Mother, with her lovely thoughtfulness, as the owner in his hour of glory went forward to shake hands, 'Do let me take your hat. You seem to be having some difficulty. Can I hold something?'

Mr Engelhard shook hands, elbows still upholding trousers. He said afterwards to Jacqueline O'Brien, 'If I'd moved my arms, my trousers would have fallen down!'

Nijinsky's next race was the Irish Derby and here he was ridden by Liam Ward, who remained the stable's first jockey in Ireland, with Piggott being number one in England. The popularity of the horse and his Irish jockey drew buzzing attention on The Curragh. During the lengthy preliminaries he showed, for the first time on a racecourse, the keyed-up characteristics which had marked his work at home. He sweated up. He was noticeably upset. But there was no repeat of the Sir Ivor defeat. The Irish crowds' voices rang out loud and long for Liam, for in this race he beat Lester Piggott into second place.

The rain hosed down and in it, after the race, stood Charlie Engelhard clutching the presentation silver chalice. It was filling to the brim with soft Irish rain. He glanced up into the leaden downpour and murmured to Jacqueline O'Brien, 'If this goes on much longer, it'll turn to wine ...' Later, pressed by journalists about the number of horses he owned and their cost in keep, he said happily, 'I can tell you one thing – all my horses will eat tonight!'

No problems beset the horse between his ninth successive victory and his return to England to attempt his toughest battle yet in Ascot's King George VI and Queen Elizabeth Stakes on 25 July. It would be the great horse's fifth race in sixteen weeks, proof positive of his magnificent constitution, the delicate timing of O'Brien's training, and the work of the staff with a horse who could, in lesser hands, have been turned into a nervous wreck. Had he fallen among the ignorant or the rough, or been trained on an American racecourse or in a large English training centre busy and bucking with hundreds of other people's horses, his temperament might have cracked. His natural nerves might have turned into sullen anger and a complete refusal to work, and he would then have been disposed of as a stallion to a lesser racing nation.

As it was, when he arrived at Ascot the unbeaten colt was being talked of in the same breath as Ribot and Sea-Bird II. His task was formidable. He was the only three year old in a field which included two previous Derby winners, the winners of the previous year's French Oaks and the Washington International, and the current holder of the Coronation Cup.

Piggott resumed the ride and rode him with a confidence which, when repeated two-and-a-half months later, contributed to Nijinsky's defeat in the Arc de Triomphe. At Ascot in July he simply sauntered to the front one furlong

(opposite above): At odds against for the first time in his life Nijinsky, bred in Canada, owned by an American, trained in Ireland easily defeats the French hope Gyr to win the Epsom Derby ... And (below) within four weeks wins the Irish Derby ridden by Liam Ward. This was Nijinsky's ninth successive victory.

(above): Phonsie left, and Maurice escort him in with his lad Tom O'Gorman who has now been with the stable for some thirty years.

After the Irish Derby in the pouring rain Nijinsky's owner Charlie Engelhard (centre) said 'If this goes on much longer the water in this chalice will turn to wine'. About to present it is Anna McGrath wife of Paddy (between them). From the left Jacqueline, David McCall, Charlie Engelhard's racing manager, Charlie's sister-in-law, Joe McGrath and Lord Donoughmore.

out and coasted home hard-held from the 1969 Derby winner, Blakeney. It was the performance of a horse outstanding not just in his year, but of his generation.

But fate had another blow to deal at the golden colt. Within a week of his return to Ballydoyle, Nijinsky was struck down by a particularly virulent form of ringworm. 'So much of his hair fell out that he was bald over most of his body,' Vincent reports. 'Of course, there was no way we could put a saddle on him. The most we could do was to lead him out and to lunge him a little.' Then Charlie Engelhard's racing manager, David McCall, got in touch with O'Brien: 'Charlie would get the greatest pleasure if we could win the Triple

Crown with Nijinsky. Do you think, Vincent, you could get him ready in time for the St Leger?'

It was a difficult request. Nijinsky's final grand goal was to be the Arc de Triomphe. The St Leger over ¼ mile further and run a month earlier was not the ideal prep race. It says much for the greatness of the horse as well, sadly, of the diminishing standard of the St Leger, that Britain's fifth classic could be considered merely a 'prep race' for a contest abroad. In the American market place, the St Leger is of little importance. To win one may even condemn a horse for lacking 1¼-mile speed. In the States, racing men rate only three European races at the top: Epsom's Derby; Ascot's 'King George VI'; and Longchamp's 'Arc'. O'Brien adds, 'And the Irish Derby, making four.'

Time was short. The horse's work had been severely held up by the ringworm. 'Even in late August,' the lads report, 'you could not ride him for ten minutes or he'd bleed.'

But no horse had won the three colts' classics since Bahram in 1935. Furthermore, O'Brien reasoned, the horse did need one prep race before the Arc. There was nothing else very suitable. With little breathing space after the ringworm the horse 'worked patchy before going over to Doncaster', the lads remember.

There did not seem much in the race. 'The opposition may not have been strong,' says Vincent, 'but they certainly set out to make it a test of stamina. He won, but I would say he wouldn't have pulled out any more. Furthermore, he lost 29 lb in weight coming back from the St Leger ...' The inference is stark: a fit horse loses very little after a race. Up till the St Leger, Nijinsky had gone through his unbeaten career of eleven victories without losing condition. Up till then he throve.

With hindsight Vincent could say, 'The Leger would not have helped his preparation for the Arc.' But he had, however, won the Triple Crown, the first horse to do so for thirty-five years, for his kindly, popular owner.

Some doubt about Lester Piggott's abounding confidence in Nijinsky's super equine powers troubled O'Brien. Ten days before the Arc, the trainer telephoned the jockey. He told him that Nijinsky's coat was coming better every day. 'The horse is working as well as ever.' Then he said, 'The records show that the winner of the Arc invariably holds a prominent position throughout the race.' He added, 'You must lie up. Few horses further back than fourth turning into the straight go on to win the Arc.'

Vincent now says, 'So I made that suggestion about riding the horse ... that he might not want to be too far out of his ground, turning into the straight – principally because of beaten horses coming back on him. Lester's exact reply to me was "I don't care if there are one hundred horses in front of me!"'

This last target for the superb horse was missed only by inches. Nijinsky

This is the only photograph we can find which shows Vincent in recent times leading in one of his winners. This is at Ascot in July 1970 when Nijinsky has won his tenth successive race, the King George VI and Queen Elizabeth Stakes beating Derby winner Blakeney.

coming from very far behind, and unable to find an opening, was forced to swing out wider and wider. He just failed to catch Sassafras by a short head. The defeat still aches, because Vincent believes it was no fault of Nijinsky's. It hurt initially because it was so desperately close that the verdict was uncertain and, while the photograph was being developed, Vincent went on hoping.

'I was a good way before the winning post watching. Everybody around me said the horse had won. I had my doubts, but I hung on the hope that maybe he had.' Then, with one of his gentle understatements, 'This made things a little tougher to take ...'

Nijinsky, the object of the racing world's attention, had been pursued by photographers round the pretty Longchamp paddock. They certainly upset him. Vincent talks about 'their mad antics. They may have taken a bit out of him. But it was hardly the real cause, though it could have made the difference of a head. Still, had the horse been right, I don't think it would have been a matter of a head.'

Nijinsky was badly drawn, too: 'Lester had him well behind,' Vincent sadly recounts, 'in fact, he was fourth from last with half a mile to go. And he wasn't getting an opening.... Still he wasn't getting any opening ... and he kept edging out – and out – and out. Meanwhile, Saint-Martin was on the inside, making the best of his way home. He knew Sassafras would get the trip. Lester hit Nijinsky once and the horse ran further left ...' The recollection after thirteen years makes O'Brien still feel wretched.

Johnny Brabston was standing 1½ furlongs before the winning post. 'I thought the horse was so far out of his ground,' he remembers, 'that he wouldn't even be placed. Then he had to come on the outside. I suppose it was the swerve away from the whip that cost him the race in the end.'

Five months after the race Vincent stated unequivocally to American turf writer, Leon Rasmussen, 'I sincerely believe that the run Lester asked Nijinsky to make was over too long a distance ... that, in the Arc, was an impossibility. The horse had shown Lester such tremendous speed in all his races that he felt he could pick them up whenever he wanted. Once again, Longchamp is different ...'

It is easy to see why, a decade later, sitting with O'Brien in that sunny room at Ballydoyle, Lester would say '... we've had some great days together – and some bloody awful days ... Longchamp and Newmarket!'

The supreme jockey requires no apologist. But some facts need repeating. In that sad Arc de Triomphe for Nijinsky, he beat Gyr, who finished fourth, further than he beat him in the Derby. And he doubled the distance by which he had beaten Blakeney in Ascot's King George VI and Queen Elizabeth Stakes. Compared with the running of those two races, he did not run below form. Indeed, he improved on it.

'Of course, Nijinsky wouldn't have gone for the Champion Stakes, if he'd won the Arc,' says Vincent crisply, 'but he seemed all right after the race. The trip hadn't caused him to lose much weight. The opposition seemed weak. It looked as if he had little to beat. And we wanted to let him finish his career on a high note: by winning.'

Until Longchamp, it had seemed certain that Nijinsky would go all through his racing days unbeaten. Well, Newmarket would erase Longchamp. But there were unluckily only thirteen days between the races.

'He looked perfectly well in the paddock at Newmarket,' Vincent O'Brien remembers, 'but as soon as he started to leave it, and go on to the course he began – for the first time – to crack under the attentions of the photographers and all his admirers and the cheering for him which broke out in the parade.' The lads recall, 'He reared up for the first time since he was a two year old. He was terribly uptight.'

And Vincent says that, after the race, Noel Murless, who was to English racing what Vincent was to Irish, told him, 'I was standing by the gate as they went out onto the course and I saw that Nijinsky was actually trembling. I said to the groundsman who was standing with me, "That horse can't win in the state he's in."'

The crowd milled round their hero even down at the start. 'I saw on the film afterwards that he was a sorry sight.' Vincent says so many years later, 'It was a sad day. Really *dreadful*.' No other race has so openly and for so long upset O'Brien. Nijinsky was beaten by Lorenzaccio, who made all the running. So ended the dreadful day. Nijinsky was retired to stud and went to join Sir Ivor at the late Bull Hancock's lovely farm Claiborne, lying above the lake and stream beyond Paris, Kentucky. Vigorous efforts had been made to raise a syndicate from England, Ireland and France to keep the great horse in Europe, but they failed to approach the value placed on him in America, which was $5½ million. Charlie Engelhard's family retained ten shares in him.

How does Vincent compare Nijinsky with all his horses? 'I would have to rate him first or second. Him or Sir Ivor. For brilliance: Nijinsky. For toughness: Sir Ivor. And Golden Fleece, for he was never tested. Does that answer your question?'

As for those other greats, Ribot and Sea-Bird II, Vincent O'Brien says quietly, 'It has to be remembered that Ribot, over three seasons, only left his homeland on three occasions, and Sea-Bird only once.

'At three years old, Nijinsky ran eight times against Sea-Bird's five. All but two of Nijinsky's three year old races were outside Ireland. He faced international competition at Newmarket, Epsom, Ascot, Doncaster, Longchamp and Newmarket again, with the Irish Derby thrown in. All in one season.'

Vincent's case for Nijinsky rests.

Nijinsky posed in the main yard at Ballydoyle. It was always very hard to get him to pose correctly as he used to like to stretch his neck forward.

14

'You should have a piece of the action'

The retirement of Nijinsky to Claiborne introduces an important figure in Vincent's life. 'Jack Mulcahy,' says Vincent, 'has had horses at Ballydoyle since 1971, when he was buying Thatch. He said to me at that time, "I can't understand you remaining *only* a *trainer*! You should have a piece of the action. You should be part owner of the horses in your yard."' Vincent concludes with feeling, 'This was the best advice I ever got.' Vincent's account of how he acted so successfully upon it is of particular interest, for it corrects some widely held impressions of the birth of the O'Brien–Sangster syndicate.

The man who gave the advice had made his own way, too, in a hard world. Jack Mulcahy left Ireland in the 1920s with very little money to emigrate to the U.S.A. He struggled through the American Depression, taking the most menial jobs to stay alive and, in the best traditions of American enterprise, studying accountancy at night school. He qualified and found a job with a steel company called Quigley. He became the confidant and friend of Mr Quigley and, on the owner's death, ran the company for his widow. 'Finally,' says Vincent, 'he wound up owning the company.'

Jack Mulcahy's connection with Vincent was through a brother, Dan, the cashier in the Munster and Leinster Bank in Cork, with whom Vincent opened an account back in 1943. 'I still have my account there and never, in all that time, was there a problem regarding the amount I was overdrawn!'

Jack Mulcahy made his fortune in America but never forgot Ireland. On the contrary, Vincent says, 'Never has an Irishman spent so much money in the promotion of his country.' He bought three big houses in Ireland including Ashford Castle, which he turned into a world-famous hotel and where President Reagan stayed in 1984, and he chartered jets to bring Americans over to see his homeland, to encourage them to set up businesses and to expand tourism. With money, leisure and energy to spare, Jack Mulcahy thought, not unusually for an Irishman, about horses.

'Bull Hancock,' Vincent recalls, 'was a very close friend of mine and one of the biggest men in the history of American thoroughbred racing and breeding. His father started Claiborne Stud and Bull built it up to be among the greatest, if not the greatest, stud in the world, with a wonderful collection of foundation mares and top stallions.

'Bull had already enjoyed great fortune in his European associations. On his

Northern Dancer, imperial founder of the dynasty.

The empress of the dynasty, Natalma, dam of Northern Dancer, 27 years young in the autumn of 1983.

Flaming Page, dam of only 3 foals, but one was Nijinsky, and another was Fleur, dam of The Minstrel; what a wonderful proud look.

The gallops of Ballydoyle, made by Vincent from ordinary farm fields. In the background stands Slievenamon, site of the ancient Irish legend. The mountain's name means 'Hill of the Woman'. On the top sat the King who chose as his bride the first woman to reach him from a level start. Selective breeding for speed plus stamina . . .

Jack Mulcahy, known as 'Uncle Jack' to the O'Brien family and the man who gave Vincent 'the best bit of advice I ever had'. Here he is congratulating Vincent's son David on training a winner.

first visit to the Newmarket sales he bought Nasrullah, probably the greatest sire ever to enter the U.S., for comparatively little money. He also bought three mares including Knight's Daughter, who subsequently bred the great racehorse, Round Table.'

He was anxious to tighten even further his association with Europe. 'Bull so much admired Vincent,' Waddell Hancock, Bull's widow from the Deep South, said recently, 'that he wanted him to come over to America and train for Claiborne. Yes I remember Bull saying to Vincent, "If you come over, you can have a farm, you can have a place at the racetrack, anything if you'd just come and train the horses."'

'Vincent did contemplate moving to the States to train,' says Jacqueline O'Brien, 'but he decided that he could not stand the hardship of training on the track; that he would never be able to do his best with the horses there.'

Jack Mulcahy, aware of the friendship between the two men, said to Vincent, 'Bull's a friend of yours, and he's got the best yearlings in America. Why don't we get a piece of his action, and ask if we can share the yearlings – buy into this year's crop.' And so was borne the idea by which some horses born, bred or raised at Claiborne would be trained by Vincent for himself and his patrons. Amongst these horses were such famous horses as Thatch, Sir Ivor, Lisadell, Apalachee, Cellini, King Pelinor, Lady Capulet and Gay Fandango.

Vincent recalls, 'I set up a meeting between Jack, Bull and myself. The three of us spent the evening together and the next day Bull said, "I was thinking about Jack in the night and the more I thought about him the more I liked him." Bull then suggested I select three or four yearlings from Claiborne and that we three should go into partnership. One of these yearlings was Thatch, who became Europe's champion miler.

'The following year, 1972, Bull Hancock proposed that we join his partnership with his old friend, Bill Perry. His idea now was that all the Claiborne yearlings be split three ways: one third to Ireland where I would train them; one third to race in the U.S. in Bill Perry's name; and one third to race in Bull's own name in the U.S. We would toss up for first pick of the yearlings. Bull Hancock, Bill Perry and Jack tossed. Jack won the toss, invoking St Patrick, which gave me first choice, and I took Apalachee, who turned out to be the champion two year old in Great Britain, and Lisadell, who won the Coronation Stakes at three years old. The horses that were to come to Ireland were valued and Jack and I each bought into them.

So it was that, six years before Robert Sangster's The Minstrel won the Derby, Vincent was already launched into the conception of 'having a piece of the action', of owning part of the horses he selected and trained, and of making top class stallions.

'It was only a few months later when Bull became very ill at the end of 1972

Laying down the new all-weather gallop. Two feet of earth are excavated, piped drains are laid then stones graduated from large at the bottom to small at the top. A special plastic which water can penetrate is put over the stones and on top of this about eight inches of wood chippings. The gallop is harrowed after each piece of work.

and died. Our happy association with him was sadly at an end. He stated in his will that the Claiborne yearlings should be sold and each year we were substantial buyers of their stock at the Keeneland sales. His son, Seth, decided after 1981 not to continue this policy, but to put the animals in training for Claiborne.'

15

'That horse won't win at Epsom'

Sir Ivor in 1968. Nijinsky in 1970. Then, in 1972, O'Brien and Piggott won their third Epsom Derby in five years when Roberto fought home by a short head from Rheingold. Like the other two, Roberto was bred in North America and he belonged to an American, for whom Vincent trained from 1968 to 1975. Mr John Galbreath, who owns Darby Dan Farm, in one of the prettiest parts of Kentucky's Bluegrass, bred the colt. He was by the classic-producing sire Hail to Reason out of a top class race mare, Bramalea, who won eight races in the States. She was by the illustrious Nashua, so the family was as strongly American as blueberry pie.

Vincent had met John Galbreath at the Saratoga sales one August. 'He asked me if I would train for him. A year or so later, he asked me would I look at his yearlings during the Keeneland sales.' The yearlings were at Columbus, Ohio, and also at Darby Dan. One of the yearlings offered to Vincent to train was Roberto. 'You wouldn't say,' Vincent comments, 'that he was one of the best-looking yearlings of his year. Like a lot of Hail to Reason's, he didn't have the best of knees. He trained all right as a two year old though. He proved a very good two year old.' He won his first three races in Ireland, including the Anglesey and the National Stakes, most impressively. His pattern followed that of an O'Brien classic colt in his two-year-old season: first run about mid-July, then a couple more before the end of the year.

He suffered two setbacks, one physical, the other psychological, on his arrival at Ballydoyle as a yearling. 'He had a virus,' Johnny Brabston remembers, 'and was quite a while in the stable with it. He had a nasal discharge for many months. And he was tempermental in the starting stalls. Not so much frightened, as objecting to them. He didn't like being shut in. We always try to coax horses in. But he had a go at the stalls. He'd try to get up on his hindlegs! So every evening through February and March I used to lead him out and through the stalls.'

After his three victories in Ireland, Roberto was being hailed as a third Sir Ivor or Nijinsky. He was rated clear top of the Madrid Free Handicap with 10 stone. But the stalls were again to cause trouble when he was sent to France for his final two year old race, the Grand Criterium.

Johnny Brabston took him over to Longchamp and was required to put him through the stalls before the day's racing to satisfy the French starter. 'He came

Roberto's breeder and owner John Galbreath with his wife Dorothy racing in America.

out all right the first time,' says Johnny, 'but the Frenchman wanted him to do it again. The boss was watching and not too happy about this. The second time Roberto reared up and fell back. He slipped coming out.' The French starter then told Johnny to do it yet again. O'Brien immediately intervened. He remonstrated with the starter as powerfully as he could, for neither could speak the other's language. O'Brien won the day. 'The boss,' says Johnny Brabston, 'was a bit angered.'

In the race Roberto came out of the stalls perfectly and settled just behind the leaders. At halfway he inexplicably but, as it would later transpire, significantly lost his place. This left him too much ground to recapture coming up the straight. He finished fourth.

'Frankly, we thought he (Lester) had ridden an ill-judged race and now that the smoke of battle has died away, we still hold to that opinion,' stated *Timeform* at the end of the year. The smoke had, of course, not cleared away. It never does by the end of a two year old's career. This race was one of the hottest Grand Criteria to be run. From the first four that day came the winners of the next year's Irish, French and English Derby's: Steel Pulse; Hard to Beat and Roberto. 'William Hill,' says Vincent, 'was present to see the race and he said Roberto was no Derby horse!'

What hindsight would also reveal was that all Roberto's disappointing races were run on right-handed tracks. He always tended to hang to the left even when galloping at home, in spite of being fitted with a special bit. He disliked going right-handed, although, as when winning the Derby and the Benson and Hedges he also drifted right in a race on a left-hand track. This is likely to have been caused by his resolution overcoming discomfort in his knees when at full stretch under pressure.

'Over that winter,' Johnny Brabston remembers, 'he got very strong. We let him forget about the stalls. He was about the only one with real classic potential that winter. He was always a wonderful mover.'

His prep race for the English Two Thousand Guineas was on April Fool's Day at Phoenix Park. Vincent says 'It rained a great deal and I had grave misgivings about running him. But finally I decided to run, because there wasn't much choice for a prep race, and because I thought that, as it had rained so much, the ground would be sloppy, not holding.'

In fact, the going at Phoenix Park did not suit Roberto at all. 'He won all right, but after the race all was not one hundred per cent with him in front. Bob Griffin expressed his opinion that Roberto was lucky to get away with it. He told me the horse would not want to run on that sort of ground again.'

The force of Bob Griffin's opinion here is important. The fact that Roberto's forelegs, particularly his knees, had seriously been threatened by sticky ground was never forgotten by his trainer. The following year, O'Brien was criticised in the press, by the public and by racing's establishment, for refusing to risk him in the Eclipse and the Benson and Hedges. He stood fast. He lost some popularity. But Roberto retired to stud having had three seasons racing without breaking down on the track. He had not been risked and this, when it came to retiring the horse to stud, was finally of great benefit to his owners.

It was a foul, wet spring. Dermot O'Brien accompanied Roberto to Newmarket a week ahead of the Two Thousand Guineas. 'I walked miles over the gallops trying to find a suitable piece of ground to work him on. It rained and it bloody well rained! In the end Tom Jones gave us a bit of ground.' Even the horse's jockey, Bill 'Weary Willie' Williamson was affected by the difficulties. 'He was not,' says Dermot, 'coming up with much enthusiasm.' The brothers conferred. Vincent urged Dermot to try to cheer Williamson up. 'It was a difficult task,' says Dermot, 'but one day it must have worked, for next morning the horse dropped a couple of points in the ante-post market. So the word must have got about!'

He started second favourite to High Top, who bowled along in front. Roberto, however, was kept at the back of the field and Johnny Brabston remembers 'Weary Willie' saying as he came in, 'I'd have won the race if I'd known the horse better. I hung too far out.' Roberto had to work his way through the ruck, encouraging some scrimmaging on his way forward. He emerged from the field in second place only a furlong from the post. High Top seemed to be coasting home. But Roberto kept on accelerating, drew closer and closer and got to High Top's girth on the line.

He could certainly have been better ridden but he showed he was tough, resolute and that he stayed. He seemed to be an excellent Derby hope and was on offer after the Guineas at an attractive 8 to 1 because the word was that, in Boucher, O'Brien had a better horse at home.

All went well with Roberto between the Guineas and the Derby, but setbacks, confusion and some acrimony beset his probable partners. First there was a possibility that Lester Piggott would ride Boucher and then, when that horse was taken out of the race, that he would ride O'Brien's Manitoulin owned by Mrs Dorothy Galbreath. Piggott had shown a preference for Manitoulin.

Vincent recalls with a smile Lester Piggott coming over to Ballydoyle to ride work on Manitoulin against Roberto. 'Roberto was a lazy horse. He'd pull himself up as soon as he passed a horse. Lester watched Roberto do that when he passed him and said "That horse won't win at Epsom!"' Something good about Roberto must however have struck Piggott, for Vincent says, 'But afterwards Lester came to me and asked me about the horse. I told him that was how he always worked.'

Piggott, with five Epsom Derbies already harvested, was searching through the current crop to find the likeliest winner for his sixth. Most of the jockeys with fancied Derby rides looked uneasily around them and slept twitchily at nights. Piggott, they knew, would not hesitate to approach owner or trainer and proffer his services. He had already put in a bid for the ride on Roberto in the Derby. Vincent smiles slightly recalling the barrage of criticism from the British press on the eve of the Derby. 'After the Guineas,' he says, 'Lester came up to me at Newmarket and said to me "If I'd ridden that horse, he'd have won." And he tried then to get on him for the Derby.'

Piggott's views thus expressed, were not particularly kind or helpful to a fellow jockey.

Bill Williamson, though booked for Roberto, was aware of Piggott's interest and could not feel blissfully secure. 'He should have felt secure,' Vincent corrects. 'He would without question have ridden the colt, had he not fallen and hurt himself.' For ten days before the Derby 'Wearie Willie's' insecurity took a different turn. He took a bad fall at Kempton, hurt his shoulder painfully, and was laid off. T. P. Burns reported 'The horse crossed his legs and gave him the mother and father of a fall. He might have been weeks off.'

A fall on the flat, though far rarer than a fall jumping, often does more damage. It's quite unexpected; the jockey is sitting perched up his horse's neck; and, when he hits the ground, the shock is greater. Furthermore, the flat-race jockey is usually more fragile, lighter and older than his jumping brothers.

Vincent O'Brien now had to make speedy contingency plans, lest Williamson's shoulder failed to recover in time. It had to be strong enough not just to support a teacup. Williamson had to be physically fit enough to ride a tough lazy horse in an exacting classic on an eccentric course. Vincent discovered that Williamson had gone for treatment to that good friend of jockeys, cricketers, and other sportsmen, kind, wise Bill Tucker, who ran his clinic in Mayfair with the shrewd geniality of a popular clubman.

'Tucker told me,' says Vincent, 'that we could really only tell if the shoulder was completely right when Bill Williamson got back and rode a horse.'

Mr John Galbreath, however, was understandably pressing O'Brien for news. It was plain that if Williamson was doubtful then the owner wanted another jockey. 'Piggott was waiting on Mrs Galbreath's horse,' Vincent adds.

O'Brien takes full responsibility for the change of jockey which brought on him a critical fusillade. 'Bearing in mind what Tucker had said, I was glad to hear that Williamson was going to ride work for an Epsom trainer on Tuesday morning, the day before the Derby. Bill Tucker had passed him fit to ride on the Monday. I thought we could leave the decision till Tuesday; till we had seen how his shoulder was when he had ridden out at Epsom.'

So it was left for one more day, to the last day before the Derby. 'Then I heard that Williamson hadn't turned up to ride work at Epsom. I was told he'd

Roberto (right) *ridden by Lester Piggott in his Tam o'Shanter walking back after working at Epsom before the Derby. Johnny Brabston rides the lead horse.*

said he had overslept. In any case, it didn't look very good. John Galbreath was now very uneasy. He asked me to get Williamson to meet us both at Claridge's.

'But when I arrived, I found Williamson already there and that Galbreath had already informed him that, in his opinion, he could not possibly be fit to ride. John Galbreath owned the Pittsburg Pirates and told Williamson that he had considerable experience of athletes' injuries and, in his opinion, Williamson could not be one hundred per cent fit to ride Roberto in the Derby. He said he wanted Piggott to ride Roberto, but that Williamson would get the same present as Piggott got if the horse won.'

The decision was ruthless, but perfectly fair. The offer was generous. Bill Williamson took this pronouncement stoically. 'No,' says Vincent, 'he'd never get livid, as you put it. He was not that kind of character.'

The British racing press, however, tore into O'Brien, Galbreath and Piggott with a splendid display of old world virtues. The public accepted the press reports and the crowd at Epsom burst into prolonged applause when Williamson rode a winner there.

Williamson, thus deposed, had to watch the Derby from the stands, but he did ride two winners of the other five races, winning the Woodcote on Captive

The desperate finish for the 1972 Epsom Derby with Lester (right) *just getting home on Roberto from Rheingold who later won the Prix de l'Arc de Triomphe.*

Dream and the Craven on Capistrano. Financially, it was a good day for Williamson. Piggott's strength and energy had, while depriving him of public glory, earned him a fat percentage. And Bill Tucker's prognosis had been proved accurate: the jockey was indeed fit enough to ride and to win, too.

But would he have proved strong enough that day to prevail on Roberto in that desperate short-head struggle over Rheingold? Piggott then was, and still remains, the strongest English jockey riding. Would a weaker jockey have succeeded?

Press comments were divided between hearty admiration of Piggott's strength and genius, and horror at the severity with which he had hammered Roberto home.

After Roberto's subsequent defeat in the Irish Derby run on the right-handed Curragh *Timeform* wondered 'how Roberto had recovered from his hiding, for hiding it was, make no mistake. Our thoughts ... were ... that it would take a long time to get over such a severe race, and we don't propose to look any further for an explanation of his defeat' (in the Irish Derby).

Some contrary pieces of evidence need presenting. Johnny Brabston said after the Epsom Derby that there was no mark on the horse. In case there was a recurrence of Roberto's old dislike of the stalls, Lester Piggott had insisted that Johnny go across the course with him to the start. 'So the Derby was over by when I got back. I could hear from the shouting that it was one of ours. Then there was twenty minutes to wait with the photograph and the Stewards enquiry and all. And Lester said afterwards that he'd have objected to Rheingold, for Rheingold had rolled onto Roberto . . .'

Furthermore, Lester reported to Jacqueline O'Brien afterwards, 'I was hardly able to hit him, because I hadn't got any room!' And Vincent reports, 'John Galbreath and I went to the stables. The horse was fine. No mark at all.'

Vincent continues: 'It's impossible to say whether Williamson would have won. But I couldn't see it.' Then he adds fairly and astutely, 'Unless, that is, the horse would have done more for Williamson than he did for Piggott. Lester rode a great race on him. He did nothing wrong. But he told me afterwards that Roberto wasn't doing much for him, he should have won much more easily . . . And apparently Roberto's mother, Bramalea, was like that – it wasn't every day she would do her best . . .'

The gentle touch can often win when hammering will not.

In the twenty minutes wait for the verdict, the O'Briens had to endure further public harassment. Two large and formidable ladies of the Turf, bitterly incensed by O'Brien's deposing of Williamson, made their views known to him like trumpets before a battle and one felt powerfully enough about it at Epsom to threaten the smaller Vincent with her umbrella. Her inside-right in the onslaught 'was a hefty lady,' says Vincent, 'who had about me, too! And she's never spoken to me since!'

In the meantime, Roberto went home to Ireland, worked well and then ran deplorably in the Irish Derby. *Timeform* said this was due to the 'hiding' it saw Roberto receive in the English Derby. Other form books, however, deduced that, since all Roberto's bad races were run on right-hand tracks, hanging left was the cause of it. Vincent O'Brien adds his own informed comment, 'Johnny Roe came in for the ride in the Irish Sweeps Derby because the arrangement was that he should ride all the stables' runners in Ireland. He rode the horse out every day between Epsom and The Curragh and he was so careful with him that the horse got wise to him. So he arrived at The Curragh in a very relaxed state of mind and never ran a race at all.'

After the Irish Derby, Roberto was given a break and then prepared for the Benson and Hedges Gold Cup. Piggott was again assessing the best partner with which he could win the race. Rheingold had been to France to win an impor-

Note the difference in styles here. Panamanian jockey Baeza scorches home in record time ahead of the hitherto unbeaten Brigadier Gerard in the Benson and Hedges Gold Cup, 1972.

tant race, the Grand Prix de Saint Cloud. Roberto had failed dismally in Ireland. Piggott, biting the hand that had recently fed him, announced that he would not ride his Derby winner at York. He would ride Rheingold. John Galbreath, the biter bit, was far from happy, and told Vincent O'Brien that he would secure and fly over the top class American jockey, Panamanian-born Braulio Baeza, of whom hardly a soul on the British circuit had ever heard.

Britons' view of American racing was even more insular and falsely superior then than it is today. The Anglo-American competitions sportingly held at Sandown, Willie Shoemaker's brilliant ride on Hawaiian Sound in the Derby, have brought a few converts. Some British racegoers can now recognise the scope of American racing and the skill and immense experience of their jockeys, many of whom are greatly superior to the general run of ours. All of them possess clocks in their heads and most have five times the actual race-riding experience of their British counterparts.

When the engagement of the mysterious Baeza was announced, some sniggering was heard in corners of the Turf's establishment. Atlases were consulted to discover Panama where, it was believed, this strange little fellow with the odd name had been riding.

Not that any jockey could seriously hope to overcome the so far undefeated darling of the people, Mr and Mrs John Hislop's Brigadier Gerard. The formidable Mrs Hislop observed Gerry leading Roberto out onto the course to work on the morning of the race. 'At least *we* don't have to lead *our* horse,' she announced. Gerry quietly replied, 'I'm not letting this fellow go till 3 o'clock this afternoon!'

O'Brien gave Baeza an extremely thorough briefing on Roberto's previous runnings, his preferences, his weaknesses and his strengths. 'Then I said, "but I leave *how* you ride him to you." '

In America there is no dawdling. Races on identical flat left-handed circuits are run at an exceptionally strong pace throughout. Winners usually come from the leading bunch. Front runners often prevail. Quick starts are universal: that dirt gritty-dry, or mucky-wet, in horses' and jockeys' faces is most unpleasant. In front, the fleet fling the muck back onto the slow.

Baeza shot Roberto out of the stalls at York like a bullet. Crouching low, American style, he kept him flying ahead. Before the horses entered the straight everything behind was off the bit and struggling with the single exception of the unconquered 'Brigadier'. A buzz of astonishment coursed through the crowds like a hive of bees disturbed and Mrs Jean Hislop was heard afterwards to mutter, 'that Roberto ran as if he'd been stung by a bee!'

Certainly the colt kept on racing at such speed that even the great Brigadier Gerard could not get within a length of him. Two furlongs out Joe Mercer's whip hand flashed up on the Brigadier. Another furlong of vain pursuit and the seemingly unconquerable was finally beaten. Brigadier Gerard dropped away and Roberto scorched home at such speed that he broke York's course record.

It was a performance which was electric. It was also in a different league to any race Roberto had run before, or would run thereafter. The ground, though officially good, was riding fast, and York is left handed: two things Roberto needed. The distance of the Benson and Hedges, 1 mile 2½ furlongs, may have really been his best distance. 1½ miles, except round easy Epsom, may have been too far. Vincent nods and adds, 'Also the dead level track, rather than the ups and down of Epsom, suited him better, probably because of his knees.'

Most important of all, especially with a colt who had grown idle with the same jockey in Ireland, was the startling change of riding styles. The dash of a new man on top came as a shock to Roberto and he ran as if galvanised. Vincent is most complimentary about Baeza's riding at York, though very critical of his later performance in the Arc de Triomphe. 'He rode a beautiful race. I remember Noel Murless saying afterwards, "Some of the English jockeys had better open their eyes and take another look at Baeza; he certainly knows how to ride!"'

Two disappointments, one small, one large, round right-handed Longchamp, ended Roberto's three year old season. His prep race for the Arc was the Prix Niel. The French Derby winner, Hard to Beat, beat Roberto a length and this time Baeza did not shoot out of the gate. He simply followed Hard to Beat and never looked like catching him. For a prep race that was not too bad. He did not need another hard battle before the major target.

So to the Arc, where surprisingly the ground was firm. So too remains O'Brien's condemnation of Baeza's tactics. 'He thought he knew how to ride Longchamp after the Prix Niel. There was no question of having a discussion, of taking advice! He had it all figured out. He'd pop him off in front and make all.'

Another top-class American jockey was also riding in the race. Lafitte Pincay, who sounds French, was riding Boucher, winner of the St Leger, also trained by O'Brien. He, too, decided to jump off and go. 'They went so fast,' says Vincent, still cross about it, 'that they did the first five furlongs in the same time it took to run the big French sprint, the Prix de L'Abbaye, that day. And they covered the first mile quicker than in the one mile Prix du Moulin also on that same day.' Both horses weakened, but Roberto was the first three year old home. He finished seventh, with Hard to Beat eighth, so the form of the two Longchamp races was close enough. Some critics were quick to say that the Arc further emphasised how extraordinary had been Roberto's victory at York. Vincent quietly replies, 'But after all, he had won the Derby and beaten Rheingold.'

John Galbreath, having bred the horse, wanted him back on his farm in Kentucky, but he decided to keep the colt in training for a four year old campaign. This was a move against the trendy tide of three year olds being whisked away as soon as they had done enough to value themselves highly, and before they could depreciate themselves. After all, with a courageously won Epsom Derby plus a vividly won Benson and Hedges, Roberto had done enough to recommend himself expensively to American breeders. It is justly rewarding that, despite the disappointments and complaints of his four year old season, he has turned out to be a very highly successful stallion indeed.

'He won the Coronation Cup at Epsom,' says Vincent, 'and he very nearly broke the course record.' But from then on almost everything went wrong. 'John Galbreath's son Dan and his wife Liz came over from America to watch the horse run in the Eclipse.' That year it was run at Kempton, because Sandown was being rebuilt. Thunderstorms soaked the ground and O'Brien, still mindful of Bob Griffin's early warnings about 'soft ground will mean

Roberto is led in after his win in the first running of the Benson and Hedges Gold Cup.

trouble in front' gloomily inspected the course. It was, he decided, too soft to risk Roberto and he withdrew the horse on the morning of the race.

'I went to Kempton and acquainted the stewards of my presence there,' he reports, 'in case they wished to talk to me. I wasn't bound to do this as the ground had changed overnight, and so I was entitled to withdraw the horse. John Hislop, one of the acting stewards, had some words to say, and I proposed that we should both go out on the track and inspect the ground.' John Hislop, a sportsman in the original meaning of the word, has always held that a good horse should be able to run on any ground. He had run his beloved home-bred Brigadier Gerard (who ran in the name of his wife) openly and hard. He had risked devaluation by keeping him in training as a four year old, thus incurring his only defeat at the hooves of Roberto at York. Finally, he had turned down large offers from the USA, in favour of standing him as a stallion in England. The temptation to molly-coddle 'The Brigadier' was tremendous but one which he overcame. He believed others should think like him and act as he had.

He, therefore, did not hold with owners withdrawing good horses from races. O'Brien accompanied him onto the course where he would prove the going was perfectly acceptable. O'Brien happily consented: he would show Hislop the ground was too bad to run his horse.

There ensued a vignette, which could have been clipped from a French comedy: two senior pillars of racing hopping about in argument on Kempton's turf – O'Brien says 'John Hislop was pretty sharp with me' – using their feet on the pocked ground to demonstrate their opposing cases. 'Hislop would press sods back to show how level it was. I'd dig my heel into the holes to make them bigger!'

Roberto did not run. The Galbreaths had come 3,500 miles for nothing. Jacqueline says, 'I was able to get two Centre Court Wimbledon tickets so they were able to watch the tennis final, which was some little consolation. They were keen tennis players.'

Their next 7,000 mile round trip was endured soon afterwards to watch their horse run in Ascot's King George VI and Queen Elizabeth Diamond Stakes. On that right-handed track he ran appallingly. 'A terrible race,' says Vincent succinctly. 'Ridden by Lester again, he dropped completely out of the race.' Less than a month passed. Once again, the Galbreaths droned expensively across the Atlantic to watch Roberto attempt a double in the Benson and Hedges. 'But the ground at York was terrible,' says Vincent, using the same strong adjective, 'I couldn't run him in it.'

Roberto was then prepared for the Champion Stakes but before the Galbreaths made a fourth transatlantic expedition, the horse pulled a ligament. He was immediately retired and went home to flourish as a stallion.

After work on the gallops. Vincent with Tommy Murphy, then the stable's Irish jockey and Vincent Rossiter, senior work rider who has been at Ballydoyle since 1961.

The main yard at Ballydoyle taken from the house on a rare day of snow.

Ascot after The Minstrel's victory in the King George VI and Queen Elizabeth Diamond Stakes. Vincent receives his trophy from the Queen. Looking on from left to right: Sir Phillip Oppenheimer, The Marquess of Abergavenny, and Lord Plummer.

The Minstrel at stud at Windfields, Maryland, in the autumn of 1983. How he has thickened since he won the Derby. There weren't many animals whose backsides he saw when he was racing!

The Galbreaths accepted their costly disappointments with their enriching triumphs. 'They've confirmed their interest in Ireland,' Jacqueline reports, 'by coming each year to shoot at Birr, the home of Lord Rosse. Vincent set the shoot up for them and it is now run by Liam Ward. Vincent took them snipe shooting on the little Galway bogs. John Galbreath, a very experienced game hunter, said, "It's the most darn difficult bird ever. I only raised my gun out of politeness to my host." '

Another new owner with much greater international impact was about to step on the stage in the reticent shape of Robert Sangster who, with Vincent O'Brien, would form one of the most remarkable and successful partnerships in the history of racing.

16

'Find the best trainer and be prepared to spend a million pounds'

Robert Sangster decided to seek the best advice before expanding his racing interests. The most famous name in the history of the British Turf had his home within a short drive of Sangster's office, the rather grim looking headquarters of Vernon's Pools on Liverpool's dismal fringe on the road to Aintree. Sangster asked the Earl of Derby if he could talk to him. Sangster recalls, 'I actually went to look at the stud at Knowsley and we had lunch together afterwards.' Lord Derby's advice was concise. 'He said to me,' Sangster clearly remembers, "If you're really interested in going in, find the best trainer, get the best advice, but be prepared to spend about a million pounds." I went back and thought about it.'

A decade later, with the once great Derby racing fortunes dwindled, Lord Derby wistfully remarked, 'If only I had taken my own advice...'

Sangster says simply, 'When I went home and thought about it, I knew the best trainer had to be Vincent O'Brien, if I could get in with him. I recognised that Vincent was a genius. I would never have invested a quarter, not even a tenth of the amount I've spent in the market without Vincent. Because he has proven results, he gives you the confidence to invest money. When he's looking at yearlings, he's visualising them as three year olds at Epsom. He can picture them. He's got a fantastic feel for a horse. I think that's his quality all the way through, from the first jumpers he ever had. You remember his Cheltenham National record. It's superb. It's instinctive with him.'

Vincent O'Brien recounts the steps which led to his association with Sangster.

'Robert was very friendly with John Magnier of Fermoy who afterwards married our daughter Sue. He and John jointly owned Sandville Sand, which was looked after by John and run in conjunction with his own stud, Castlehyde. Our first venture together was when they bought Boone's Cabin which I had in training here. Through Tim Rogers, Robert also bought a share in Blood Royal which won the Ascot Gold Vase for us. At the end of 1974, Robert and I bought six mares together.

'I was also in the stud business. In 1973 I bought two-thirds of a stud farm near Ballydoyle called Coolmore. It was owned by Tim Vigors, the famous Battle of Britain pilot, bloodstock agent and international horseman. Tim had done a wonderful job transforming his father's farm to a top stud. He built

John Magnier who runs Coolmore, one of the largest stud complexes in Europe and where many of Vincent's best horses stand at stud.

boxes and laid out paddocks and barns. But he did not want to continue managing the stud, which then included stallions such as Home Guard, King's Emperor, Gala Performance, Thatch, and at the end of 1973, Rheingold, for whom a million pounds had been paid after winning the Arc. Tim and I decided that we would approach John Magnier to run Coolmore. In our opinion, he was the most capable young man in Europe for the job.

'The Magniers had for many years been good friends of ours. John's mother had been matron of honour at our wedding; and at this time John and Sue were engaged. I suggested first John manage Coolmore, then afterwards we talked about the amalgamation of his stud in Fermoy with ours. Robert was prepared to come in and bring the capital needed for such an undertaking.

'John, Tim and I eventually decided to pool our resources and Robert joined us. Castlehyde and Coolmore were amalgamated, and Tim remained with us for some years.'

John Magnier has continued to build up Coolmore which is now among the top studs in the world. Intense, cigar-smoking, dark head jutting forward, mind clicking like a computer, he looks older than his years. (He was born only in 1948.) He lives his life at a tremendous rate, pacing about dictating memoranda, grabbing telephones for calls across the world, organising the continuing expansion of the Coolmore stud empire. He has the reputation of being ruthless.

'You can say if you must that I look fifty,' he says, 'but I'm not ruthless. I've hardly lost a client over the years, except Lord Weinstock, and now he is back with us, and we have several of his best mares at Coolmore.'

Vincent says of his son-in-law, 'He is a young man of exceptional ability; he thinks big, deals shrewdly, and is most knowledgeable about blood lines and everything to do with the stud business. Among other stallions at his Grange Stud, his grandfather stood Cottage – probably the greatest jumping sire of all time. When his father died at a very early age, John, with his mother, took over the running of the stud, and he has never lost his interest in breeding jumpers. He has brought many of his original jumping clients into flat racing.

'John is so able I feel he would have reached the top of whatever profession he chose, and our very close association has been the greatest pleasure to me – it is a joy to work with someone of his calibre.'

And so it came about that in 1975 a racing syndicate was formed which would swoop down on the Keeneland Sales and bring back to Britain and Ireland so much of the bloodlines lost to America. A number of people joined Sangster and O'Brien to provide the necessary funds.

'I feel there have been a number of reasons for the success of their syndicate,' says Jacqueline O'Brien. 'They went to America where most of the best blood was; they chose syndicate members so that they had plenty of capital to spend,

Robert Sangster multi-millionaire head of Vernon's Pools and one of the great racehorse owners.

which meant that they could go for top quality, and in most markets the top end holds its value in good times and bad. Vincent bought the Northern Dancer line before anyone else recognised its potential. The group were able to spread their risk so that they had a dozen potentially top class yearlings out of which one or two might come; and then Vincent chose yearlings so successfully. Perhaps one could say too that the timing was good. Syndicates were unusual in 1975. Buying in America practically unheard of, and competition was not as fierce as now when Arab money has put up prices.

'Another factor which made things easy was that the first year was a great success so they could go back with confidence. It was like a win in the casino early in the night, so that you are playing for the rest of the evening with casino money. You can be more courageous.'

The members of the syndicate have changed over the years but the principals have remained the same. The buying has a strong back-up team. But Robert Sangster declares, 'To be honest, it's ninety per cent, or even ninety-nine per cent, Vincent. The team are really just to confirm his judgement, to make it easier for him, to get the horses pulled out for him.

'John Magnier takes all the notes and then we go through them in the evening before the sale to discuss every horse Vincent's seen. Like any other genius you wait for him to tell you. It might take quite a long time for it to come out. Then, suddenly, he'll make an announcement and we're all listening to what he says. We've got vets, of course, but the one that makes the difference is Vincent. I've probably got four vets and advisors at the sales, but Vincent makes the decisions. If he says "Yes", we go ahead and buy the horse.'

Vincent says warmly, 'The association has not only been most successful, but a very happy one. We all get on together and respect each other's functions and opinions.'

17

'If you run him, I'll ride him'

'The best laid schemes o' mice an' men gang aft a-gley-and certainly wi' horses.' It therefore seemed unlikely that the syndicate's plan would immediately pay dividends. But they at once struck oil. From the first crop of yearlings bought by the group came the Derby winner, The Minstrel, the Eclipse winner Artaius, and Be My Guest, bought at Goffs in Ireland. The double Arc winner, Alleged, joined the group as a two year old.

On paper, The Minstrel's attractions for Vincent O'Brien were plain. He was not only by the same sire, Northern Dancer, as Nijinsky. His dam was Fleur, daughter of Nijinsky's dam, Flaming Page, and thus Nijinsky's half-sister. The chestnut three-parts brother which the O'Brien team kept looking at on those steamy July days at Keeneland, in 1975, had been bred by the same man, E. P. Taylor.

The team kept reappraising the colt. Because of his size O'Brien kept going back to look at him in his stall in the long lines of barns, decked out in vendors' colours and blazoned with breeding boards. 'I was definitely concerned about his height. I remember going back to his box more than once to see if I could make myself feel any easier about it. But he was certainly small. He did grow in the end. He finished just short of 15.3 hands, which was big enough. But again,' Vincent adds, 'this Northern Dancer breed was something new in the racehorse world. They don't have to be big to be good.'

It was impossible to forecast this because of the novelty of the Northern Dancer blood. For reasons of size Vincent rejected Lyphard, who would turn out so well in France and then go right to the top in America as a sire. 'He has proved a successful stallion, tops in fact with his fillies, but I didn't bid for him as a yearling when he came into the ring at Newmarket. Tim Rogers had bought him as a foal at Keeneland, then put him up at Newmarket. I looked at him and I thought: he's too small. You couldn't, you just couldn't buy him. He was led out of the ring unsold, although Tim had only the same reserve as the price he'd bought him for as a foal. Tim came to an arrangement with Alec Head, who took him and trained him, and he turned out a very good miler.'

It is refreshing to hear a man at the top of his profession honestly confess to doubt. The picture lingers of O'Brien in his short-sleeved shirt and straw hat, catalogue in hand, sunglasses in his top left pocket, immaculate in the sweating humidity trying to evaluate the small colt.

The Minstrel ridden by Tommy Murphy working at home with Malinowski (Johnny Brabston) on the all-weather gallop in the spring of 1977. The Minstrel had finished his two-year old season unbeaten.

The fact that the chestnut in no way resembled the mighty Nijinsky would put off most buyers. You have had a brilliant Northern Dancer who is big and bay. Here is his small relation; a chestnut with, as Vincent says, 'An awful lot of white about him ...' You could expect that if one was good, the other, so different, would not be. Such a supposition would not have proved inaccurate, for The Minstrel at home, in training, and on the racecourse was quite different from Nijinsky. Where Nijinsky was highly strung, difficult, temperamental and had brilliant speed, The Minstrel was tough, brave, sound and possessed of great stamina. One thing they shared which was a symptom of a good Northern Dancer: they both sweated a lot.

Few people then wanted to pay big money for a small Northern Dancer and many people would not want a flashy chestnut with four white stockings and a huge white blaze at any price. People say that chestnuts tend to be temperamental, they tend to be hot, and 'as for white legs,' says Vincent, 'they are prone to infection and unsoundness.' 'One buy; two try; three doubt; four go home without,' goes the jingle.

Even the following morning after he had bought him for just over $200,000, O'Brien was back looking at the colt again. 'Did we, or did we not, make a good buy? He was small and compact, with not much scope. Chestnuts with a lot of white are not usually attributed with the greatest complement of courage, either. Strange, for I'd say he was one of the toughest horses I've ever

Alleged and The Minstrel, the two great colts whose paths so nearly crossed in their three-year-old season. On the left is Johnny Brabston, the stable's headman. On the right, Gus Burke with Alleged. They're just at the back of the stables.

(Below) Going down to the start of the old gallops at Ballydoyle, Alleged (Johnny Brabston) leads two companions. In the days of the jumpers, the schooling fences were here.

(Inset) Alleged going out for the last race of his career: his second successive victory in the Prix de l'Arc de Triomphe. Lester adjusts his leathers even shorter. Travelling headman, Gerry Gallagher, leads the way.

Another shot of the gallops from Vincent's helicopter.

(Inset) Storm Bird, the unbeaten two year old, a winter favourite for the classics with one of Vincent's five grandsons, Sean McClory.

(Inset below) *Storm Bird's private country house at Ashford, Kentucky. The first foals of this unlucky horse were outstanding.*

Epsom after Golden Fleece's dazzling Derby – in the fastest time since Mahmoud. From the left, the happy owners, Danny Schwartz from California, Vincent, Jean-Pierre Binet from France, and Robert Sangster.

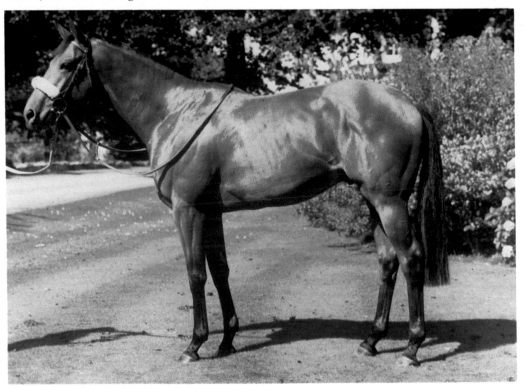

Golden Fleece in the garden at Ballydoyle.

trained! And he was a very lucky horse. He never had any setbacks. Though he didn't have quite the brilliant early career of Sir Ivor or Nijinsky.'

This judgement simply illustrates the height of quality at Ballydoyle. In almost every other stable in Europe, The Minstrel's two year old career would have been the subject of rapture. He was unbeaten in his three starts. He started his racing life later than most of O'Brien's classic hopefuls. Instead of 'coming up for' his first race in early July, he did not appear until 8 September, 1976. John Gosden, then Vincent's assistant at Ballydoyle, before starting on

Lester and Vincent leaning against one of the straw divisions in the large barns. The horses can be exercised in these in bad weather trotting and hack-cantering under cover.

his own so successfully in America, says of The Minstrel, 'No trouble in training except that he'd get worked up before the start of a race. I always led him with the jockey on his back. And you had to be careful not to overdo the training with him.'

Both as a two year old and as a three year old, he needed time, which was what you would expect of something big and gangly like Alleged. You would not expect a small, compact colt to require age to improve. But this, like a good claret from a small vineyard, was the case with The Minstrel.

Not particularly noted in England, The Minstrel won his first race, the Moy Stakes at The Curragh, by an easy five lengths. Unchallenged, he still broke the track record. Less than three weeks later he went to Leopardstown and won yet another race named after an alumnus of Dr O'Brien's academy, the Larkspur Stakes. Three weeks' break and he arrived at Newmarket for the Dewhurst Stakes. 'He did wind up as a two year old winning the Dewhurst well, but,' O'Brien considers, 'not as impressively as Nijinsky.' He did, however, win comfortably by four lengths. At that stage, he was still not receiving rave notices in the British racing press. *Timeform* was one of the few organs prepared to trumpet out its praise. 'How he comes to receive only 8st 13lb in the two year old Free Handicap,' it boomed, 'we cannot imagine.' Putting its rating where its lips were, it rated The Minstrel exceptionally high with 116 at the end of his first season. Next year, it could afford to be smug about its perspicacity.

The Minstrel escaped ailments and setbacks and through the winter continued to thrive. This would prove the fortunate pattern of his life. He was not only as hard and tough as a middleweight professional boxer, taking a series of hard fights in his stride, but he kept improving his physique. He was that rarity, an easy horse to train. This should not detract from his trainer and his staff who prepared him for his targets and picked them correctly. Nothing can diminish the power of Piggott's riding of the little chestnut. The image shimmers on of the tall grey-faced man, bent over the small white-faced chestnut, the jockey with his whip held aloft, and the battling colt with his head heroically stuck forward.

The Minstrel's first outing as a three year old proved the point on his visit to Ascot for the Two Thousand Guineas Trial. 'The ground was barely raceable,' says O'Brien, 'so bad, they couldn't use the starting stalls, and had to start by flag. He won all right, but most of the opposition never won a race again. The going finished them.' Here was another proof of The Minstrel's courage and of his exceptional ability to act with equal speed and lack of strain on ground varying between glutinous and rattling.

Still unbeaten, The Minstrel with the filly Cloonlara went off to Newmarket for the Two Thousand Guineas and the One Thousand Guineas. Those were two bad days for the O'Briens. Both horses started hot favourites. Both got beaten. 'It was a gloomy ride home,' Jacqueline O'Brien remembers, 'for we thought we had a great chance of bringing off the double.' The Minstrel was beaten two lengths into third place. He went back to Ireland and then in the Irish Two Thousand Guineas was beaten only a short head to be second, but in front of Nebbiolo, who had beaten him in the English Two Thousand Guineas. Nebbiolo hampered him at a tricky instant at The Curragh, and The Minstrel could not quite beat Pampapaul.

'He was a bit unlucky,' says Vincent. 'Lester thought he would have won. But the question then was whether he'd run in the Derby.' No excuses, no spilt milk tears. Onto the next target. Would The Minstrel be ready to do himself justice at Epsom? Should he wait till the Irish Derby, giving him more time to recover? 'But I had a discussion with Lester that night,' Vincent recalls. 'I could see he'd considered what other likely rides he might have. He was in favour of running him. He said to me, "If you run him, I'll ride him."' And Dermot O'Brien comments drily, 'which was better than any question or answer!'

In the eight weeks between that Ascot bog and the Epsom Derby, The Minstrel had endured three particularly punishing races. Many English experts expected the small chestnut to appear at Epsom looking like an over-raced rabbit.

The racing world knew, however, that he was strongly fancied by his stable. Robert Sangster's co-owners in the horse were Vincent O'Brien and, rather unusually, the Hon. Simon Fraser. Mr Fraser, entitled The Master of Lovat, is a Scottish landowner and son of the legendary commando hero, Lord Lovat, DSO, MC, Croix de Guerre, whose title goes back among the Highland mists to 1458. There were a number of others too, including tycoon Charles Clore's French-based son, Alan, and David Ackroyd. Racing makes unlikely bed-fellows.

But the owners were united when, a week before the Derby, they received a bid of £1 million for their colt. They firmly refused it and, by so doing, enriched themselves jointly after the race by some $4.5 million dollars. The refusal of the bid, and Piggott's selection of The Minstrel, told the world of the confidence at Ballydoyle. The stable ran two others: Be My Guest and Valinsky.

The French invader, Blushing Groom, started favourite, though the herd of English chauvinists who are convinced that 'no Frog can ride Epsom' gave him no chance. His jockey, Samani, was thought by them to be vastly inferior to better-known names like Freddy Head and Yves Saint-Martin, and yet Head had always had a hapless time round Epsom. Blushing Groom was beaten, but not through any misjudgement. Like a number of others in a slightly sub-standard Derby field, he failed to stay. Because The Minstrel was inclined to sweat up before a race Vincent was afraid the long parade, noise and general hurdy-gurdy atmosphere would distress him. He plugged the horse's ears with cotton wool so he would not be able to hear too much and John Gosden, the assistant trainer, walked down to the start to remove it before the race. It worked, and was another example of how a good trainer can anticipate the likely problems.

Piggott, the *sans pareil* round those extraordinary Downs, had The Minstrel exquisitely placed. Only Hot Grove and Blushing Groom had a chance in the straight. It took The Minstrel nearly three furlongs to draw up with Hot Grove, to struggle along upsides him under the full force of Piggott, and to get just in front as the winning post loomed up.

'But he had to run hard to win,' says Vincent. 'He proved himself very game.'

Piggott had seemed desperately hard on him, harder, in most observers' eyes, than he had been on Roberto. He had more room to be so. He was on the outside of Hot Grove and his whip could wheel and whirl and crack all the way to the line. By comparison, certainly in the last decisive strides, Hot Grove escaped such punishment.

'Lester had to be hard on him,' says Vincent, 'I'd certainly say he needed all Lester's power and skill on him at Epsom that day.'

Such a hammering, the experts decided, would now finish The Minstrel. But not at all. He went home, ate up and flourished to such an extent that O'Brien decided to run him in the Irish Derby, three and a half weeks later, the race which had originally been his alternative to Epsom. He kept in mind, additionally, Ascot's great race in July, to which its decorous sponsors De Beers had now appended a modest 'Diamond' to 'King George VI and Queen Elizabeth.'

The decision to go for the Irish Derby with The Minstrel illustrates a trainer's dilemma when he has more than one star horse with different owners. The decision caused bad feeling from another patron of Ballydoyle. This was Bob Fluor in whose name and colours ran The Minstrel's stable mate, Alleged, bought by Sangster as a two year old in California. Fluor was a Californian friend of Sangster. 'I don't think,' says Sangster, 'that Bob takes racing quite as professionally as we do! But the Fluor Corporation is the tenth largest company in the world.' The inference here is that when the head of such an empire wished a horse to run, run it would, where, when and how he chose.

Sangster fills in the background to the Irish Derby controversy. 'We worked Alleged with The Minstrel after the Epsom Derby – I'm still not saying who

The Minstrel goes to post before the start of the Derby.

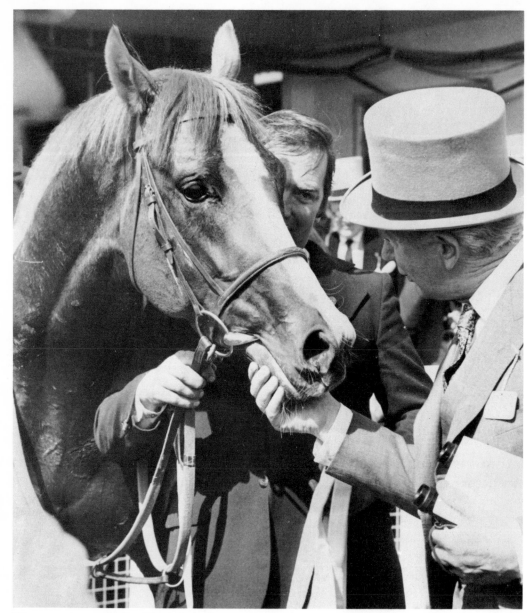

Vincent congratulating The Minstrel on winning the 1977 Epsom Derby. This clearly shows the affection of the man for the horse.

won the gallop – but we then knew we'd got an exceptional horse. So we put him away, because we still had The Minstrel who was a very hot property. But Bob Fluor had invited all his executives and relations to fly over to The Curragh to watch Alleged run in the Irish Derby. I could see that Vincent was very edgy all the way through Ascot.' (Between the two Derby's). 'I knew something was worrying him. It was that he didn't want to run Alleged in the

The Minstrel veers across the course when winning the Irish Derby.

Irish Derby: he didn't feel he'd perform at his best on hard ground. He wanted to run The Minstrel. As I owned forty per cent in both horses, and between the European co-owners we had seventy per cent, I said, "to hell with it. We'll run The Minstrel!" Bob Fluor didn't take this very happily. I think he understood in the end. In fact, I said I would buy him out, valuing Alleged for a million pounds. He sold most of his share, but I think he retained five per cent. So he was still happy when Alleged won the "Arc"!'

The Irish Derby was The Minstrel's easiest victory of the year, which puts into perspective the difficulty of the others. For although he won by 1½ lengths, he was objected to by the second horse, Lucky Sovereign (who had been well behind him at Epsom), and the Stewards also enquired into possible interference. He had once again to be driven out to win and, in so doing, began to hang outwards across the course.

The victory made him favourite for Ascot on 23 July, his sixth contest in sixteen weeks, an intensity of programme which few top class flat racehorses stand these days. But his appearance under the trees at Ascot's sloping paddock drew a hum of admiration. The cynosure of all the experts had actually developed and thickened since Epsom.

The faces of trainer and owner Robert Sangster tell the story of the winning of the Irish Derby.

Susan Sangster leads in The Minstrel after winning the Irish Derby. His lad in the smart blazer is Tom O'Gorman.

This time Vincent O'Brien, so full of praise for Lester Piggott in the English Derby, was more critical. 'Lester struck the front quite early – too soon, I'd say, for the horse. All these American horses are not out-and-out stayers. Coming to the front too early exposed him to the risk of getting beaten by an out-and-out stayer.'

O'Brien's view is that The Minstrel might not have been a true mile and a half horse. His public form in the Irish Derby and at Ascot contradicts this, allowing for Epsom's eccentricities. But every stop had to be pulled out by Piggott at Ascot. On the minus side, the horse was very slowly away in a field which included five major classic winners, the only other three year old, Crystal Palace (French Derby), and the four year olds, Excellor, Crow, Orange Bay and Bruni. On the plus side, Piggott typically stole a smooth run up on the inside turning for home.

In Vincent's view, his horse having hit the front too soon, was stopping at the finish, and holding on only by courage plus Piggott's strength from Orange Bay, who was fighting back at him all the way to the post. 'He won by the shortest of short heads. Perhaps 3 inches. And after that,' says Vincent simply, 'we decided not to run him any more. He'd done enough.'

At the point of his retirement, The Minstrel had proved himself in a succession of hard battles to be the best middle distance horse in Europe. His breeder

The closest finish in all The Minstrel's hard races – 'about 3 inches' says Vincent – as the colt gets home under Lester Piggott to win the King George VI and Queen Elizabeth Stakes, his last race.

and vendor, E. P. Taylor, had followed his triple peak of victories with satisfaction and strategic thinking. One day, and probably soon, he would need a replacement for Northern Dancer, who was thirteen years older than The Minstrel. Mr Taylor wanted to buy back half of the little chestnut and did so at a price which valued The Minstrel at $9 million. In the space of two years, one of the first crops of the syndicate had appreciated in value forty-five times.

It was the pattern of the colt's racing to win under pressure and often at the last stride. His manner of leaving Ireland to return to America reflected this. With the scourge of equine metritis rampant, the American authorities were poised to ban all imported horses from Europe. The O'Brien intelligence service swiftly got wind of the impending clampdown and The Minstrel was whisked out of Ireland and into the States with only hours to spare.

Where would O'Brien rate this winner of two Derbies and a 'King George'

A posed picture of the Minstrel taken the day before he left to take up his stud duties on the farm where he was bred in Maryland.

who, in nine races, had never been unplaced nor beaten more than two lengths?

'I'd say he would not rate with Sir Ivor or Nijinsky.' Then in March, 1984, with the news of Golden Fleece's tragic death still fresh, Vincent adds, 'Nor with Golden Fleece, but he was a very tough and genuine racehorse.'

18

'A case of mission accomplished'

There is no such thing as 'an O'Brien type'. His winners come in all sizes, colours and shapes. Nijinsky and The Minstrel, though so closely related, were different in almost every aspect, save for their ability to win classics. Dapper little Larkspur could not have looked more different from the huge Golden Fleece, who had the build of a Cheltenham Gold Cup favourite. But both won their Derbies, too.

And Alleged, whose career overlapped The Minstrel's, was a totally different type to the small, flashy chestnut. Robert Sangster describes him as 'a different cup of tea'. But that was because, though Alleged was part of the syndicate's first year's operation, he was bought not as a yearling, not at Keeneland, Kentucky, and not by Vincent O'Brien.

'I actually bought him myself,' says Robert, 'as a two year old in training at a sale in California, for $165,000 in the ring.'

'Alleged was going to be trained out in California by Tom Pratt. I went up and saw him a week later and thought he'd best be trained by Vincent in Ireland. So I sent him across to Vincent. And after that, he only lost one race in his whole career!'

The advice which Sangster took in California was that Alleged's knees might well not stand up to the extra strain of racing on dirt out there. They had already had to be blistered. The horse was in full training to such an extent that he was doing 'time trials' on the track. His knees did not appreciate this. Ironically, it was the ability of American horses to stand their tougher racing conditions which was one of their earliest attractions for O'Brien. 'They were raced hard on dirt,' he said, 'so I believed their stock would stand up well to racing in Europe.'

When Alleged arrived at Ballydoyle, he was greeted by the staff without much enthusiasm for the bargain. No one there thought a world-beater had come to join them. The best they could say was that he was 'moderate'. Even with the benefit of hindsight, the staff are frank: 'Very scrawny; looked terrible,' says one. 'Never carried much condition,' opines another. Willie Fogarty declares, 'He was weak and backward. He never carried what we call the Ballydoyle condition. He was very slack over his loins.'

Vincent disagrees, 'He was a nice horse, who needed time.' And T. P. Burns opined when the two year old arrived, 'I see no objections to him. I think he'll

A conformation shot of Alleged – what a head and what a shoulder.

be all right.' They all agree that Alleged had a very good head and outlook. This is one aspect found in every O'Brien horse, at least over the last thirty years. They come in different types, sizes and colours. But they all give you the same bold handsome look from head and eyes and ears. As mankind judges one another, so does the wise judge of horses pick them by the look they give you. The perfectly made equine machine is no good without that invisible motor of courage and the will to win. Alleged did not prove to be a favourite in his stable. Jacqueline O'Brien remembers, 'The boys said he was not an easy horse in the box. He was often cross, a little like his great-grandfather, Ribot.'

One of the best young trainers now in America, John Gosden, was then with Vincent as his assistant. He said of Alleged in 1984, 'He was kind, but if you were silly enough to bend over in his box he'd have a go at you. He was a masculine horse, aggressive in the stable. He had a wonderful head, strong and powerful, very broad between the eyes. He was not nasty. He was straight-forward. He meant business.'

One thing still puzzles O'Brien about Alleged. The colt had originally come up for sale as a yearling at the Keeneland sales the previous July. 'But I can never quite recall him myself. Yet I must have seen him, because with the pedigree he had, he was a horse I would have looked at.' The bay colt, foaled in 1974, the same year as The Minstrel, was by Hoist the Flag (a grandson of Ribot by the good American horse, Tom Rolfe). He was the first living foal of his dam, Princess Pout (by Prince John). But she had excellent form as a race mare which would prove significant. She was four years old before she won her first stakes race, and she won three more stakes races as a five year old. All were on grass and she demonstrated that she needed time to mature.

Hoist the Flag was saved for stud by the skill of American veterinary science and surgery. Having won five of his first six races, he fractured a hind pastern when being wound up for the Kentucky Derby. He might easily have been destroyed on the spot. But he underwent a major operation in which a piece of his hip-bone was cut out and transplanted as a bone graft into the broken pastern.

O'Brien shakes his head over those sales. 'Apparently, Alleged was very immature-looking at the time and he wasn't well presented. A chap from California called Monty Roberts bought him for around $40,000 for re-sale in California as a two year old.'

Vincent remembers, 'When he arrived I did see that his legs were already showing slight signs of trouble. So I decided that I'd take my time with him. They'd prepared him for what they call their Horses in Training sale. So they get the two year olds ready and they ask them to find some speed – which is a bit unusual at that time of year.' It would certainly be exceptional for any potentially good horse in Europe. Apart from the low-class early runners who must try to earn their oats as soon as the flat season yawns awake in March, nothing of any consequence is doing more than quiet canters at Newmarket in January. Yet in the red dawns over Los Angeles, the big two year old Alleged was being whizzed round the dirt track of Hollywood Park.

The sun nearly always shines in California. Even in January, the horses start working on the tracks at 6 am because, by 11 am when the last of a trainer's six or seven 'sets' has finished, the weather is as warm as an English June. Alleged certainly felt the cold when he arrived at Ballydoyle, for the sun scarcely shines in Ireland in February. 'He was a little slow in conditioning. I suppose the change of climate had something to do with it. So I gave him most of the year and brought him along only in the autumn. He did no serious work before August. I just got him up to a run right at the end of the season – actually in the first week of November. He won at The Curragh and you'd like the way he won: he was going away at the end, very nicely.

Lester Piggott having his first ride on Alleged wins the Gallinule Stakes at The Curragh in May 1971 at 11 to 10. In his previous race Alleged had startled the stable by winning at 33 to 1 ridden by Peadar Matthews.

'I didn't at first think we'd run him at all as a two year old. His knees looked as if they'd give trouble. He was never a very robust horse in training – which was just as well, as he was that bit lighter on his legs. The stock of his sire, Hoist the Flag, give a lot of trouble with their legs – knees and joints usually. It's a question of bone structure.'

In the spring of Alleged's three-year-old season, the staff recall him working 'really well'. They were the more disappointed, therefore, when, as they put it, 'he just scraped home in his first race, the Ballydoyle Stakes at Leopardstown, towards the end of April.'

O'Brien says, 'He didn't show me a great deal early on, and I didn't press him. He only just won that first race and there was nothing very exciting about winning it. So I talked myself out of pressing on with him. I decided to give him a little bit more time and a chance to improve more.'

Like all else in life, training is timing. But the trainer of good flat race horses is locked into an inflexible calendar. Where a jumping man may have three or four cracks at steeplechasing's single classic, the Cheltenham Gold Cup, the man on the flat has only three dates for his three-year-old classic colt. It is no good only getting your Derby hope ready in July.

In Alleged's case, O'Brien had long ago abandoned any notion of early successes. The Epsom Derby was never on his schedule. 'I didn't run him again until the Royal Whip at The Curragh in the middle of May and then he was only one of three to run from here. Alleged was ridden by Peadar Matthews, the work rider here. Valinsky was ridden by Lester as he had won very impressively as a two year old.'

Against this, Alleged started the complete outsider at 33 to 1, although as the lads remember, 'Tommy Murphy wanted to ride him but he rode Meneval, a four year old.' Vincent goes on, 'Valinsky struck the front as they came into the straight and looked as though he'd won. Then this horse Alleged cruised up to him and beat him quite comfortably. Then I realised he was a pretty nice horse. We knew we had a good horse.' The lads remember the day clearly, 'The crowds were dumbfounded!'

It was, however, the year of The Minstrel, too. So came the decision, resented by Alleged's American co-owner, the tycoon from California, Bob Fluor, that Alleged would not go for the Irish Derby. O'Brien's decision was affected by four factors: Alleged still needed time; he did not want hard ground; The Minstrel had recovered so quickly from Epsom that he could win the Irish Derby; and, twinkling ahead, lay the lure of the Arc de Triomphe for Alleged.

'I took my time with him,' Vincent repeats, 'and I didn't run him between the Gallinule Stakes on The Curragh on 28 May and York in August, nearly three months.'

The race chosen was the Great Voltigeur Stakes which produced a very

York, August 1977, Alleged hacks up with Lester Piggott in the Great Voltigeur Stakes with the field trailing.

strong field, including several horses like Hot Grove, Lucky Sovereign and Classic Example, who had been placed behind The Minstrel in the English and Irish Derbies. These were left gasping when Alleged accelerated dramatically three furlongs from home, and won with complete disdain for his pursuers by eight lengths. 'I must say,' Vincent comments, 'he surprised me. He just simply trotted up!'

Timeform Annual went into eulogies about this performance even when compiling their notes in the cold of winter. Though 1977 had already been enriched by the victories of The Minstrel in his two Derbies and in Ascot's 'Diamond' Stakes, *Timeform* pronounced that Alleged's Voltigeur victory was 'the most dramatic race of the season ... It changed the face of European racing for the year.'

O'Brien was more occupied in mapping out a programme than polishing up the panegyrics. 'Then he was in the Arc and I thought: "August to the first week in October. He needed a race in between." There wasn't really any suitable prep race for him except the Leger. And I really wasn't keen to run him in the Leger before the Arc ... I always think it's a bad prep for the Arc for a three year old, to run him over a mile and three quarters. It's almost two

In the winner's enclosure at York: Susan Sangster and Bob Fluor in whose colours the horse ran.

miles, because it's a big galloping course and a long run-in ... But anyhow there wasn't any other race to run him in.'

Horses are not alone in remembering places and races. Nijinsky's race for the St Leger, giving him the Triple Crown, had been hard won, and contributed to his defeat in the Arc. Such thoughts loomed large in O'Brien's mind as he weighed the pro's and con's. Even the same phrases used over Nijinsky's St Leger came up again for Alleged's. 'I thought, well, the opposition didn't look too strong. He didn't seem to have all that to beat. I thought that I'd take a chance. I thought he'd probably have an easy race. But it didn't work out quite like that.'

Everything is relative. To most stables the presence of the Queen's Oaks-winning filly, Dunfermline, accompanied by her pacemaker, Gregarious, would pose at least a threat. Pat Eddery on Classic Example could be dangerous. But Alleged (Lester Piggott) in the colours of Mr Fluor, started at 4 to 1. Dunfermline ridden by the engaging Willie Carson was a 10 to 1 chance. The Queen would have dearly loved to have been at Doncaster to see her homebred, classic-winning filly run. She was up at Balmoral on her Scottish holiday. She would certainly have come down to Town Moor, but Mr Harold Wilson was staying to discuss affairs of State. Duty as usual came first ahead of the Queen's special pleasure.

The glorious day she missed was one of sadness and frustration for the O'Brien raiders. Their horse had been hot favourite for the St Leger since York. 'There was great confidence here,' the lads recall.

Vincent comments, 'The Queen's filly had her pacemaker. He set a good pace, a strong pace. But Lester quite early moved up second and had Dunfermline behind him! And when the filly's pacemaker was finished with, Lester went on with Alleged. Well, he looked as if he was going to win – but just inside the last furlong, the filly came on. She just outstayed him, and duly she got up to beat him ... What was he thinking about? I don't know ...' and Vincent shakes his head. The Ballydoyle staff are less diplomatic. They declare robustly, 'Well, Dunfermline had *two* pacemakers that day, didn't she? Her own and Alleged! If Alleged had been held up, he'd never have been beat. Never.' They remember, however, that 'he came out of the Leger very well – he'd just been kept ticking over between the Voltigeur and the Leger.' But T. P. Burns comments, 'He grew peevish.' Willie Fogarty grins, 'You wouldn't want to be in

Vincent's favourite picture of Alleged. Winning the 1977 Prix de l'Arc de Triomphe – 'He looks a real horse'.

the box with him!' The others add, 'But once you were up, there was no trouble. And he never needed much work.'

The St Leger would prove Alleged's solitary defeat in three years and ten races: Her Majesty's Dunfermline, beat Mr Fluor's Alleged (USA) by one and a half lengths. Colonel F. Hue-Williams' Classic Example was ten lengths further behind in third. That baldly was that.

On to the Arc and O'Brien praises Piggott: 'Lester rode a wonderful race on the horse. Having a chat with Lester beforehand,' Vincent goes on, 'he said he didn't think they'd go a great pace, which turned out to be correct. Lester thought that because it was a pretty open race, a lot of the jockeys would think they had a chance. Therefore, they wouldn't go crazy. He was right.

'So Lester lay pretty close to the pace. Coming down the hill he was second and when they started to turn for home, he took up the running and went on from there.'

The lads still have the impression that 'he made it all. And we were disappointed to see him leading that early, for the Arc is not a race you would want to be making all in!' Their early fears were swiftly confounded. Alleged quickened so brilliantly that nothing else could match him. He came home an easy 1½ lengths winner from the top-class New Zealand horse, Balmarino, who had been sent to England to campaign that year. Alleged was the first three year old to win the Arc since San San in 1972, five years earlier.

'The horse won really well,' Vincent sums up, 'and then we decided to keep him on and train him as a four year old and aim him at the Arc again.'

One sentence covers weeks of discussions, of heart searchings, financial calculations and prognostications of what 1978 should bring. The temptations were juicy to retire him then and capitalise him at several million dollars as a stallion. He had easily won Europe's greatest race. His Voltigeur victory had drawn rave notices. Backward though he had been, he had been sufficiently advanced to win as a two year old. All these things would count richly with breeders. O'Brien came under pressure from his co-owners to take the enormous profit which awaited them. He had cost only $165,000. The Minstrel had been syndicated for $9 million. Alleged would make as much. There, dangling like great sacks of gold, jangled a profit of well over $8 million. And a racehorse can go wrong anytime. Surely, it was better to sell while he was sound and safe and victorious? In straight money talk the deal was obvious: Alleged's age meant he could not win a classic. Therefore, unless he won a second Arc de Triomphe, he could hardly enhance his value by staying in training as a four year old, unless by winning Ascot's 'Diamond' Stakes, perhaps. The actuarial odds against winning two 'Arcs' were enormous. You had to go back more than twenty years to the supreme Ribot in 1955 and 1956 to find the previous double winner.

Passing the post in 1977 (above) and (below) in 1978 – the first double winner since the great Ribot.

O'Brien quietly, unsurprisingly, had his way. He pointed out that Alleged had done very little racing in his life – 'he was a fresh horse.' He reminded his co-owners that, though a second 'Arc' would be his supreme objective, there were a number of attractive, important and rich races to be picked up on the way. Provided that the ground did not turn too firm next summer, there was the King George VI and Queen Elizabeth Diamond Stakes. If The Minstrel had won it, so could Alleged. There were the Eclipse and the Benson and Hedges. Earlier, the Coronation Cup at Epsom and Ascot's Hardwicke Stakes were possibilities.

While Alleged's future was debated by his shareholders, there was no doubt at all in the minds of the staff working at Ballydoyle. 'We all knew he'd stay in training as a four year old!'

But once again, as it nearly always is with horses, it was a question of 'man proposes; God disposes,' as Thomas à Kempis wrote in Latin five hundred years ago. Although Alleged did quite well over the winter – 'he never looked that great,' say the lads, 'he always had that rather dry skin' – things began to go wrong in the spring and summer of 1978. The ground grew firm. He again ran in and won the Royal Whip on The Curragh. The race jarred his knees. 'He was short in his action,' the lads remember. 'He had to be rested and we treated his knees.' Davy Walsh, the blacksmith, recalls, 'the horse was also lame behind and not in his foot.' Then Alleged went down with a virus that plagued O'Brien's stable that summer. 'He got it pretty heavily,' says Vincent, 'and we had to be prepared to sit back with him and wait, and give him plenty of time to get over it.'

The weeks fled past. All those tempting prizes which had been Alleged's targets last autumn were being lost. Human doubts muttered. Had it not proved a disastrous decision to keep him in training? He had, by the end of August, won one little race in Ireland. Had he gone to stud in Kentucky he would have earned more than one million dollars already ...

'We had to wait,' says Vincent calmly, 'and it was September before I got him up to a race again. There was nothing available in Ireland or England, so I had to send him to France.' He flew from Shannon to Paris to run at Longchamp in the Prix du Prince d'Orange. The lads report that he flew alone, without a lead horse. 'He didn't need friends.'

After nearly a year with only one race, the expectations were that he would be in urgent need of this race. 'Actually,' says O'Brien, 'he broke the track record for that race and distance, which was quite something after not having a run since May.' The turn of phrase is itself quite something for the modest and controlled O'Brien. It needs to be said that this race alone was a magnificent feat of training. Yet it was only the final stepping stone to a sort of immortality among the racehorses of the world.

Alleged flew back to Shannon. Twelve days later he was again back in France to attempt the principal purpose of all that season: his second 'Arc'. To the delays in his training was now added a further change. In 1977, the ground

What John and Sue Magnier call 'An Alleged Connection'. On the left is Billy McDonald who bought the horse in California as a two-year-old on behalf of Robert Sangster, with the trainer and jockey having a celebratory drink after the Arc.

had ridden fast. Piggott had then foxed the opposition by keeping at half-throttle in front before suddenly losing them by a surge of speed which could only be unleashed on fast turf. This time, it had rained for two days. The going turned soft; too soft, some thought, for Alleged's speed. And on this ground, too, another doubt was aired. Might Lester Piggott keep Alleged too far back as he had done with Nijinsky and Park Top?

But all turned out as smooth as silk. 'Lester rode a somewhat similar race,' says Vincent, 'not quite as prominent as he'd been the year before, but still not too far off the pace. The horse had a very clear run and, again, when he hit the straight he was quickly in front. There was nothing to catch him from there home.'

Since the 1914–18 war only five horses had previously won two Prix de l'Arc de Triomphes: Ksar in 1921 and '22; then the strange Motrico, who came up from France's south-west to win it in 1930 as a five year old, and then in 1932 as a seven year old. Corrida won it at four and at five in 1936 and 1937; and before Ribot, there was only Tantième, at three and four in 1950 and 1951.

T. P. Burns, sitting in his office on a chill winter's afternoon, overlooking the grey stable yard at Ballydoyle five years later, lets a smile warm his face in

Vincent at home with Alleged.

contemplation of that great day at Longchamp. He sums it up simply. 'It was a case of Mission Accomplished,' he says.

Robert Sangster, in the July after the famous victory stood shirtsleeved among the sale barn at Keeneland and put the business aspect of the operation. 'After the second Arc, we syndicated him here in Kentucky for roughly $13 million. This may seem an unbelievable figure but, in fact, it's quite simple. It's based on his earning capacity in that the horse stands at $80,000 and he can cover forty mares. So he earns $3.2 million a year. And a horse is normally valued on a four year purchase of his earnings.'

During the same sales Vincent O'Brien took time off to drive out of Lexington, north-east up the straight but dangerously undulating Paris Pike to turn off it at Walmac Farm to visit Alleged. 'He looks wonderfully well for a horse just at the end of his first season. How's he been with his mares?' he asks Kenny, the stallion man, who had looked after the 1975 Epsom Derby winnner Grundy at Britain's National Stud.

Golden Fleece arriving at Coolmore, eight miles east of Ballydoyle, to start his career at stud.

Vincent and stable jockey Pat Eddery weighing up proposals on the sawdust ring by the gallops. Pat flies over a lot in the spring.

'Sir, you couldn't ask for a better breeding stallion. He's really great.'

Vincent looks pleased. 'That's marvellous. No problems?'

'Well, he's just a little anxious!' says Kenny, grinning. 'He squeals like a pig the whole time he's . . .,' and Kenny modestly breaks off.

At the end of 1980 Lester Piggott ceased riding for Vincent O'Brien and he accepted a retainer from Henry Cecil who was on his doorstep at Newmarket. Thus ended one of racing's most powerful partnerships between two great professionals. Their victories since 1957 had given great pleasure to racegoers in four countries. O'Brien says of Lester, 'He must be the greatest jockey of his generation, or indeed, any generation. He is cool, shrewd, a great judge of pace, and is capable of riding brilliant races, in particular the big ones.

'He revolutionised race-riding by being able to dictate the pace from in front, and he has won many races that way. There can be few jockeys who give as much thought to how best to ride a horse – many Ribot horses for example were notoriously difficult. Lester discovered that they resented being asked to find early pace, and he allowed them to lope along in the rear until he felt that they were beginning to take more interest. He could get them

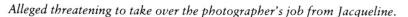

Alleged threatening to take over the photographer's job from Jacqueline.

Pat Eddery's grandfather Jack Moylan, a well-known jockey who rode for Vincent in the early days. This photograph was taken during the war – note all the bicycles in the years of petrol rationing.

running from there and persuade them to put their heads in front before the winning post.

'We had wonderful days together. And as he once said "Some bloody awful ones too – when things went wrong."

'Pat Eddery was retained by the stable in 1981 and the partnership quickly developed into a most successful association. He's already ridden numerous brilliant races for the stable.

'I knew Pat's grandfather, Jack Moylan, who was one of the top jockeys riding in Ireland in the twenties up into the forties. He used to ride for my father and then rode for me when I started to train.'

19

'He was a real man!'

Not everybody was enchanted by Golden Fleece as a yearling. That good Newmarket trainer, 'Tom' Jones took a look at him at Keeneland. Harry Thomson Jones had the finance available to buy an expensive colt or two for the Maktoum brothers. But he did not want to spend their money on this Nijinsky yearling. 'Didn't like him at all! Thought him a great big boat of a horse,' he says cheerfully, watching Touching Wood, the double classic winner he bought instead, being exercised at stud at Newmarket.

Tom laughs, and it's a big man at the top of his profession who can do so in these circumstances. For two years later, Touching Wood was overwhelmed in the Epsom Derby by that whirlwind run of Golden Fleece, which so nearly clipped the old course record. But Touching Wood proved very well bought, for after his second to Golden Fleece, he won the St Leger in the fastest time since Triple Crown winner, Bahram, back in 1935, and then won the Irish St Leger.

As Tom Jones looked at Golden Fleece and turned away, so must O'Brien and his attendants have looked at Touching Wood, for the latter was by O'Brien's Derby winner, Roberto, out of a mare by Vaguely Noble. Golden Fleece, the Nijinsky colt, was also out of a Vaguely Noble mare, but a better-bred one. His dam, Exotic Treat, was half-sister to America's champion three-year-old filly, What a Treat, dam of several winners, including the O'Brien-trained Be My Guest.

'Putting it in business terminology,' said Sangster at Keeneland, 'the yearling is really the raw material. What we're seeing here is the product. Vincent is the production line, as it were. We certainly jacked up the market enormously here. It's like any commodity market. There's a shortage. A lot of people in the past have thought that buying expensive horses is a ludicrous hobby and a rich man's whim.'

Vincent comments, 'That is *exactly* what it was. The reason being that the top-priced yearling each year rarely proved worth what they cost.' Jacqueline adds quietly, 'I believe Vincent changed that trend.' But with all the talk of the yearlings that succeed there are very many costly ones which don't. 'Each year it is a great relief to find a good enough horse to pay for the moderate ones.'

In the May before the July sales, Tom Cooper goes round all the farms in Kentucky, Maryland and Pennsylvania, (an area of 96,000 square miles, nearly

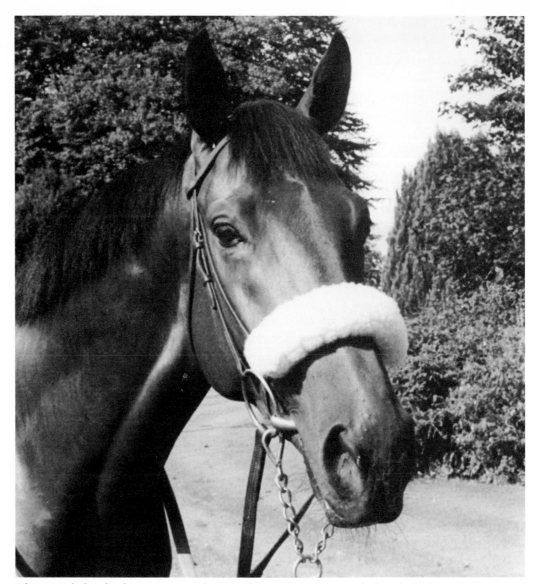

The superb head of a very great horse who was never extended and died tragically young eighteen months after winning the Derby.

twice the size of England), which are likely to have yearlings of the quality the syndicate seeks.

'I'll probably see three hundred yearlings in the three weeks,' says Tom Cooper. 'They take quite a lot of getting round! I bring a dictaphone and do a report in note form for Vincent. I'll try to see the yearlings on their farms, turned out in the paddocks in the early mornings to see how they move cantering.'

While Tom is looking at the individuals in America, back in Tipperary Vincent is poring over his advance copies of the catalogue, picking out the blue blood he requires, and the families he likes.

Then, at Keeneland, Vincent O'Brien starts to go quietly through his shortened list of 'possibles', looking first at heads, eyes and ears to give him the first impression of character. The team usually flies into Lexington on the Wednesday before the sales begin on Monday. They work eight to ten hours a day, inspecting from Thursday to Sunday.

The wise vet, Bob Griffin, whose association with O'Brien goes back forty years, is going round, too, checking the possible yearlings for defects. 'My job,' says Bob, 'is to express an opinion as to the yearlings' prospects of standing up to racing. I start off from the head and go from there to the tail. Then from the body down to the legs. It's a complete examination – the same as for any horse. I examine everything to see there are no conditions likely to cause lameness. Eyes and heart, of course – heart is very important.'

He leans over, stethoscope plugged into his ears, and onto a yearling's heart. He listens to the beat, then looks up over the horse's withers at O'Brien and gives that famous nod and smile. 'Wish mine were as good.'

Equally, he will murmur to Vincent, 'I wouldn't touch that.' Between them, they try not to allow any tiny defects to escape notice. But in the misty areas of hazy doubts heads come together and there are murmured discussions. Sangster and the rest of the syndicate wait upon the decision of the maestro. 'I wouldn't quite like those knees ... on the other hand, he is a very good mover.' Conformation is gone over. Snatches of conversation escape from the earnest group of millionaires seeking their next investments from fragile, four-legged creatures who may never run fast enough to catch a cold.

'Probably the best pedigree in the catalogue ... he's a good looking colt ... Quite a big horse, or will be. He's got a lot to like about him. Walks well ... Fractionally overshot of his mouth, but I think it's more he puts his lip out – makes it look worse than it is. This one's quite nice, not very big. He looks a sharp individual. I can see him coming early to hand...'

A particular yearling is crossed out as a reject, marked as a possible, or specially marked to join a short list of a dozen. Out of this, the syndicate will finally pick about half. On these, they will spend 10 or 12 million dollars in a babble of hectic minutes.

'The biggest problem besetting the bloodstock industry at the moment,' says Vincent, 'is that *we* must pay cash at the sales. But no stallion is paid for with instant cash. They are sold on terms covering four or five years. There's a long gap between buying the yearling and getting your money back, *even* if he turns out very good!'

City financiers, huge institutions, and international merchant bankers, do not plunge millions of pounds into companies without a close study of profit records, future prospects and management. A thoroughbred yearling has no profit record. His future prospects are uncertain hopes. Only management, the skill of the trainer, is there to be measured. The responsibility resting on O'Brien is awesome. The feeling that he might finally pick six yearlings who would all fail abysmally is always present. No one in racing is infallible. The loss of his investment stake would hurt him far less than the dent his reputation would suffer. Yet each year, the magic touch continues. His ability to see far deeper than most people into a yearling's frame and mind remains.

Jacqueline O'Brien declares, 'One of the reasons for his success is that he's a great judge of a horse, and he says himself, "I feel I get better each year from experience. I'm always a learner. I never think the moment's arrived when I think I know all there is to know."'

As the hour of the sale approaches, slacks and sports shirts yield to dark suits, white shirts and French silk ties, and the debate continues. Vincent O'Brien, carefully, quietly sums up.

Of one 'possible', beautifully bred: 'The one with conformation problems is the Nijinsky...'

Of another one, on the small side: 'He's a very late foal, born 20 May. You've got to take that into account...'

'He looks backward. Nothing like the majority of colts we've seen here.'

Of another: 'He doesn't have the best of forelegs. If he was bred other than he is, I wouldn't consider him!'

Of another, showing the length of vision required, 'I think you'd want to count him out as a two year old, and not do too much with him next year, hoping he'd develop, given extra time. That's the only consideration on which I would agree to have him.'

Meanwhile, the syndicate has been masterminding the disguised attacks. 'People can tell what we're likely to be after,' Sangster says, 'but they don't know the final selection. Most consignors have probably got twelve animals in the sale. We may only look at six, then narrow it down to three. But we'll probably put a couple of "fourth ones" in to have them vetted. We'll probably bring those out more often than the ones we're really interested in, just so we don't alert the vendor as to which is our selection.'

After such labours, feints and crafty bidding, Golden Fleece made his 775,000 dollars and came over, a glorious looking great yearling, to Ballydoyle. His reception was markedly different from that given by the staff to Alleged. 'Big strong colt,' they say. T.P. Burns comments, 'He was a top "store type",' meaning that he had the size and strength as well as the quality to make into a top class steeplechaser. Certainly from the moment of his purchase in July, 1980, he particularly pleased the eye of racing enthusiasts who love the jumping game. He was big but balanced, weighty but quick in action, 'like a male ballet dancer' as O'Brien once described the correct make of a jumper.

'No problems with him as a two year old,' say the lads. 'Until the end of the season.'

As part of his preparation for his first race at Leopardstown in September, Golden Fleece went twice to The Curragh with some stable companions to work after racing. He travelled up without difficulty, worked very satisfactorily, and then as calmly returned home. There were no signs of anxiety in the horsebox.

He won his one mile maiden race so commandingly that his name was being buzzed all round Ireland. Once again he completed the long haul from Tipperary up to Leopardstown and back calmly. But no one, except perhaps Vincent O'Brien's young son, David, knew how much Golden Fleece had beaten that day. The runner-up was the two year old Assert, one of David's first horses to train on his own.

The plan then was for Golden Fleece to run in the Larkspur Stakes. To this end he was taken over to Thomastown Castle, the nearby stud and training quarters formerly occupied by Vincent's brother, Phonsie, whose daughter, Gillian, has now made a successful start as a trainer. Using Thomastown from time to time gives the Ballydoyle horses a change of scene and practice in travelling, working, loading and unloading, all helpful rehearsals for race days proper. No trainer worth his fee runs a valuable newcomer without a dummy run.

Gerry Gallagher, the travelling headman, took him over. Golden Fleece did his work. 'He had only normal space in the box,' Gerry explains, 'then, on our way back, he suddenly got into a panic. It was fear of being shut in, for he was such a big horse. But he broke out sweating and he kicked and kicked against the back of the box. He was covered white with sweat and there were cuts inside both his hindlegs from where he'd kicked himself.'

The colt had suffered a bad bout of claustrophobia. Horses connect things and places with feelings. The next sight of the horsebox with its ramp down might again spur panic. If this fear could not be conquered, the colt would not be able to travel; and few racehorses outside Newmarket and The Curragh can be led to a racecourse. There was certainly no question of that down in the mountain-ringed countryside of remote Tipperary.

So began the long process of rehabilitation. To restore Golden Fleece's confidence he would be taken out in the horsebox with stalls removed so that he had double room. He would go out twice every week all winter long from October to April. He was driven first a little way and then unloaded. Then further. Then for little jaunts along the lanes which climb up and wind down the small hills round Ballydoyle. By such patient small steps, he completed the

The horse who was big enough to win a Cheltenham Gold Cup as a three year old going down to the start at Leopardstown.

(right) Golden Fleece, ridden in all his four races by Pat Eddery, coming home at Leopardstown.

full stride to recovery. But it had been a very anxious winter. And there loomed ahead the doubts whether he could ever be taken to England.

The same dislike of being shut in affected Golden Fleece in the starting stalls. So he practised there, too, twice weekly throughout that winter. All the time he was being particularly watched for any further signs of that tense temperament shown by his sire, Nijinsky, which might have been inherited by his big bay son. In the hour of triumph the following June, O'Brien immediately told the press what they might not have guessed. He wanted it recorded straight, 'how much I owe to the care and patience of my staff.'

The seeds of another likely complication over plans for Golden Fleece lay unexpectedly on the door step, where Vincent's eldest son, David, had just made his remarkably successful start as a trainer. Having finished his studies early in accountancy in Dublin he came home to assist his father, an extremely difficult task. Then David set himself up on the opposite side of the sweeping gallops. He used Vincent's original isolation yard as a base and expanded from there, building further lines of boxes and a neat office. A bachelor until May 1984 he lived before that with his parents, rising at 5.30 am to go across to his own stables to feed all his horses himself. He used his father's gallops but his horses were worked quite separately from the Ballydoyle ones and at different times. He would jest, 'I want to get mine off the gallops before the boss sees them!'

Young David kept his cards very close to his chest. This now became very important because his colt, Assert, the same age as Golden Fleece, but bought

very inexpensively for £16,000 in France, had sharply improved on his first run behind Golden Fleece at Leopardstown. He had gone on to win the Beresford Stakes at The Curragh very easily. Then David had thought so highly of him that he sent him across to run in the William Hill Futurity at Doncaster. Although he was a fine looking colt, he failed to attract much attention from the English. He got bumped about a bit in the race and lost his action around a quarter of a mile from home and finished eighth. David was very disappointed at Doncaster with the run, but well pleased with the horse. By the spring of 1982, Assert seemed to him something quite out of the ordinary. He was to prove so nearly the equal of Golden Fleece that only one pound would separate them at the end of that golden year.

Assert had been one of a flock of two-year-old winners produced by David in his first season. Now, as their three-year-old seasons opened, it would be difficult to prevent him meeting Golden Fleece. They were each owned principally by Robert Sangster, a situation which, if he had owned all of both, might have helped. As it was, he gave David *carte blanche* to plot Assert's programme without regard to Golden Fleece. Neither David nor his father would discuss plans for each other's classic hopes. For this Golden Fleece and Assert certainly were. Yet the O'Briens, father and son, would sit over lunch amicably chatting but never asking each other even if their rival horse was going to take them on.

Once, at lunch in the spring of Golden Fleece and Assert's classic year, Vincent left the room to take a telephone call. David took advantage of his

Looking from the kitchen window towards the stable yard.

father's brief absence to ask his mother, 'Would he be running that horse at The Curragh, do you think?'

'I really don't know,' said Jacqueline, who probably didn't. 'I should ask him.'

'Oh, I wouldn't do that,' said David, giving one of his shy smiles, 'I wouldn't want to show my hand.'

England is a long way from Tipperary and the uninformed impression across the water was that David O'Brien was still assistant to his father, running a secondary yard, though in his own name but nevertheless subservient to paternal control. Nothing was further from the truth. David, beneath his mop of flopping hair and behind his languid eyes, has a burning ambition to prove himself. Vincent preserves the normal attitude of a proud but competitive father. In the case of the two good colts, he longed for David to succeed but not, he hoped, at his expense.

Golden Fleece's first prep race for the 1982 Derby was only the second of his career. The way he won the Ballymoss Stakes at The Curragh in mid-April was with such ludicrous ease that certainly one professional English observer of racing was positive he had witnessed a wonder horse, and was bold enough to recommend him to the readers of his Sunday column.

Pat Eddery reported after The Curragh, 'He ran away with me well before the straight. I told the boss he needed a pacemaker to get him off the bridle.'

The horse, at the start of the season, had been a 25 to 1 shot for the Derby. After that classic, Pat announced, 'The Derby was the first time I could hold him!' He added eighteen months later, 'Golden Fleece was the best horse by a long way I have ever ridden.'

The horse had brilliant speed. Not since his sire, Nijinsky, had there been even in O'Brien's yard a horse bred to stay 1½ miles and yet possessed of such astonishing acceleration. Some doubt had to exist in the trainer's mind. He said that spring, 'When a horse is as fast as this, you would have to wonder whether he will really stay, and,' he added, 'he has *such* speed!' using for him singular emphasis.

Golden Fleece's next race brought him and Assert together on the same course, Leopardstown, where they had met the previous autumn. Once again, the big bay won with derisory ease with Pat Eddery 'sitting against him', as if on the training grounds, where O'Brien might have told him, 'Just go steady. Don't let him off the bit.' Pat reported, 'We had two pacemakers and still I couldn't hold him! I shouted to Vincent Rossiter to go on, but he couldn't go any faster!'

It was a spectacular performance for any judge of horseflesh. But form book experts looked at the race sceptically. Golden Fleece's nearest pursuer was Assert, who was making his first appearance of the season and seemed to the cynics to be enjoying an unarduous outing. To this Vincent replies, 'I thought Assert put up an excellent performance to finish second to Golden Fleece, beaten two and a half lengths. Golden Fleece was being eased inside the last furlong. Before this, Assert had been making ground. His jockey rightly did not give him a hard race when he saw he had no hope of the catching the winner.'

Third was another Ballydoyle horse, Lords, an expensive purchase running in the colours of the Californian tycoon, Danny Schwartz, a member of the syndicate. Not every million dollar yearling they buy automatically succeeds. As Vincent points out, 'It's no good just talking about the big prices we finally get for *some*. Remember the others.'

After Leopardstown's Nijinsky Stakes in early May, which was to be Golden Fleece's last run before the Epsom Derby, and the penultimate race of his life, cynics who had not witnessed Golden Fleece in action, were not one whit as impressed by his form as those who had watched him in Ireland.

We had no sooner returned to England with these glowing reports than mishaps, such is the way of the world, began to befall our hero. 'At the time of the Irish Two Thousand Guineas,' says T.P. Burns ruefully, 'Golden Fleece whipped round and dropped me on the gallops at home.' His leap and twist must have been great to decant that former top jockey on the flat and over hurdles.

Pat Eddery reported after riding him at home, 'Golden Fleece was a highly-strung horse; he didn't like patting on the neck or being fussed with. Riding out, if he did anything silly you wouldn't want to give him a slap, or he wouldn't go well. You had to *coax* him along. He was a horse you had to watch all the time. You couldn't ride him with a long rein or you'd be on the floor! Very quick at spinning round, he was. For a big horse he was very sharp. He was a real man!'

In that fall poor T.P. Burns broke his ankle painfully and Golden Fleece got loose on the gallops. Nothing is more alarming. At Newmarket, until they railed most of the roadsides, horses often got killed. A loose horse, alarmed or excited by flapping stirrup leathers and irons acting like a jockey's kicking heels, and bewildered by trailing reins, can often slip over or crash into fences, breaking a leg. Golden Fleece returned safely to the yard at Ballydoyle. He had no roads to cross. He had not travelled a tenth of the distance wildly traversed by the 1981 Derby winner, Shergar, who had been more than five miles down roads round Newmarket till caught, unharmed, by a nimble milkman in an astonished village. 'T.P.', like Brer Rabbit, laid low and said nuffin'. The bookmakers' intelligence service had a mole somewhere around Ballydoyle. This was the sort of news they needed, but the mole did not report.

Then, only ten days before the Derby, Golden Fleece's off-hind hock swelled up. 'He was not quite sound,' O'Brien stresses, 'and we suspected a small spavin. Bob Griffin moved in once more.'

Such a mishap so close to the classic put the colt's contention in doubt. David O'Brien had already been considering whether to take on his father with Assert, and Robert Sangster had given him free rein to do so. Up till Golden Fleece's setback, David had inclined to go for the French 'Derby', the Prix du Jockey Club, run four days after the Epsom race and then come back to Ireland for the Irish Derby. This latter race had been in Vincent's mind for Golden Fleece, too, if all went well in the English Derby.

Since following Golden Fleece home at Leopardstown, Assert had massacred a good field for the Gallinule Stakes at The Curragh. The fourth horse there, nearly 15 lengths behind him, had been second the time before to Golden Fleece, beaten only three lengths. Assert was plainly improving quickly enough to put him in the same class as Golden Fleece. '*Nearly* in,' says Vincent. Assert was a likely classic winner, if not at Epsom, then in France or Ireland. If Golden Fleece did not recover in time for Epsom, Sangster had a superb deputy in Assert.

Cabinet discussion: Pat Eddery listens while Vincent and Robert Sangster interrogate Dermot Hogan about how the horses worked.

Davy the blacksmith, had already been taking precautionary measures with Golden Fleece to help support the massive colt's hindlegs. He had started to shoe him with raised heels behind, which would just tilt the foot a fraction forward, taking a little strain off the hock. 'I made the shoes so that they got deeper towards the back and curled round.'

Jacqueline O'Brien was in the King Edward VII hospital in London and sought advice from the three physiotherapists there. The treatment prescribed was ice-packs and ultrasonics and this was carried out. Meanwhile, though they couldn't ride the horse, it was necessary to keep him moving.

'Was he fresh!' T.P. repeats. 'He was a very fresh horse, anyway!' He was led out twice a day for three days. It was like watching a clock ticking away. 'We were running out of time,' T.P. remembers grimly, 'On the fourth day, we were on his back again.'

Between then and his due departure for Epsom, which would be on the Saturday before Wednesday, 2 June, Pat Eddery came over twice to ride the Derby favourite. The lads remember Golden Fleece working on 26 May with his two expensive workmates, Lords, who had cost just over one million dollars, and Pilgrim, who cost one and a quarter million dollars. Lords went past Pilgrim, and Pat Eddery on Golden Fleece went past Lords and dropped his hands. Vincent asked Eddery, 'Did he do enough?' The lads recall with glee, 'Lords went out the back door!'

'The second piece of work,' says Vincent, 'was on the Friday with Pilgrim. Golden Fleece drew ten lengths away and Pat was very pleased.'

The decision to run at Epsom was made. For a little longer, David O'Brien remained uncertain whether to take on the favourite with Assert. He came under no pressure from either his father or from Robert Sangster. 'He finally decided,' Vincent reports, 'that his colt's action was more suited to a good galloping course: Chantilly, rather than Epsom.' Then it was heard that Persepolis, probably the best French 1½ mile colt, would run at Epsom instead of at Chantilly in the Prix du Jockey Club. This would give Golden Fleece a harder task but make the French 'Derby' easier. David O'Brien decided to go to Chantilly, although no foreign-trained horse had ever won that race on the beautiful French course below the Château. Jalmood and Peacetime were, like Persepolis, also fancied to beat Golden Fleece at Epsom. The latter's hold-up had not improved his chances.

There also remained some doubt about Golden Fleece's flight to England. It would be his first experience of air travel. The 'Skyvan', built by Short and Harland in Belfast and used from the airstrip built like a road along the bottom of the Ballydoyle gallops, was not considered large enough. 'He'd not fit in!' says T.P. The Skyvan was bought and converted, at O'Brien's suggestion, to take two horses standing side by side, loaded from the rear, with their heads over the pilot's. Commuters from New York up to Albany (the airport for Saratoga Springs) use the same aircraft. The snag is its low roof space for a big horse. Vincent decided to charter a CL44 from Shannon to Gatwick. Golden Fleece would travel with his lead horse, General Custer. As a precaution against an outbreak of the previous year's panic, Vincent had plugs put in Golden Fleece's ears, and a hood put over his head. He also had the customs officers at Gatwick alerted so that there would be minimal delay. Gerry says, 'The customs were waiting for us. They looked after us very well.'

The flight had passed without a hitch and the Derby favourite arrived safely in the racecourse stables four days before the race. He had overcome getting loose; he had recovered from his holdup. His trainer seemed dexterously to have caught up the lost days' work. All seemed bright and shining. But now another threat was poised to break out. The colt, at the worst possible moment, was about to cough.

On the Sunday, Golden Fleece walked out twice at Epsom. O'Brien thought the big horse might still be short of exercise. On the following day, he obtained special permission to work on the course itself and that day the horse went to the Derby start and worked fast over five furlongs at a nice speed. 'Pat rode

A crisis is about to brew. Golden Fleece ridden by Pat Eddery on the morning before the Derby has coughed several times. On the near side is Gerry Gallagher on his lead horse General Custer.

him,' says Vincent, 'from the 1½ mile gate to the seven furlong starting gate.'

On Tuesday morning, thirty hours before the Derby, Golden Fleece and General Custer went to the start again, worked two furlongs at half-speed and then quickened for the final two furlongs. O'Brien was, as usual, out to watch and listen. As the two horses were pulled up to walk down Tattenham Hill and round Tattenham Corner, Golden Fleece coughed a number of times.

Normally, the O'Brien horses canter quietly on under the grandstand side of the course and pull up at the winning post. A group of photographers and racing journalists were standing there watching. Pat Eddery and Gerry, who was riding the lead horse, decided to canter on along the stands side, as if all was well, and not to pull up at the winning post in front of the photographers and journalists.

They took the horses up to the stables and Pat got off to let Golden Fleece's lad lead him into the stables. Pat waited anxiously to talk to Vincent who came hurrying up. They had an urgent, troubled discussion. Bob Griffin was telephoned at once with what seemed like another version of Nijinsky's pre-race drama. But the colt, he was told, had no discharge from his nose. More important, he was not running a temperature. It was a question again of cross fingers and pray. No medication, even had it been allowed by the Rules of Racing, could have averted the onset of a fever.

'Is he hot?' Bob Griffin asked, 'Is he sweating?'

He was a little hot. But it was a very hot day. Bob Griffin said, reassuringly, 'It could be the heat that caused some dehydration and made him cough.' Griffin's calm accuracy was now proverbial at Ballydoyle. It was fervently hoped that he would prove right again. Should they now announce to the waiting world what had happened? Suppose the horse coughed in the race, ran deplorably, had even to be pulled up?

The O'Brien camp resolved to make no announcement for the moment but to wait and see what would happen. A man was stationed outside Golden Fleece's box all day 'to ascertain,' as Vincent puts it, 'if the colt might cough again.' The horse, to their blessed relief, did not. And in the world outside, no one caught even a whisper that anything might be amiss with the Derby favourite.

Vincent comments, 'Over the years I do agonise about how much one should announce publicly when minor mishaps occur to the horses. Unless you are associated with a racehorse, you've no idea how many little things go wrong. If a trainer keeps making announcements every time a horse gets say, a stone bruise, we'd get the public thoroughly confused because the troubles can clear up within hours. After all a lame horse at breakfast can easily be sound by tea-time. The existence of ante-post betting makes trainers' lives a hell coming up to a big race. Either way, whether you make announcements or don't, you're likely to be wrong.'

The colt had not impressed everyone who had watched him in action at Epsom before the race. This was the first occasion he had set foot in England. Some observers got up early to sneak a previous glimpse of him. Were those reports of his Irish victories to be fully believed? No one, outside the stables of the O'Briens of course, yet knew how good Assert was. Not even David O'Brien could have said in May that his colt would win two Derbies.

A reporter then with the *Sporting Life* called John McCririck declared on raceday morning on the front page of that mighty organ, 'Watching Golden Fleece in his spin with General Custer, I can't remember seeing a leading Derby contender with a more scratchy action in his faster paces.' To support this unusual view – knowledgeable racing observers always found Golden Fleece, a tremendous galloper – the reporter produced a 'quote' from an unnamed 'local trainer' who said 'he thought the Irish star lumbered along like a great tank!'

Lomond, *winner of the 1983 2,000 Guineas, waits to board his private Skyvan from Ballydoyle to Newmarket.*

El Gran Senor, *champion two year old and winner of the 1984 2,000 Guineas and Irish Sweeps Derby. Vincent's three grandchildren are, David and Jamie Myerscough and Sean McClory.*

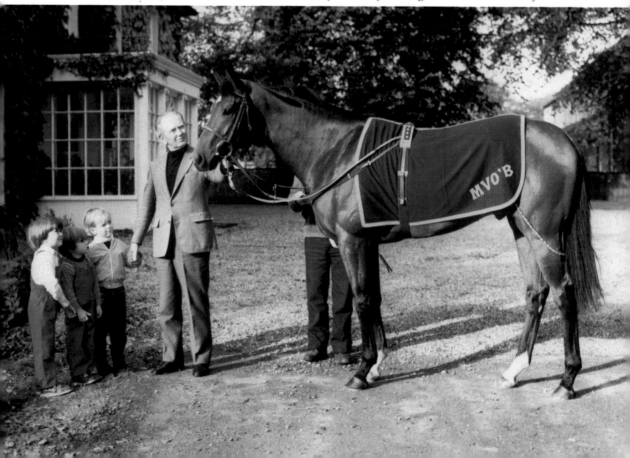

Golden Fleece at Coolmore with
some of his friends from Ballydoyle,
including King's Lake, Try My Best
and Be My Guest. Coolmore, run by
Vincent's son-in-law John Magnier,
is still rapidly expanding. It is now
the biggest stud complex in Europe.

The hope for the future – a filly foal
by Nijinsky out of Fish Bar.

Headman Johnny Brabston preparing the feeds.

Some tank. Some lumber. Some observer ... To right the balance, three of the *Sporting Life's* swarm of real tipsters buzzed loud for Golden Fleece. Michael O'Hehir, the jolly Irish commentator, was one of those who had been so impressed by Golden Fleece winning at Leopardstown the race named after his sire. 'Augur' made him a confident selection, though referring mysteriously to 'his alleged bad temper'. No one at Ballydoyle found him bad tempered. The *Sporting Life's* ratings man, Dick Whitford, said succinctly, 'any recipe for a potential Derby winner would call for the exact credentials possessed by Golden Fleece.'

None of these gentlemen could know their selection had started to cough on the eve of the race. Those who quizzed Vincent O'Brien were puzzled that he did not show unbridled optimism. Such is never his form. And in this instance there would be no way of knowing whether the cough might not break out again in the paddock, at the start, during the race. Tension triggers diseases. Heat accelerates a fever.

So O'Brien repeated his assessment of the favourite. The colt had brilliant speed – such brilliant speed – that he just hoped he would also stay 1½ miles. 'I'm hopeful,' he repeated again and again to press men, tongues out for something firmer and juicier with which to appease their hungry sports editors.

Older racegoers would have recalled, had they known of O'Brien's problems, the anxieties of Captain Cecil Boyd-Rochfort (as he was then) struggling with liberal doses of cod liver oil to get his great filly, Meld, to the post for the 1955 St Leger to win the fillies' Triple Crown. She had coughed on the day and yet she won.

The tension gripped Robert Sangster who, like Vincent O'Brien, disguises emotion behind a mask of calm.

O'Brien was at Epsom in the thick of things. Sangster stayed in the Isle of Man, playing golf most of Tuesday. He told a friend he couldn't bear to go to Epsom till the last minute. He did not arrive until the morning of the race. His three sons by his first wife, Guy, then a stockbroker, and Ben and Adam, still at school, came to the races. The two oldest had touched trouble at Harrow for betting. Both said they had not even had a pound on Golden Fleece, who had been 25 to 1 in April and 33 to 1 at the start of the year. He would start 3 to 1 with the bookies, with 4 to 1 paid by the Tote.

The Downs being free at Epsom, no one really knew how many people came to Derby Day. Three quarters of a million was a figure bandied about among those in the more exclusive but quaint and elderly stands. Racegoers there included the Queen, Prince Philip and Princess Anne, as well as Joe Gormley, an ardent racing man just retired from the chair of the National Union of Mineworkers. There were also actor Albert Finney, the new American Ambassador, John Louis, actress Britt Ekland, and two famous brothers from Dubai, Sheikh Mohammed who, among sixty horses in England, owned the much fancied Derby hope, Jalmood, and his seven years older brother, Maktoum al Maktoum, who was running the horse Tom Jones had preferred as a Keeneland yearling to Golden Fleece: the tough colt, Touching Wood.

And in the television perch in the stands, pale, wrinkled, with a light jacket over his colours for another, lesser race, was the famous man who would have ridden Golden Fleece had he continued his links with Ballydoyle. Lester Piggott, the best Derby rider of the century and probably of all time, was without a ride in the race. He would have been on Simply Great for his new stable, Henry Cecil's, at Newmarket. This once so promising colt was a late withdrawal and the housewives of Britain, who make 'Piggott in the Derby' their annual flutter, were saved a loser. Instead, Lester was making comments about the runners to Brough Scott, tossing his locks in front of the ITV cameras.

Like the fox with the grapes, Piggott was critical of Golden Fleece...

In his old seat in the saddle was his replacement, the thirty year old Pat Eddery, whose wife Carolyn had produced their first child, Nicola Jane, on the Saturday Golden Fleece flew over. She watched the race on ITV. She saw that, in spite of the sweltering day, Golden Fleece sweated less than many in the paddock. The thunderstorm which drenched the course before racing took the sting out of the firm Epsom turf but left the air as humid as Kentucky where O'Brien had bought him 22 months before. Golden Fleece looked magnificent. He proceeded calmly along that extraordinary track which, as scruffy as an old livery stable trail, leads the most valuable horses in Europe past broken bottles, cans, orange peel, kids on ponies, goggling gypsies and boozing day trippers, across to the Derby start.

Pat Eddery reported, 'For the Derby the boss decided to use a sheepskin noseband.' Expert observers in the press thought this was the first time O'Brien had ever used one in the Derby. 'With this on, he really settled and relaxed, though he was sweating at the start.'

Golden Fleece entered the gate like a warm bishop into his cathedral stall. At 3.38 pm (three minutes late) when the starter let them go, he sprang off with the leading bunch up that quite steep, right-turning bend past the wood. With O'Brien's doubt about his horse's stamina, Eddery had been told to settle him towards the back of the field. Pat Eddery comments, 'It could have helped that he'd had those two mornings' slow cantering from the start – which he'd enjoyed. Golden Fleece helped himself to win the Derby because he relaxed so well.' He settled to such effect that he was almost last going down Tattenham Hill. There were only three horses behind him at the bottom of the Hill as the leaders rushed round Tattenham Corner and swung into the straight.

There then occurred a sight which far transcended even that of Shergar's devastating victory of the year before. For Golden Fleece, coming from the back of his field, shot through them like a bullet. Once he had sped through the ruck, Pat Eddery moved him leisurely towards the outside. Ahead on the rails galloped Norwick, Peacetime and Silver Hawk with Touching Wood battling through them.

Eddery then seemed calmly to pause as the driver of a Ferrari might glance at Minis as he swept by. Then the speed of Golden Fleece's astonishing acceleration quickened again and he was clear and striding home unchallenged. 'He's won the world's greatest race,' said Pat Eddery, still amazed as he rode in, 'and he still has to be extended!' Pat said, aglow, 'He's learned to race. He'll have no problems now.' He was longing to ride him in all the big races ahead. 'On the way home, I said to Mum and Terry, "Think what's to come!"' Terry Ellis is Pat's brother-in-law and manager.

In none of Golden Fleece's four races had he ever been exerted. His speed

Golden Fleece still unextended in his last race wins the 1982 Epsom Derby in the fastest time since Mahmoud in 1936.

for the Derby 1½ miles in 2 min 34.27 sec set the record since electrical timing was introduced in 1964, nearly twenty years earlier. It almost equalled Mahmoud's hand-timed (and so still suspect) record set at 2 min 33.8 sec on 27 May, 1936.

In the glow of victory, Vincent O'Brien declared that he would have to rank Golden Fleece with Nijinsky and Sir Ivor at the top of the six Epsom Derby winners he had so far trained. He has not changed his view. And eighteen months later, Pat Eddery remained adamant that the horse was the best he had ridden.

No sooner was the race over than the trainers of the second, third and fourth horses announced that they had no intention of trying to take on this spectacular winner in the Irish Derby. As a result, Golden Fleece was quoted 3 to

An overjoyed Susan Sangster leads in Golden Fleece after his devastating victory.

1 *on* for that race which would, without Assert, have proved another cantering conquest for him.

Would Assert take him on? The official assessments for the season's end placed the two colts, trained by O'Brien father and son, clear at the top of their trees. In the Free Handicap, Golden Fleece was given 10 st followed by Assert at 9 st 13 lb. Next came Awaasif at 9 st 7 lb and Touching Wood (winner of the two St Legers) on 9 st 6 lb.

The International Classification compiled jointly by the official handicappers of France, Great Britain and Ireland gave Golden Fleece 94, Assert 93, level with Green Forest, and Akiyda, winner of the Arc de Triomphe, on 89.

Assert made 1982 the *annus mirabilis* for the syndicate and the Sangster colours. Four days after Golden Fleece's Derby, Assert won the French Derby and then the Irish Derby – making the rest look rubbish on The Curragh. He was just beaten in Ascot's King George VI and Queen Elizabeth Diamond Stakes and then cantered home, clearly the easiest winner to date, of the Benson and Hedges Gold Cup at York.

No one who saw Golden Fleece's electric spurt to his Derby victory will ever forget it. But it was to be his last race. The slender thread by which the fortunes of even the greatest racehorses tenuously hang, began to fray, then snap.

Those dread coughs on the eve of the Derby were not a transient threat. Within ten days of that tremendous race, Golden Fleece was down with a cold and Demi O'Byrne, Ballydoyle's regular vet, was there to attend him. Golden Fleece's cold dragged on for three weeks. Plans for him to run in the Irish Sweeps Derby had been quickly abandoned. And then, when his cold finally dried up and he was eased back into work, his other hindleg swelled up, just as its pair had done ten days before the Derby. 'By the time that had gone down,' says Vincent O'Brien resignedly, 'it would have taken another six weeks just to get him ready.'

It was too late. Golden Fleece was retired to stud. His valuation was similar to that of Assert's, about $25 million. But, as Robert Sangster on one of the only occasions he has shown public excitement, burst out after the Derby, 'We're talking about a great horse and a great race! Why spoil it talking about money?'

Golden Fleece was not exported to stand in Kentucky but was retained at Coolmore. There, only eighteen months after his Derby triumph, came the catastrophe. In December, 1983, the great horse was struck down with cancer. A team of American surgeons were flown over to operate on him. The operation seemed successful. Then, in late February, 1984, he began to sicken again. He fought for life with immense courage, but in vain. Before the flat race season of 1984 had begun, the glory of 1982 was dead.

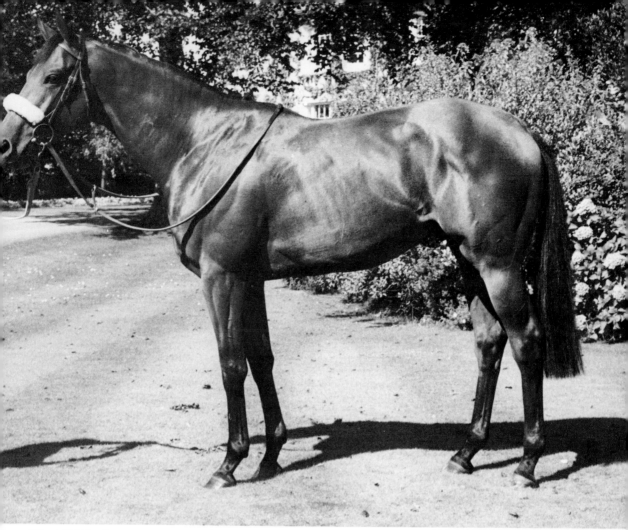

The 1982 Derby winner wearing his special sheepskin noseband photographed in the garden at Ballydoyle before he went to stud seven miles away at Coolmore for his tragically short career as a stallion.

O'Brien's comment after his sixth Epsom Derby win was in keeping with his character. The man who began with the Good Days – Drybob gamble back in the dark years of the war, murmured about Golden Fleece, 'I'm delighted, naturally, and privileged to have been associated with a really great horse.'

The thread that has linked O'Brien's great horses together had, in the case of Golden Fleece, been broken cruelly soon.

O'Brien, as is his nature, briskly shook off vain regrets. His eyes in April were turned towards the future and the new season. Pat Eddery came in smiling from the sunlit gallops at Ballydoyle, and Vincent said quietly, 'I'm pleased with the way the horses are working.'

20

'I'm absolutely thrilled for my son'

In the spring of 1980 the mare Sex Appeal conceived a colt foal by Northern Dancer at Windfields Farm, Maryland. Sex Appeal, by the good staying sire Buckpasser, was then still partly owned by E.P. Taylor from whom Vincent had bought the fabulous Northern Dancer yearling, Nijinsky. After weaning, the foal came to O'Brien's Lyonstown Stud near Ballydoyle where he grew, developed and was broken.

In June, 1984, the power of Northern Dancer was dramatically and doubly emphasised on Epsom Downs. The 1984 Derby furthermore had the resonance of Greek classical drama where kings come into conflict with their sons. For the trainer and part-owner of Sex Appeal's son, El Gran Senor, was Vincent, and one of the few colts who seemed any sort of threat to him was trained in the same remote corner of Tipperary by Vincent's twenty-seven year old son David. This was Secreto, another son of Northern Dancer.

El Gran Senor had been named by Vincent after that brilliant and romantic trainer from South America, Horatio Luro, who had trained Northern Dancer and was making his first visit to Epsom to watch his namesake run. By a further coincidence Secreto had been bought by another South American senor, Luigi Miglietti, who had emigrated from Italy and founded a coach company and a fortune in Caracas, Venezuela, and had built up a thoroughbred stud there.

He had bought Secreto himself as a yearling at the world famous Keeneland Sales, that Kentuckian treasure trove where Vincent since the mid 1970s has picked out so many golden nuggets.

In 1982 Secreto was on Vincent's list of 'possibles', but the colt did not attract the really big bidders, some of whom thought that he was heavy topped. He may not have been an impressive yearling, but on his first visit to England he showed in the Epsom paddock great presence and depth, and was a wonderful walker. Senor Miglietti was able to buy him for 340,000 dollars in a sale when yearlings were fetching millions. The price was below the sales average and less than the cost of a nomination to Northern Dancer.

The South American had no other horses in training in Europe. Not surprisingly he knew the name O'Brien, and took advice from American bloodstock experts, one of whom knew David well and had admired his establishment at Ballydoyle. It was the year in which David won the French and Irish

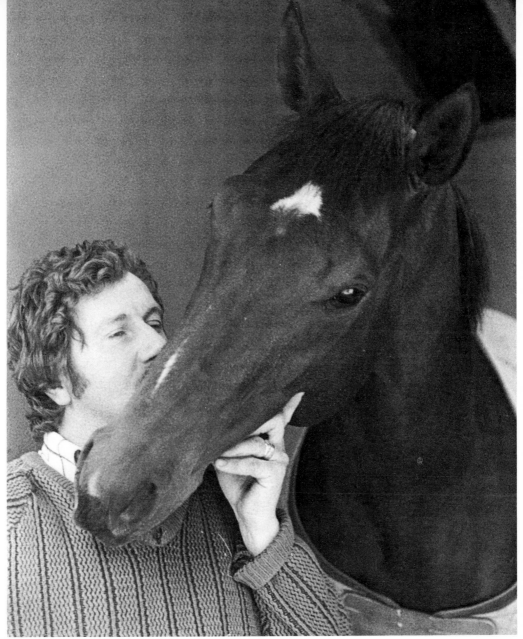

El Gran Senor's lovable temperament has endeared him to all at Ballydoyle. He is seen here with his lad Willie Burke.

Derby's with Assert and it was easy for the American friend to say that David was 'very professional', a phrase which lingered in the Migliettis' minds after the Derby ... They were advised that the colt might well do better in Europe than in America and they sent him over in December, still unbroken, to David's stables on the other side of Vincent's gallops at Ballydoyle.

Vincent did not have to buy El Gran Senor. Together with Robert Sangster and his group he had bought two-thirds of the colt's dam, Sex Appeal, from E.P. Taylor after Try My Best, El Gran Senor's full brother, had won the

Dewhurst Stakes and proved himself the top two year old of 1977. Eddie Taylor retained his third in Sex Appeal until the winter of 1983. The mare returned every year to Northern Dancer, the horse whom Vincent had discovered and whom he had made in the words of that great breeding expert Tony Morris of the *Sporting Life* – 'simply the best there is'.

'The Senor' turned out like his full brother to be unbeatable as a two year old, and came over to Newmarket in October 1983 to start favourite for the Dewhurst. English race-goers had their first sight of him. They found him beautifully made, slightly smaller than average, of an excellent hard bay colour, and with a brow as broad as an intellectual's, and an expression as calmly benign as a saint's. Even if he had possessed little ability his lovable temperament had particularly endeared him to the O'Brien family and to all the staff at Ballydoyle. In their 1983 Christmas card you can see him standing as quietly as a hunter at their front door.

In the Dewhurst he had quite a tussle over the last furlong to beat the highly regarded Rainbow Quest, but did so bravely by half a length. At the season's end he was Champion European two year old. At Ballydoyle there were the highest hopes for him for the English classics.

As the 2,000 Guineas approached in an abnormally dry spring, The Senor had already won at The Curragh beating his stable companion Sadler's Wells. His winnings rose to just under £100,000. For once, all racing observers agreed that this was a particularly high-class Guineas which would take a great deal of winning.

One image lingers, indicative of El Gran Senor's character. There was a delay down at the start. Pat Eddery slipped off his back to rest him. The colt gently lowered his head and Pat, flinging one arm loosely across the horse's neck, leaned against his shoulder, legs nonchalantly crossed as a child stands with a loved and gentle pony.

The billed 'clash of giants' produced one giant and a gaggle of ordinary horses. El Gran Senor did a most difficult thing with the greatest of ease; he made two separate challenges during the course of a hard-run race. He won going away from Chief Singer, Lear Fan and Rainbow Quest. He was unextended, ears pricked above that handsome head, to win in nearly two seconds under standard time.

'He was in a class of his own,' Vincent said quietly as the colt came in. The press besought him to compare this horse with the greatest of his previous six Derby winners. 'I believe,' he said 'that his Guineas performance today is on a level with Nijinsky's and Sir Ivor's. If he wins at Epsom next month he could be the best I've trained....'

Doubts about The Senor's stamina were immediately put forward. But Vincent pointed out three factors: the colt's relaxed style of running – 'I could,'

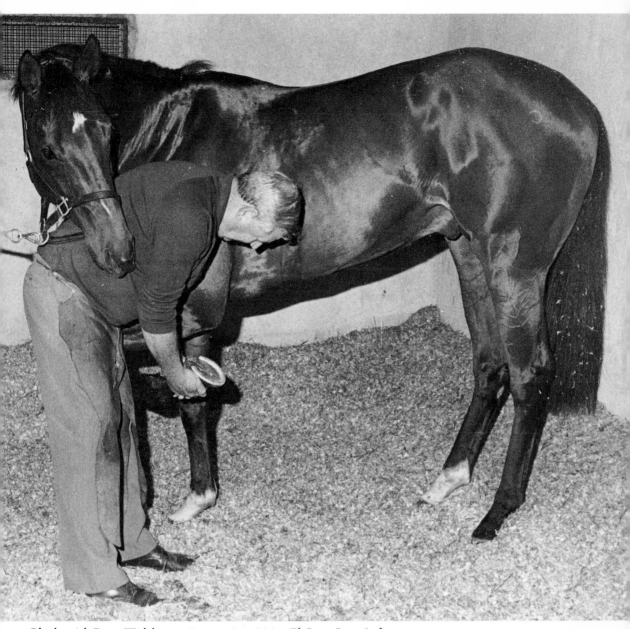

Blacksmith Davy Walsh examines an inquisitive El Gran Senor's feet.

said Pat Eddery, 'put him anywhere in a race at any time'; the fact that his dam was by Buckpasser; and added 'Mile-and-a-quarter horses possessed with outstanding speed can win the Derby.'

As El Gran Senor sailed past the post at Newmarket he was instantly installed red-hot favourite for the Derby which, Vincent announced, would be his next race. Between the Guineas and the Derby all went without a hitch.

This was the even tenor of his life. No one at Ballydoyle can remember anything going wrong with him before the Derby. On the contrary, his work at home was phenomenal. Jacqueline reported, 'I can't ever remember any horse here doing so well.'

Rain fell spasmodically at Epsom in the weeks before the Derby, and heavily at times on the Monday and Tuesday before the race. Vincent stayed close to the course at the RAC's Woodcote Park where he had spent all his previous Derby visits. He was out on the Tuesday morning with his daughter Sue Magnier facing the press and television cameras outside the stable block. He did not, as was his usual custom with Derby contenders, work El Gran Senor on the course. He said, 'The horse did a good bit of work at home on Monday before he left.' He produced the odds-on favourite for the cameras. The colt regarded the crowd sleepily, strolled around the yard, and retired to his box.

'Would the rain-softened going affect the favourite's chances?' Vincent was repeatedly asked. He explained patiently that the colt acted on any going, but the softer it was the more it became a test of stamina.

Remembering Vincent's views just before Golden Fleece's Derby two years earlier, journalists asked 'Are you hopeful or confident?' He had said about Golden Fleece that he was 'hopeful', an adjective which he uses quite often. Few could recall him declaring in public that he was confident. This time he replied with a small smile, head tilted, 'I'm confident.'

David did not travel Secreto from Ireland on the large aircraft which was hired for El Gran Senor on Monday. He had sufficient confidence in his horse to justify the expense of taking the same plane a day earlier. He wanted to work his horse on the track round Tattenham Corner. Secreto impressed observers that wet Tuesday morning and his young trainer said he handled the corner well.

During the race before the Derby the crowds were thicker around the pre-parade paddock than at any time in the previous decade. The star drew his admirers down the long walk from the grandstands like a magnet attracting a thousand multi-coloured needles. Guarded by Gerry Gallagher on his inside, and by Matt Fogarty, son of Willie, between him and the crowd pressing over the white rails, El Gran Senor showed only a trace of tension. His tail flicked. Occasionally he gave a slight stamp of a hoof. But in the long parade up the course in front of the stands he was more relaxed.

Vincent's instructions to Pat Eddery before the 2,000 Guineas had been, 'The longer you wait, the further you will win.'

'Before the Derby,' Pat says, 'the guv'nor didn't give me any more instructions.'

Since the only possible flaw in the favourite lay in his stamina, the opposition in the shape of Tom Jones and Guy Harwood ran pacemakers to ensure a really strong gallop for respectively Ilium and Alphabatim who started second favourite at 11 to 2. Of the small field of seventeen, ten horses started at 50 to 1 or longer.

The horses had reached the start before Vincent and his party, including Robert Sangster and John Magnier, came quietly through the gates into the enclosure, and climbed up a few steps below the television platform. Watching from the stands was Charles Taylor, who, with his father, had bred both the two O'Brien horses.

Soon after the start Eddery could be seen poised confidently about the middle of the field with plenty of room around him. Turning down the Hill Claude Monet began to improve and El Gran Senor moved easily forward to track him. Tom Jones' pacemaker At Talaq, who had led from soon after the mile starting gate, was still ahead as the field pursued him round Tattenham Corner and into the straight.

Then the most astonishing sight became so plain to the colossal crowd that a hum surged like surf across the Downs: Pat Eddery, still just behind Claude Monet in fifth place was sitting up, as if riding work with 'a double handful'. His hands seemed to be resting on The Senor's withers, and the colt was

Secreto and El Gran Senor race neck and neck to the finish of the 1984 Derby.

lobbing along on the bit, apparently cantering while all around whips rose and cracked, and heels and elbows pumped.

'The favourite will win six lengths,' shouted a veteran of the Press Box, 'when Pat lets him go!'

To emphasise the ease with which he was coasting along Eddery turned and looked steadily to his right at the jockey who, exerting extreme pressure, was forcing his colt alongside. Riding with the busyness of a man racing to the post was Pat's fellow Irishman, Christy Roche. The horse was Secreto, evidently fully extended. It looked as if Pat was laughing at his rival and he said afterwards, 'I thought I had a stone in hand there.'

At that instant Claude Monet choked and stopped so quickly that Pat had to switch El Gran Senor outside him. 'Suddenly I had nothing in front of me,' he said. He still kept a firm hold on the favourite, while Christy Roche, a rider with a lot of action anyway, pushed and shoved and drove Secreto along. Pat said, 'The horse on the outside was just getting going.'

Christy commented, 'It was the thought of El Gran Senor not staying that kept me going. If I'd been sure that he'd stay a mile and a half,' he said smiling, 'I'd have dropped my hands wouldn't I? I was really happy to see that little rise in the ground.'

For as Epsom's final rise began, the expected surge forward by El Gran Senor simply did not happen. A long horrified moan arose from the crowd. It was as if no-one wanted to believe this amazing turn of the tide of battle. The favourite, who had been going so easily, was not pulling away. As Pat Eddery at last began to ride him furiously he did edge half a length ahead but Secreto and Christy Roche kept on coming. They began to claw back that slight lead. The two colts from Tipperary, stride for stride, heads nodding alternately, came close together and touched, and still battled on and on. Up to the very last stride of the race it seemed that El Gran Senor would grimly, gallantly, just hold on. But on the line, Secreto's muzzle, held fractionally higher than the favourite's (and thus a little in front) was four inches, the width of a nostril, ahead.

Pat Eddery dejectedly reflected, 'Just up the hill I started to get after my horse, and I still thought I'd win. But the horse on the outside just kept fighting. His horse is quite tough, and he just got me on the line.' He added philosophically, 'If the short head had gone the other way, you'd have said my colt stayed.'

As he rode in he leaned down and said to Vincent, 'I've never been going so easy in a race two furlongs out – and got beat!'

Vincent with Charles Taylor of Windfields Farm where both Secreto and El Gran Senor were bred.

Two days later he was still repeating, 'I can't believe it. The more I think of it, the more I can't believe it.'

The first shock – that the wonder horse, the hot favourite, had been beaten – had no sooner rushed through the crowd than another followed it like a wave. All around people burst out, 'Do you see what beat him? It's David O'Brien's horse! My God! He's beaten his father!'

As a result of the photo finish was announced, everybody's eyes turned on the principals. When the colts battled past the post, the hatless David had cast his head forward like a triumphant athlete at the end of his own race. Now, intensely moved, he went forward onto the course to greet Christy Roche and Secreto. He walked back with them into the winner's circle to the roars of the crowd. This was an amazingly warm reception in view of the fact that the shortest priced Derby loser for thirty-seven years had just been beaten.

With David was Catherine, his wife of just ten days: what a marvellous wedding present.

Out on the course Vincent and a large party surrounded El Gran Senor. Jacqueline O'Brien, festooned with her cameras, darted into the winners circle to congratulate her son.

'I'm sorry,' said David.

'For goodness sake don't apologise!' she exclaimed, hugging him, 'we're so thrilled.'

At that instant came the announcement: 'Stewards' Enquiry.' This provoked further outbreaks of speculation among the crowd. Worse was to come. To almost everybody's amazement, and particularly to that of the entire O'Brien family, Pat Eddery decided to lodge an objection against the winner 'for leaning on me'.

Out on the course, Vincent was visibly shaken by this announcement. But after ten minutes consultation the Stewards declared that the result stood. There was a further eruption of cheering.

Brough Scott pulled Vincent from the crowd to be interviewed. He, too, seemed shaken by the result. He introduced Vincent on ITV neatly as 'losing trainer, winning father,' but then asked how Vincent felt about El Gran Senor's value dramatically plummeting by millions of pounds.

Vincent replied, 'The money simply doesn't matter. I'm absolutely thrilled for my son.' Paternal pride was again emphasised when he said, 'I'm glad the objection went the way it did. I'd never have got over it, if the race had been taken from my son.'

When David came before the camera he was asked how it felt to have beaten

El Gran Senor surveys the scene after his victory in the Irish Sweeps Derby, 30 June 1984.

'*Losing trainer, winning father.*' *Vincent and David are interviewed on television by Brough Scott after the Epsom Derby, 1984.*

his father. He answered roundly, 'It was nothing to do with beating father. It was winning the Derby. It's a wonderful day.' At this point Vincent was looking steadily across at David with real pride.

Asked if he had fancied his horse before the race David replied, 'I wouldn't have brought him over if I didn't give him a good chance on his home work.'

Did he remember his father's early Derbies?

'I remember Larkspur very well,' said David fondly, 'I was six years old and I remember sitting in the room at home watching it.'

Jacqueline O'Brien was plainly split between triumphant joy for her son and the greatest sympathy for her husband. Similar emotions swung Vincent one way and another, and you could see them in his face. More than any horse over the last thirty years he seemed to love the brilliant El Gran Senor. Yet his pride in his son was even greater.

The Queen Mother with her marvellous sensitivity understood the dramatic events which had just taken place below her. She immediately sent the Queen's Racing Manager, Lord Porchester, down to the course with a message. Leaning over the rails towards Vincent and Jacqueline, Henry Porchester said, 'The Queen Mother would like you *all* to come up to the Royal Box, because it is such a *family* affair.'

Epilogue

No man, it used to be said, was ever a hero to his valet. Not many a racehorse trainer can play the hero to his wife for she, unlike the wives of millions who wave husbands off to the factories and offices, spends the long days with his problems, his setbacks, his defeats.

So one spring day in the garden at Ballydoyle, Jacqueline O'Brien talked about what made Vincent tick, about the daemons driving him onwards.

'People are always asking me "What's the secret of his success?" It's a very hard thing to answer even if you've lived with someone for more than thirty years. I'm sure even when he was born he had that hunger in him to get places. It's an ambition and a drive which hasn't lessened over the years; in fact I'd say it's got worse! He can never stay in bed in the morning. He can never *not* come home after a race-meeting. He can never sit peacefully anywhere. He must always be working.

'I remember once he and Dermot went for a holiday to fish in the west of Ireland. I thought they would have five days sitting in a boat in the sun, and that he would come back refreshed and very good-humoured! Instead of that they returned exhausted. The fish were running, and he would never let Dermot sit down for one second. They fished as hard as they would have worked here, and the point of the holiday was rather lost.

'He is completely dedicated and has tremendous ability to concentrate on whatever he's doing. If he has something on his mind, he can sit quite peacefully through meals and never hear what anyone's saying or see what's happening around him. He pays great attention to detail, but more than that, nothing is ever good enough. If he wins the Derby, or the Arc de Triomphe he can come straight home and all that's behind him, except that he's relieved to have it over. The only thing that matters is what will happen in the race at The Curragh next week, and who hasn't been doing what while he was away!

'Vincent is a very quiet and private person who doesn't like a lot of people around him. He's very fond of his family and has always been marvellous with children. He's not very social and is most happy here at home. He likes to fish, or play golf, but mostly he likes walking round the gallops, and the yard, supervising the farm, looking at the horses and just paying attention to what's happening.

'One thing I notice over the years is how much more he seems to love his horses. There's nothing he wouldn't do to make life more comfortable for them or their training less arduous. He gets tremendous satisfaction from going round all the stock – mares, foals and yearlings – as much as the horses in training.

'But I think Vincent would have made a great success of whatever he'd done. It was only a matter of chance that he was a trainer. If he'd been a butcher as he'd once thought of, or a vet, or in finance, or in any other kind of a job, he would have got to the top, because he simply could never have sat at the bottom. And he would have pulled up the people around him whether they wanted to go or not! I wish that after he wins an Arc de Triomphe, or three consecutive Nationals or other great victories, he would sit down and say, "Wasn't that marvellous! and didn't we have a wonderful day? Wasn't it worthwhile working so hard?" I wish he'd feel satisfied and get more fun out of it all. But perhaps the people that get the fun don't get the places. . . .

'His ambitions are just to do everything better. To improve the gallops. To have more supervision over the horses. To get better ways of transporting them. To have better veterinary facilities so that when the horses get injured or laid up they can be cured more easily. He wants everything to go more smoothly. He's a perfectionist – and it is rather hard to ever feel you've reached perfection!

'With the horses he always plans backwards. He never considers running a horse that is only "nearly ready". He fixes the eventual objective – say the Derby – and then works out how many races – and when – the horse will need before it. In many cases the whole two year old career is planned with the classics in mind. He has tremendous patience with horses and will never run one more quickly than he feels is right for the horse's own good. As the work of a horse increases, if he shows the slightest signs of stress, like being restless in his box, or not eating up, Vincent goes right back to slow exercise again and waits until the horse gets his confidence back.

'I feel that Vincent has tremendous common sense, and can always think of an answer, whatever the problem. For instance if things go wrong in the house and I can't think what to do – if I've got to drive to Dublin and fit in three other things in different directions, and I say to him "How will I manage?" he can always think what's the best solution. He seems to be able to get order into my chaos.

'When the farmlands at Ballydoyle were being drained, an expert came from Dublin to find the lines of the old drains so that they could be used again to take away water. He spent a fruitless two days, and went home again, and still nobody knew. Then Vincent in his Land Rover drove out, looked round and said, "These look the lines where the drains should be running," and when the men got their shovels and opened up, there of course were all the drains.

'After we were first married he used to drive quite quickly past donkeys and herds of milking cows going home along the roads, and I never could understand how he knew which way they'd move. But he'd say, "Anybody would know that those cows won't come out into the road, they'll go right not left." It was simply by studying the animals' heads. I never knew him to be mistaken. It's a sort of instinct for the correct solution to any problem.

'He's terribly flexible in his thinking and he never, ever will decide anything definitely. And that's quite difficult when you're running a family, a house and entertaining; he never will make a plan! So that he might or might not run Alleged, let's say, in the St Leger until the very last minute. Everything gets a bit crowded at the end, because he keeps his mind absolutely flexible. He says with horses you have no alternative, and I am sure he has won many races he might have lost if he had stuck to rigid plans.

'Vincent doesn't discuss things much with outside people, because he's not a very extrovert person. But he'll discuss them with his family – not that he expects to get any correct answers from us – but he uses us as a sounding board. He talks over ideas with John Magnier, and with the people that are close to him. He will even listen patiently to all sorts of people who tell him about horses, and give him their ideas about training! He always hopes he'll learn something new. Among his owners have been a number of the world's top businessmen. They may not know about training horses, but he recognises that they're very good at weighing up decisions. Very often when he has a choice that's 48% grey rather than definitely black and white, he gets a lot of help from the men who make decisions in big industries.

'He talks about the horses with the people most intimately connected with them. Every morning after work, any jockeys who are riding out here and the work-riders come into his office, and they all have a discussion about what's happened. They go over each horse's work in a lot of detail.

'Vincent is always drawing in pieces of information from all sorts of sources. They come together in his head. He weighs them up so carefully. And then he eventually decides what to do.'

It could fairly be said that no trainer in the western world this century has more frequently decided the right things to do.

Appendix 1 – Roll of Honour

NATIONAL HUNT

ENGLAND

Grand National	*Cheltenham Gold Cup*	*Champion Hurdle*
1953 Early Mist	1948 Cottage Rake	1949 Hatton's Grace
1954 Royal Tan	1949 Cottage Rake	1950 Hatton's Grace
1955 Quare Times	1950 Cottage Rake	1951 Hatton's Grace
	1953 Knock Hard	

IRELAND

Grand National
1952 Alberoni

FLAT

ENGLAND

Derby	*2000 Gns*	*Oaks*
1962 Larkspur	1968 Sir Ivor	1965 Long Look
1968 Sir Ivor	1970 Nijinsky	1966 Valoris
1970 Nijinsky	1983 Lomond	*St Leger*
1972 Roberto	1984 El Gran Senor	1957 Ballymoss
1977 The Minstrel	*1000 Gns*	1970 Nijinsky
1982 Golden Fleece	1966 Glad Rags	1972 Boucher

King George VI and
Queen Elizabeth Diamond Stakes
1958 Ballymoss
1970 Nijinsky
1977 The Minstrel

Benson and Hedges Gold Cup
1972 Roberto

Sussex Stakes
1973 Thatch
1977 Artaius
1978 Jaazeiro
1981 Kings Lake

Eclipse Stakes
1958 Ballymoss
1966 Pieces of Eight
1977 Artaius
1984 Sadler's Wells

Champion Stakes
1966 Pieces of Eight
1968 Sir Ivor

Coronation Cup
1958 Ballymoss
1973 Roberto

Dewhurst Stakes
1969 Nijinsky
1973 Cellini
1976 The Minstrel
1977 Try My Best
1979 Monteverdi
1980 Storm Bird
1983 El Gran Senor

Ascot Gold Cup
1958 Gladness
Gold Vase
1958 Even Money
1975 Blood Royal
Goodwood Cup
1958 Gladness
Ebor Handicap
1958 Gladness

Futurity Stakes
1973 Apalachee

Middle Park Stakes
1978 Junius

Cheveley Park Stakes
1967 Lalibela
1981 Woodstream

IRELAND

Derby
1953 Chamier
1957 Ballymoss
1970 Nijinsky
1977 The Minstrel
1984 El Gran Senor

2000 Gns
1959 El Toro
1978 Jaazeiro
1981 Kings Lake
1984 Sadler's Wells

1000 Gns
1966 Valoris
1977 Lady Capulet
1979 Godetia

Oaks
1964 Ancastra
1965 Aurabella
1969 Gaia
1979 Godetia

St Leger
1959 Barclay
1966 White Gloves
1969 Reindeer
1975 Caucasus
1976 Meneval
1977 Transworld
1980 Gonzales

Joe McGrath Memorial Stakes
1978 Inkerman
1979 Fordham
1980 Gregorian
1981 Kings Lake
Phoenix Stakes
1976 Cloonlara
1981 Achieved

FRANCE

Prix du Jockey Club
1983 Caerleon
Grand Criterium
1967 Sir Ivor

Prix de L'Arc de Triomphe
1958 Ballymoss
1977 Alleged
1978 Alleged

U.S.A.

Washington International
1968 Sir Ivor

Appendix 2 – Career records

These statistics have been compiled by *Raceform*'s senior racereader, John Sharrat. His principal source was *Raceform*, the official Form Book, which is such an essential work of reference for all who are engaged in and follow racing. For their assistance, the publishers are indebted both to John Sharrat and Raceform Ltd, 2 York Road, London SW11 3PZ.

COTTAGE RAKE

Date	Course	Race	Dist	Value	Weight	Jockey	Price	Place
			1945–46 Season					
Mar 1	Thurles	Corinthian Plate	2m	£74	11.9	Mr T. Bennett	100/8	unpl
Dec 27	Limerick	County Mdn Hurdle	2m	£178	11.0	D. O'Sullivan	10/1	won
			1946–47 Season					
Feb 16	Leopardstown	Corinthian Mdn Plate	2m	£96 10s	12.0	Mr P.P. Hogan	Evens	won
Oct 31	Limerick	Emly H'cap	2m 4f	£222	9.5	N. Brennan	7/1	unpl
Nov 9	Curragh	Irish Cesarewitch	2m	£740	7.7	N. Brennan	100/7	unpl
Nov 23	Naas	Naas November H'cap	12f	£370	7.12	J. Tyrrell	3/1	won
Dec 26	Leopardstown	Carrickmines Chase	2m 4f	£296	12.3	A. Brabazon	4/7	won
Apl 5	Phoenix Park	Castleknock Welter H'cap	2m	£370	9.2	M. Wing	7/4	unpl
Apl 7	Fairyhouse	Maiden Chase	2m 2f	£444	12.0	E. Newman	4/1	won
Apl 18	Dundalk	'Mickey MacCardle' Memorial Cup Chase	2m	£296	13.0	E. Newman	2/1	won
Apl 26	Naas	Champion Novice Chase	2m 40y	£296	13.0	D. Morgan	6/4	3rd
			1947–48 Season					
Sept 27	Phoenix Park	Tallaght H'cap Hurdle	2m	£222	11.0	E. Kennedy	20/1	unpl
Oct 30	Limerick	Garryowen Plate	12f	£111 10s	10.12	G. Wells	4/5	2nd
Nov 8	Curragh	Irish Cesarewitch	2m	£740	8.2	G. Wells	5/1	won
Nov 22	Naas	Naas November H'cap	12f	£370	9.1	G. Wells	7/2	unpl
Dec 27	Leopardstown	December H'cap Chase	2m 175y	£296	12.0	A. Brabazon	11/8	won
Feb 14	Leopardstown	Leopardstown H'cap Chase	3m 100y	£468 5s	12.7	A. Brabazon	5/4	fell
Mar 4	Cheltenham	Cheltenham Gold Cup	3m 2f	£1,911	12.0	A. Brabazon	10/1	won
Mar 29	Fairyhouse	Irish Grand National	3m 4f	£1,467 10s	12.7	A. Brabazon	6/4	2nd
			1948–49 Season					
Oct 21	Limerick	Croom H'cap Chase	3m	£268 10s	12.7	A. Brabazon	Evens	won
Nov 6	Curragh	Irish Cesarewitch	2m	£740	9.3	A. Brabazon	20/1	unpl
Nov 19	Manchester	Emblem H'cap Chase	3m	£1,616 5s	12.7	A. Brabazon	3/1	won
Dec 28	Kempton	King George VI Chase	3m	£2,486 10s	12.6	A. Brabazon	13/8	won
Apl 11	Cheltenham	Cheltenham Gold Cup	3m 2f	£2,817 10s	12.0	A. Brabazon	4/6	won

Date	Course	Race	Dist	Value	Weight	Jockey	Price	Place
			1949-50 Season					
Oct 20	Limerick	Croom H'cap Chase	3m	£256 10s	12.8	A. Brabazon	1/4	won
Nov 5	Curragh	Irish Cesarewitch	2m	£740	9.0	A. Brabazon	33/1	unpl
Nov 25	Sandown	Withington Stayers Chase	3m 125y	£690	12.7	A. Brabazon	1/3	won
Dec 26	Kempton	King George VI Chase	3m	£2,179	12.7	A. Brabazon	4/6	2nd
Feb 18	Leopardstown	Leopardstown H'cap Chase	3m 5f	£740	12.7	Mr J. Cox	6/4	brt dwn
Mar 9	Cheltenham	Cheltenham Gold Cup	3m 2f	£2,936	12.0	A. Brabazon	5/6	won
Apl 10	Fairyhouse	Irish Grand National	3m 4f	£1,485	12.7	A. Brabazon	Evens	4th
June 29	Limerick	Santon Cup (H'cap)	1m 6f	£129 10s	10.7	A. Brabazon	10/1	unpl
			1950-51 Season					
July 15	Leopardstown	Leopardstown H'cap Hurdle	2m	£478 15s	12.0	R.J. O'Ryan	10/1	unpl
Aug 2	Galway	Galway Plate (H'cap Chase)	2m 5f 60y	£1,110	12.7	A. Brabazon	2/1	unpl
			1951-52 Season					
Dec 27	Leopardstown	Shankill Hurdle	2m	£202	11.7	A. Brabazon	6/1	3rd
			1952-53 Season					
Apl 15	Cheltenham	Painswick Hurdle	2m	£204	11.3	G. Kelly	100/7	2nd
May 25	Hurst Park	Queen Elizabeth H'cap Chase	3m	£3,735	11.9	A. Brabazon	100/6	fell
			1953-54 Season					
Nov 5	Wincanton	Newquay Chase	2m	£136	12.0	O.B. Marshall	6/1	2nd
Dec 8	Wolverhampton	Shrewsbury Chase	3m	£204	11.10	R. Francis	9/4	3rd

HATTON'S GRACE

Date	Course	Race	Dist	Value	Weight	Jockey	Price	Place
			1946-47 Season					
July 3	Bellewstown	Bellewstown Plate	2m	£74 5s	12.0	Mr D. Corry	1/2	won
Aug 10	Phoenix Park	Naul Plate	2m	£223	12.7	Mr P.J. Leneham	4/5	won
Oct 5	Curragh	Irish Cambridgeshire	8f	£740	9.7	B. Duffy	25/1	unpl
Oct 12	Leopardstown	Holywood H'cap	8f	£222	9.9	B. Duffy	20/1	unpl
Oct 19	Curragh	Curragh October H'cap	10f	£444	9.7	B. Duffy	20/1	unpl
Nov 1	Naas	Sallins H'cap	6f	£132	9.5	B. Duffy	20/1	unpl
Nov 23	Naas	Naas November H'cap	12f	£370	9.0	T.P. Burns	20/1	unpl
			1947-48 Season					
Apl 9	Curragh	Irish Lincolnshire H'cap	8f	£518	8.10	T.P. Burns	6/1	unpl
Apl 26	Naas	Dublin Mdn Hurdle	2m	£222	11.7	J. Brogan	3/1	unpl
May 3	Phoenix Park	Eglington Mdn Hurdle	2m	£222	12.0	J. Brogan	6/4	won
July 30	Galway	Galway H'cap Hurdle	2m	£740	12.0	M. Molony	10/1	unpl
Aug 30	Dundalk	Mountain Bay Plate	12f	£286 10s	9.13	M. McCourt	5/2	4th
Sept 18	Curragh	J.T. Rogers Memorial Cup (H'cap)	2m	£296	8.9	John Power	2/1	unpl

Oct 18	Phoenix Park	Ward H'cap Hurdle	2m	£222	11.11	M. McCourt	100/8	unpl
Nov 8	Curragh	Irish Cesarewitch	2m	£740	8.3	John Doyle	33/1	unpl
Nov 22	Naas	Park H'cap Hurdle	2m	£222	10.1	D. Morgan	100/8	unpl
Dec 27	Leopardstown	Tower H'cap Hurdle	2m	£222	11.9	J. Brogan	3/1	won
Jan 3	Naas	Liffey H'cap Hurdle	2m	£222	11.2	J. Brogan	4/5	won
Feb 18	Mullingar	Kilbeggan H'cap Hurdle	2m 2f	£222	12.7	D.L. Moore	6/1	fell
Mar 2	Cheltenham	Champion Hurdle	2m	£2,068 10s	12.0	M. Molony	20/1	unpl
Mar 27	Phoenix Park	Rank Cup H'cap Hurdle	2m	£380	12.7	E. Newman	100/8	unpl

1948–49 Season

July 7	Curragh	Kildare H'cap	1m 6f	£202	8.3	G. Wells	40/1	unpl
July 28	Galway	Galway H'cap Hurdle	2m	£740	12.0	R.J. O'Ryan	40/1	unpl
Jan 8	Naas	Liffey H'cap Hurdle	2m	£202	12.7	A. Brabazon	20/1	unpl
Feb 5	Naas	Rathcoole H'cap Hurdle	2m	£202	12.7	A. Brabazon	7/4	won
Mar 8	Cheltenham	Champion Hurdle	2m	£2,299 15s	12.0	A. Brabazon	100/7	won
Apl 2	Curragh	Irish Lincolnshire H'cap	8f	£518	9.0	M. Wing	6/1	won
Apl 20	Curragh	Rossmore Plate	12f	£370	9.10	M. Wing	7/4	unpl

1949–50 Season

Sept 17	Phoenix Park	Tallaght H'cap Hurdle	2m	£286	12.7	E. Kennedy	20/1	unpl
Oct 1	Curragh	Irish Cambridgeshire	8f	£740	8.8	M. Wing	7/1	unpl
Nov 5	Curragh	Irish Cesarewitch	2m	£740	9.2	M. Molony	8/1	won
Dec 27	Leopardstown	Shankill Hurdle	2m	£202	12.7	A. Brabazon	1/3	won
Feb 18	Leopardstown	Scalp H'cap Hurdle	2m	£202	12.7	R.J. O'Ryan	5/4	won
Mar 7	Cheltenham	Champion Hurdle	2m	£2,427 5s	12.0	A. Brabazon	5/2	won
Apl 8	Phoenix Park	Rank Challenge Cup (H'cap) Hurdle)	2m	£380	12.7	A. Brabazon	4/6	2nd
Apl 19	Curragh	Rossmore Plate	12f	£370	9.12	Herbert Holmes	4/5	won

1950–51 Season

Sept 16	Phoenix Park	Tallaght H'cap Hurdle	2m	£286	12.7	A. Brabazon	10/1	unpl
Sept 30	Curragh	Irish Cambridgeshire	8f	£740	9.9	A. Brabazon	13/2	unpl
Nov 4	Curragh	Irish Cesarewitch	2m	£740	10.0	M. Molony	10/1	won
Dec 27	Leopardstown	Shankill Hurdle	2m	£202	12.7	M. Molony	4/6	won
Feb 17	Leopardstown	Scalp H'cap Hurdle	2m	£202	12.7	M. Molony	Evens	4th
Mar 6	Cheltenham	Champion Hurdle	2m	£3,615	12.0	T. Molony	4/1	won

1951–52 Season

Nov 17	Naas	Naas November H'cap	12f	£740	10.10	E.J. Kennedy	25/1	unpl
Dec 8	Naas	Rathbridge H'cap Hurdle	2m	£202	12.7	Mr A. O'Brien	4/1	4th
Dec 27	Leopardstown	Shankill Hurdle	2m	£202	12.7	Mr A. O'Brien	2/5	won
Feb 2	Naas	Rathcoole H'cap Hurdle	2m	£286	12.7	Mr A. O'Brien	Evens	unpl
Mar 4	Cheltenham	Champion Hurdle	2m	£3,632	12.0	Mr A. O'Brien	13/2	unpl
Mar 15	Sandown	Imperial Cup (H'cap Hurdle)	2m	£1,741	12.5	Mr A. O'Brien	10/1	unpl
Apl 26	Naas	Champion Chase Challenge Cup	2m 40y	£286	11.9	Mr A. O'Brien	2/1	2nd

Nov 29	Leopardstown	Rathfarnham H'cap Chase	2m 3f	£286	12.7	Mr A. O'Brien	20/1	unpl
Dec 20	Hurst Park	Henry VIII Chase	3m	£680	11.4	F. Winter	100/30	unpl
Jan 24	Leopardstown	Dundrum Chase	2m 3f	£202	11.11	P. J. Doyle	5/2	won

KNOCK HARD

Date	Course	Race	Dist	Value	Weight	Jockey	Price	Place
				1948-49 Season				
Dec 11	Mullingar	Kinnegad Mdn Hurdle	1m 4f	£100	11.7	E. Kennedy	20/1	4th
Jan 8	Naas	Dodder Mdn Plate	2m	£100	11.10	Mr D. J. Lane	2/1	won
May 11	Leopardstown	Dargle Plate	1m 4f	£286	10.0	Herbert Holmes	100/7	4th
				1949-50 Season				
Sept 14	Curragh	Turf Club H'cap	1m 2f	£202	9.9	Herbert Holmes	20/1	unpl
Sept 24	Baldoyle	Kinsealy Plate	2m	£133 10s	12.7	Lord Mildmay	8/13	2nd
Nov 5	Curragh	Irish Cesarewitch	2m	£740	8.3	Herbert Holmes	Evens	2nd
Dec 27	Leopardstown	Shankill Hurdle	2m	£202	11.7	R. J. O'Ryan	7/1	2nd
Mar 11	Leopardstown	Dundrum Chase	2m 2f 166y	£202	11.11	M. Molony	2/5	won
Mar 17	Baldoyle	St Patricks Day Chase	2m 2f	£286	12.2	A. Brabazon	4/7	won
Apl 1	Curragh	Irish Lincolnshire	1m	£518	8.12	T. P. Burns	2/1	won
Apl 22	Naas	Champion Chase (Challenge Cup)	2m 40y	£286	12.5	A. Brabazon	2/5	won
				1950-51 Season				
Oct 7	Leopardstown	Johnstown H'cap Chase	3m	£202	11.8	Mr A. O'Brien	10/1	unpl
Oct 26	Limerick Junction	Croom H'cap Chase	3m	£286	12.0	M. Molony	2/5	won
Nov 18	Naas	Blessington H'cap Chase	3m 76y	£202	12.0	A. Brabazon	8/11	2nd
Dec 26	Kempton	King George VI Chase	3m	£2,150	11.9	J. Dowdeswell	100/30	fell
Mar 31	Naas	Clane H'cap Chase	3m 76y	202	12.12	T. Molony	10/1	2nd
				1951-52 Season				
Sept 22	Phoenix Park	Ward H'cap Hurdle	2m	£202	12.12	Mr A. O'Brien	20/1	unpl
Oct 25	Limerick Junction	Croom H'cap Chase	3m	£273	13.0	Mr A. O'Brien	6/4	won
Nov 19	Birmingham	Nuneaton Hurdle	2m	£340	11.0	T. Molony	4/7	won
Dec 8	Naas	Maddenstown H'cap Chase	3m 76y	£286	12.7	Mr A. O'Brien	9/4	unpl
Feb 16	Baldoyle	Baldoyle H'cap Chase	2m 1f 120y	£370	12.7	Mr A. O'Brien	8/1	4th
Mar 6	Cheltenham	Cheltenham Gold Cup	3m 2f	£3,232 10s	12.0	Mr A. O'Brien	5/1	fell
Apl 4	Liverpool	Liverpool H'cap Hurdle	2m 1f	£860	12.5	Mr A. O'Brien	11/2	2nd
May 15	Newmarket	Shelford Stakes	2m	£467 2s	9.5	W. H. Carr	8/1	4th
				1952-53 Season				
June 10	Lewes	Southdown Plte (Am. Rdrs)	1m 4f	£138	11.4	Mr A. O'Brien	2/7	won

Date	Course	Race	Dist	Value	Weight	Jockey	Price	Place
June 21	Worcester	Coventry Plte (Am. Rdrs)	1m 2f	£138	11.8	Mr A. O'Brien	11/8	won
Oct 18	Curragh	Autumn Scurry H'cap	6f	£202	10.1	T. P. Burns	100/6	unpl
Nov 7	Liverpool	Autumn Cup (H'cap)	1m 2f 170y	£1,294	8.7	H. Holmes	7/1	3rd
Nov 15	Manchester	Manchester November H'cap	1m 4f	£1,967 12s	8.6	W. Nevett	9/1	2nd
Dec 26	Kempton	King George VI Chase	3m	£2,158 10s	11.9	T. Molony	100/30	3rd
Jan 24	Leopardstown	Ticknock H'cap Chase	3m	£286	12.7	P. J. Doyle	5/2	4th
Feb 7	Doncaster	Gt Yorkshire H'cap Chase	3m 40y	£2,037	11.7	T. Molony	5/1	won
Mar 5	Cheltenham	Cheltenham Gold Cup	3m 2f	£3,258	12.0	T. Molony	11/2	won
		1953–54 Season						
Nov 7	Curragh	Irish Cesarewitch	2m	£740	9.12	E. J. Kennedy	20/1	unpl
Nov 28	Leopardstown	Blackrock H'cap Hurdle	2m 3f	£202	13.4	D. O'Sullivan	100/7	unpl
Dec 9	Sandown	Milburn Hurdle	2m	£469	11.9	B. Marshall	9/4	2nd
Jan 2	Baldoyle	Feltrim H'cap Hurdle	3m	£286	11.6	P. Taaffe	1/2	2nd
Feb 6	Leopardstown	Leopardstown H'cap Chase	3m 5f	£740	12.7	T. Molony	8/1	4th
Mar 4	Cheltenham	Cheltenham Gold Cup	3m 2f	£3,576	12.0	T. Molony	9/4	unpl
Apl 17	Phoenix Park	Rank Cup (H'cap Hurdle)	2m	£380	12.2	D. O'Sullivan	20/1	unpl
Apl 24	Naas	An Tostal H'cap Hurdle	3m	£740	12.3	B. Marshall	4/1	unpl
		1954–55 Season						
Apl 9	Phoenix Park	Rank Cup (H'cap Hurdle)	2m	£380	11.12	Mr A. O'Brien	4/1	unpl
May 30	Hurst Park	Queen Elizabeth H'cap Chase	3m	£3,460	11.8	B. Marshall	10/1	unpl

ROYAL TAN

Date	Course	Race	Dist	Value	Weight	Jockey	Price	Place
		1948–49 Season						
Sept 29	Listowel	Abbeyfeale Hurdle	1m 4f	£100	11.2	J. Burke	10/1	4th
Oct 21	Limerick Junction	Bansha Mdn Hurdle	1m 4f	£133 10s	11.2	J. Burke	10/1	unpl
Nov 4	Powerstown Park	Killenaule Plate	2m	£100	11.10	Mr B. Whelan	3/1	unpl
Feb 16	Mullingar	Winter Mdn Hurdle	2m	£100	11.1	J. Burke	25/1	2nd
Mar 26	Naas	Kildare Chase	2m 40y	£286	10.10	J. Burke	100/6	3rd
Apl 9	Leopardstown	Silverpark Chase	2m 4f	£370	11.5	J. Burke	100/7	3rd
		1949–50 Season						
Dec 27	Leopardstown	Shankill Hurdle	2m	£202	11.2	P. Cox	25/1	4th
Jan 14	Leopardstown	Kerrymount H'cap Chase	2m 2f 166y	£286	12.2	D. O'Sullivan	100/6	unpl
Feb 18	Leopardstown	Milltown Nov. Chase	2m	£202	12.3	R. J. O'Ryan	10/11	won
Mar 8	Cheltenham	National Hunt Chase (Am Rdrs)	4m	£977 7s	12.7	Mr A. O'Brien	9/2	fell
Mar 25	Naas	Kildare Chase	2m 40y	£286	12.2	G. Wells	6/4	2nd

Date	Course	Race	Distance	Prize	Weight	Jockey	Odds	Result
Apl 10	Ward Union Hunt (Fairyhouse)	Maiden Chase	2m 2f	£444	12.2	A. Brabazon	6/4	won

1950–51 Season

Date	Course	Race	Distance	Prize	Weight	Jockey	Odds	Result
Oct 7	Leopardstown	Johnstown H'cap Chase	3m	£202	11.2	M. Browne	8/1	3rd
Oct 28	Naas	Maddenstown H'cap Chase	3m 76y	£202	10.12	A. Brabazon	4/6	2nd
Nov 11	Leopardstown	Dodder H'cap Chase	3m	£202	12.0	E. Newman	4/6	won
Jan 13	Leopardstown	Kerrymount H'cap Chase	2m 3f	£286	11.10	Mr A. O'Brien	5/1	3rd
Feb 17	Leopardstown	Leopardstown H'cap Chase	3m 5f	£740	11.3	Mr A. O'Brien	8/1	unpl
Feb 28	Leopardstown	Kilcoole H'cap Chase	2m 5f	£286	11.13	Mr A. O'Brien	3/1	won
Mar 26	Ward Union Hunt (Fairyhouse)	Irish Grand National	3m 2f	£1,485	11.12	Mr A. O'Brien	100/8	2nd
Apl 7	Liverpool	Grand National	4m 856y	£8,815	10.13	Mr A. O'Brien	22/1	2nd

1951–52 Season

Date	Course	Race	Distance	Prize	Weight	Jockey	Odds	Result
Sept 22	Phoenix Park	Ward H'cap Hurdle	2m	£202	11.0	E. Kennedy	20/1	unpl
Oct 4	Listowel	Newcastle West Plate (Mdns) (Am Rdrs)	2m	£100	12.0	Mr A. O'Brien	1/3	won
Nov 24	Cheltenham	Cowley Nov. Hurdle	3m	£204	11.5	Mr A. O'Brien	11/10	won
Jan 12	Leopardstown	Kerrymount H'cap Chase	2m 3f	£286	11.4	Mr A. O'Brien	5/4	4th
Feb 9	Leopardstown	Leopardstown H'cap Chase	3m 5f	£740	11.8	Mr A. O'Brien	3/1	unpl
Mar 5	Cheltenham	National Hunt Chase (H'cap)	3m	£685	11.6	Mr A. O'Brien	7/2	won
Apl 5	Liverpool	Grand National	4m 856y	£9,268 12s 6d	11.6	Mr A. O'Brien	22/1	fell

1952–53 Season

Nil

1953–54 Season

Date	Course	Race	Distance	Prize	Weight	Jockey	Odds	Result
Oct 8	Limerick	Adare H'cap Hurdle	2m	£133	12.10	Mr A. O'Brien	100/7	unpl
Oct 31	Naas	Blessington H'cap Chase	3m 76y	£202	12.7	B. Marshall	4/1	unpl
Jan 9	Leopardstown	Kilternan H'cap Hurdle	2m	£202	10.13	B. Marshall	20/1	unpl
Jan 21	Gowran Park	Thyestes H'cap Chase	3m 1f	£286	11.7	B. Marshall	6/1	fell
Feb 20	Baldoyle	Baldoyle H'cap Chase	2m 1f 120y	£370	11.7	B.Marshall	7/1	unpl
Mar 3	Cheltenham	National Hunt H'cap Chase	3m	£1,025	11.11	P. Taaffe	10/1	2nd
Mar 27	Liverpool	Grand National	4m 856y	£8,571 10s	11.7	B. Marshall	8/1	won

1954–55 Season

Date	Course	Race	Distance	Prize	Weight	Jockey	Odds	Result
Jan 1	Baldoyle	Feltrim H'cap Hurdle	3m	£286	11.12	D. O'Sullivan	100/6	unpl
Jan 26	Gowran Park	Thyestes H'cap Chase	3m 1f	£286	12.6	P.Taaffe	5/1	3rd
Feb 12	Lingfield	Manifesto H'cap Chase	3m	£769	11.12	D. V. Dick	9/2	unpl
Mar 1	Leopardstown	Leopardstown H'cap Chase	3m 5f	£740	12.7	D. V. Dick	100/8	fell
Mar 26	Liverpool	Grand National	4m 856y	£8,934 10s	12.4	D. V. Dick	28/1	unpl
Apl 23	Bogside	Scottish Grand National	3m 7f	£1,030	12.6	B. Marshall	10/1	unpl

1955–56 Season

Date	Course	Race	Dist	Value	Weight	Jockey	Price	Place
Nov 12	Manchester	Emblem H'cap Chase	3m	£1,786 5s	11.10	D. V. Dick	20/1	unpl
Dec 27	Limerick	Mid-Winter Chase	2m 1f 16y	£100	11.7	T. Taaffe	11/10	won
Mar 3	Naas	Newlands H'cap Chase	3m 76y	£370	12.4	T. Taaffe	100/7	unpl
Mar 24	Liverpool	Grand National	4m 856y	£8,695 5s	12.1	T. Taaffe	28/1	3rd

1956–57 Season

Date	Course	Race	Dist	Value	Weight	Jockey	Price	Place
Nov 24	Leopardstown	BlackRock H'cap Hurdle	2m 3f	£133	11.9	J. Stapleton	100/7	unpl
Jan 12	Leopardstown	Ticknock H'cap Chase	3m	£360 10s	12.0	T. Taaffe	10/1	unpl
Mar 2	Naas	Newlands H'cap Chase	3m 76y	£375 10s	11.10	T. Taaffe	7/4	unpl
Mar 29	Liverpool	Grand National	4m 856y	£8,868 10s	11.12	T. Taaffe	28/1	ref

EARLY MIST

Date	Course	Race	Dist	Value	Weight	Jockey	Price	Place

1949–50 Season

Date	Course	Race	Dist	Value	Weight	Jockey	Price	Place
Apl 15	Leopardstown	Corinthian Plate	2m	£133 10s	11.7	Mr W. Taaffe	100/7	won
May 6	Down Royal	Whinny-Hill Mdn Hurdle	2m	£100	12.2	M. Molony	2/1	won

1950–51 Season

Date	Course	Race	Dist	Value	Weight	Jockey	Price	Place
Nov 25	Navan	Boyne Chase	2m	£133 10s	11.8	M. Molony	4/6	won
Dec 26	Leopardstown	Carrickmines Chase	2m 3f	£286	11.10	M. Molony	4/6	won
Feb 28	Leopardstown	Kilcoole H'cap Chase	2m 5f	£286	11.1	E. Newman	7/4	fell
Mar 3	Naas	Newlands H'cap Chase	3m 76y	£370	10.12	E. Newman	11/10	won
Mar 27	Fairyhouse (Ward Union Hunt)	Dunshaughlin Chase	3m	£202	12.10	M. Molony	4/7	won

1951–52 Season

Date	Course	Race	Dist	Value	Weight	Jockey	Price	Place
Nov 24	Navan	Second Autumn H'cap Hurdle	3m	£133 10s	12.7	P. Taaffe	10/1	unpl
Dec 1	Leopardstown	Rathfarnham H'cap Chase	2m 3f	£286	11.2	P. Taaffe	5/4	unpl
Dec 26	Leopardstown	Christmas H'cap Chase	3m	£370	10.3	P. Taaffe	2/1	won
Feb 9	Leopardstown	Leopardstown H'cap Chase	3m 5f	£740	11.1	P. Taaffe	3/1	unpl
Mar 15	Baldoyle	Stapolin Chase	2m 2f	£202	12.7	P. Taaffe	2/1	won
Apl 5	Liverpool	Grand National	4m 856y	£9,268 12s 6d	10.11	P. Taaffe	18/1	fell

1952–53 Season

Date	Course	Race	Dist	Value	Weight	Jockey	Price	Place
Feb 7	Leopardstown	Scalp H'cap Hurdle	2m	£202	11.12	P. J. Doyle	100/8	unpl
Feb 21	Baldoyle	Baldoyle H'cap Chase	2m 1f 120y	£370	11.12	P. J. Doyle	5/1	unpl
Mar 7	Naas	Newlands H'cap Chase	3m 76y	£370	12.3	P. J. Doyle	4/7	won: disq
Mar 28	Liverpool	Grand National	4m 856y	£9,330 10s	11.2	B. Marshall	20/1	won
May 25	Hurst Park	Queen Elizabeth H'cap Chase	3m	£3,735	11.6	B. Marshall	7/2	unpl

1953–54 Season

Date	Course	Race	Dist	Value	Weight	Jockey	Price	Place
Nov 28	Leopardstown	Blackrock H'cap Hurdle	2m 3f	£202	11.13	Mr A. O'Brien	100/7	unpl
Dec 26	Leopardstown	Bray Chase	3m	£202	12.7	B. Marshall	2/5	won

			1954–55 Season					
Jan 15	Leopardstown	Delgany Hurdle	2m	£133	12.2	D. O'Sullivan	100/7	2nd
Mar 10	Cheltenham	Cheltenham Gold Cup	3m 2f	£3,775 15s	12.0	B Marshall	5/1	4th
Mar 26	Liverpool	Grand National	4m 856y	£8,934 10s	12.3	B. Marshall	9/1	unpl
May 6	Leopardstown	Glenview Hurdle	2m	£133	12.7	T. P. Burns	2/1	unpl
May 21	Naas	Carlow H'cap Hurdle	2m 1f	£202	12.3	T. P. Burns	3/1	unpl
			1955–56 Season					
June 4	Auteuil	Prix Saint-Sauveur (H'cap Chase)	3m 110y	£910	11.5	P. Taaffe	—	unpl
June 19	Auteuil	Grand Steeplechase de Paris	4m 110y	£9,057	10.1	P. Taaffe	—	unpl
Mar 1	Ludlow	Torbra Gold Cup (H'cap Chase)	3m 3f	£342	12.7	B. Marshall	100/7	unpl
Mar 10	Hurst Park	Black Vine H'cap Chase	3m	£204	12.9	B. Marshall	100/7	3rd
Mar 24	Liverpool	Grand National	4m 856y	£8,695 5s	12.2	B. Marshall	25/1	fell
Apl 2	Wincanton	Amesbury H'cap Chase	3m 1f	£170	12.7	B. Marshall	6/4	3rd
			1956–57 Season					
Oct 8	Fontwell	Chichester H'cap Chase	3m 2f	£244 16s	12.7	B. Marshall	7/2	4th
Nov 30	Windsor	Brocas Chase	3m	£170	11.0	M. Scudamore	10/1	won
Dec 13	Sandown	Ewell Chase	3m 125y	£371 12s	11.9	B. Marshall	9/4	2nd
Jan 19	Sandown	Mildmay Memorial Chase (H'cap)	3m 5f 25y	£2,097	11.13	B. Marshall	100/6	unpl
Mar 2	Sandown	Grand International H'cap Chase	3m 125y	£749 13s	11.11	B. Marshall	10/1	p.u.

QUARE TIMES

Date	Course	Race	Dist	Value	Weight	Jockey	Price	Place
			1951–52 Season					
Apl 26	Naas	Rathcoole Mdn Plate (Am. Rdrs)	2m	£99 10s	12.0	Mr A. O'Brien	10/1	unpl
May 15	Limerick Junction	Knockalong Mdn Hurdle	2m	£99 10s	11.9	E. Kennedy	100/8	unpl
			1952–53 Season					
Nov 13	Thurles	Amateur Mdn Hurdle	2m	£100	11.4	Mr J. O'Dwyer	10/1	unpl
Nov 27	Gowran Park	Carrickshock Nov Chase	2m 4f	£133	11.12	D. Kinane	100/8	fell
Dec 26	Limerick	Rineanna Mdn Plate	2m	£100	12.0	Mr A. O'Brien	5/4	4th
Jan 24	Leopardstown	Dundrum Chase	2m 3f	£202	11.6	D. O'Sullivan	20/1	unpl
Feb 21	Baldoyle	Portmarnock Nov. Chase	2m 4f 130y	£133	11.12	D. O'Sullivan	100/8	unpl
Mar 19	Gowran Park	Birchfield Mdn Plate (Am. Rdrs)	2m	£100	12.0	Mr A. O'Brien	3/1	2nd
Mar 26	Powerstown Park (Clonmel)	Sportsman's Plate (Mdns) (Am. Rdrs)	2m	£100	12.0	Mr A. O'Brien	5/4	2nd
May 8	Leopardstown	Kilcoole H'cap Chase	2m 3f	£286	9.4	D. O'Sullivan	20/1	fell

1953–54 Season

Date	Course	Race	Dist	Value	Weight	Jockey	Price	Place
Jan 2	Baldoyle	Portmarnock Nov. Chase	2m 1f 120y	£202	12.3	P. J. Doyle	8/1	unpl
Jan 21	Gowran Park	Shaun Goilin Nov. Chase	2m 4f	£100	12.3	B. Marshall	5/2	won
Feb 6	Leopardstown	Sandyford H'cap Chase	2m 3f	£133	11.1	Mr J. R. Cox	2/1	fell
Mar 3	Cheltenham	National Hunt Chase (Am. Rdrs)	4m	£2,245	12.4	Mr J. R. Cox	5/2	won

1954–55 Season

Date	Course	Race	Dist	Value	Weight	Jockey	Price	Place
Jan 8	Naas	Boyne H'cap Chase	3m 76y	£286	10.5	P. Taaffe	10/1	3rd
Jan 29	Naas	Celbridge H'cap Chase	3m 76y	£133	11.12	P. Taafe	4/7	won
Feb 9	Haydock	National Trial Chase (H'cap)	3m 4f	£980	11.11	P. Taaffe	7/4	4th
Mar 10	Cheltenham	National Hunt H'cap Chase	3m	£1,025	11.1	P. Taaffe	2/1	2nd
Mar 26	Liverpool	Grand National	4m 856y	£8,934 10s	11.0	P. Taaffe	100/9	won
May 6	Leopardstown	Glenview Hurdle	2m	£133	11.11	P. Taaffe	4/1	won
May 30	Hurst Park	Queen Elizabeth Chase (H'cap)	3m	£3,460	11.0	P. Taaffe	11/2	unpl

1955–56 Season

Date	Course	Race	Dist	Value	Weight	Jockey	Price	Place
Nov 19	Naas	Maddenstown H'cap Chase	3m 76y	£202	12.9	D. O'Sullivan	100/8	unpl
Dec 26	Leopardstown	Bray Chase	3m	£237	12.7	P. Taaffe	2/7	won
Jan 25	Leopardstown	Delgany Hurdle	2m	£133	12.7	P. Taaffe	4/9	unpl
Feb 8	Haydock	National Trial Chase (H'cap)	3m 4f	£1,055	12.7	P. Taaffe	7/2	2nd

1956–57 Season

Nil

1957–58 Season

Date	Course	Race	Dist	Value	Weight	Jockey	Price	Place
Jan 11	Leopardstown	Ticknock H'cap Chase	3m	£333 10s	12.7	T. Taaffe	100/7	unpl
Feb 1	Naas	Celbridge H'cap Chase	3m 76y	£359	12.7	T. Taaffe	3/1	unpl

BALLYMOSS

Date	Course	Race	Dist	Value	Weight	Jockey	Price	Place
			1956 Season					
July 21	Curragh	Lagan Mdn Plate	6f	£202	9.0	G. Gallagher	100/7	unpl
Sept 12	Mallow	Kilfinane Mdn Plate	5f	£133	9.0	T. P. Burns	2/1	2nd
Sept 29	Leopardstown	Laragh Mdn Plate	7f	£202	9.0	T. P. Burns	3/1	won
Oct 20	Curragh	Stayers Plate	7f	£202	9.1	T. P. Burns	5/4	2nd
			1957 Season					
Apl 6	Curragh	Madrid Free H'cap	7f	£850	8.11	T. P. Burns	20/1	unpl
May 10	Leopardstown	Trigo Stakes	12f	£772 15s	8.2	John Power	20/1	won
June 5	Epsom	Derby Stakes	12f	£18,659 10s	9.0	T. P. Burns	33/1	2nd
June 26	Curragh	Irish Derby Stakes	12f	£6,790	9.0	T. P. Burns	4/9	won
Aug 21	York	Great Voltigeur Stakes	12f	£8,264	9.0	T. P. Burns	7/4	2nd

Date	Course	Race	Dist	Value	Weight	Jockey	Price	Place
Sept 11	Doncaster	St Leger Stakes	14f 132y	£14,575 5s	9.0	T. P. Burns	8/1	won
Oct 17	Newmarket	Champion Stakes	10f	£4,965	8.7	T. P. Burns	11/8	unpl
		1958 Season						
May 8	Chester	Ormonde Stakes	13f 75y	£2,418 15s	8.9	T. P. Burns	9/4	2nd
June 5	Epsom	Coronation Cup	12f	£3,371 5s	8.7	A. Breasley	Evens	won
July 12	Sandown	Eclipse Stakes	10f	£11,672 10s	9.7	A. Breasley	8/11	won
July 19	Ascot	King Geo and Queen Elizabeth Stakes	12f	£23,642 10s	9.7	A. Breasley	7/4	won
Oct 5	Longchamp	Prix de l'Arc de Triomphe	12f	£46,439	9.6	A. Breasley	—	won

GLADNESS

Date	Course	Race	Dist	Value	Weight	Jockey	Price	Place
		1955 Season						
Nov 5	Curragh	Swilly Mdn Plate	6f	£202	8.6	T. Bryson	100/8	unpl
		1956 Season						
Nov 16	Manchester	Broughton Mdn Plate	12f	£207	8.7	T. P. Burns	8/11	won
		1957 Season						
Apl 6	Curragh	Irish Lincolnshire H'cap	8f	£1,000 5s	10.0	T. Taaffe	25/1	2nd
May 10	Leopardstown	Trigo Stakes	12f	£472 15s	9.4	T. P. Burns	10/11	unpl
July 20	Ascot	Sunninghill Park Stakes	16f	£1,178 10s	8.4	A. Breasley	13/8	won
Sept 19	Curragh	Leinster H'cap	14f	£486 5s	9.12	T. P. Burns	4/5	won
Oct 6	Longchamp	Prix de l'Arc de Triomphe	12f	£55,158	9.3	T. P. Burns	—	unpl
Oct 19	Curragh	Champion Stakes	14f	£667	9.4	T. P. Burns	2/9	won
		1958 Season						
Apl 12	Curragh	Irish Lincolnshire H'cap	8f	£1,015 5s	10.10	T. Taaffe	25/1	unpl
May 11	Longchamp	Prix du Cadran	20f	£11,496	9.3	T. P. Burns	—	2nd
June 19	Ascot	Ascot Gold Cup	20f	£10,950	8.11	L. Piggott	3/1	won
July 31	Goodwood	Goodwood Cup	21f	£3,413 15s	8.11	L. Piggott	1/2	won
Aug 20	York	Ebor H'cap	14f	£10,214 15s	9.7	L. Piggott	5/1	won
		1959 Season						
Apl 11	Phoenix Park	Glendalough Stakes	9f	£411 10s	10.1	L. Piggott	1/2	won
May 10	Longchamp	Prix du Cadran	20f	£8,234	9.3	L. Piggott	—	unpl
July 18	Ascot	King Geo and Queen Elizabeth Stakes	12f	£23,642 10s	9.4	G. Bougoure	9/2	2nd

LARKSPUR

Date	Course	Race	Dist	Value	Weight	Jockey	Price	Place
		1961 Season						
May 10	Curragh	Barow Mdn Plate	5f	£202	9.0	B. Swift	100/7	unpl
Sept 16	Leopardstown	Laragh Mdn Stakes	7f	£518	8.7	G. Bougoure	100/8	won

Date	Course	Race	Dist	Value	Weight	Jockey	Price	Place
Oct 7	Curragh	National Stakes	7f	£2,531 5s	9.0	G. Bougoure	100/30	3rd
Oct 21	Doncaster	Timeform Gold Cup	8f	£21,893 15s	8.12	T. Gosling	10/1	unpl
		1962 Season						
Apl 7	Curragh	Madrid Free H'cap	7f	£874	8.11	L. Piggott	9/1	unpl
May 4	Leopardstown	Wills Gold Flake Stakes	12f	£2,776 5s	8.2	P. Glennon	6/4	won
June 6	Epsom	Derby Stakes	12f	£34,786	9.0	N. Sellwood	22/1	won
June 30	Curragh	Irish Derby	12f	£50,027 10s	9.0	A. Breasley	9/4	4th
Sept 1	Curragh	Blandford Stakes	12f	£921	9.3	N. Sellwood	1/2	2nd
Sept 12	Doncaster	St Leger Stakes	14f 132y	£31,407	9.0	N. Sellwood	8/1	unpl

SIR IVOR

Date	Course	Race	Dist	Value	Weight	Jockey	Price	Place
		1967 Season						
July 1	Curragh	Tyros Stakes	6f	£1,203 15s	8.7	L. Ward	3/1	unpl
July 29	Curragh	Probationers' Stakes	7f	£1,122	8.7	L. Ward	9/4	won
Sept 16	Curragh	National Stakes	7f	£4,460	9.0	L. Ward	5/2	won
Oct 15	Longchamp	Grand Criterium	8f	£30,108 10s	8.12	L. Piggott	—	won
		1968 Season						
Apl 5	Ascot	Ascot Two Thousand Guineas Trial Stakes	7f	£1,290	9.0	L. Piggott	8/15	won
May 1	Newmarket	2,000 Guineas Stakes	8f	£22,586 14s	9.0	L. Piggott	11/8	won
May 29	Epsom	Derby Stakes	12f	£58,525 10s	9.0	L. Piggott	4/5	won
June 29	Curragh	Irish Sweeps Derby	12f	£55,340	9.0	L. Ward	1/3	2nd
July 6	Sandown	Eclipse Stakes	10f	£3,167 10s	8.7	L. Piggott	4/5	3rd
Sept 29	Longchamp	Prix Henry Delamarre	11f	£14,309	9.6	L. Piggott	—	2nd
Oct 6	Longchamp	Prix de l'Arc de Triomphe	12f	£96,685 15s	8.10	L. Piggott	—	2nd
Oct 19	Newmarket	Champion Stakes	10f	£14,673 10s	8.7	L. Piggott	8/11	won
Nov 11	Laurel Park	Washington DC International	12f	£37,190	8.8	L. Piggott	—	won

NIJINSKY

Date	Course	Race	Dist	Value	Weight	Jockey	Price	Place
		1969 Season						
July 12	Curragh	Erne Stakes	6f	£842 15s	9.0	L. Ward	4/11	won
Aug 16	Curragh	Railway Stakes	6f 63y	£2,140	8.7	L. Ward	4/9	won
Aug 30	Curragh	Anglesey Stakes	6f 63y	£2,185	9.0	L. Ward	4/9	won
Sept 27	Curragh	Beresford Stakes	8f	£4,272 10s	9.0	L. Ward	2/7	won
Oct 17	Newmarket	Dewhurst Stakes	7f	£10,576 4s	8.12	L. Piggott	1/3	won
		1970 Season						
Apl 4	Curragh	Gladness Stakes	7f	£2,025	8.10	L. Ward	4/6	won
Apl 29	Newmarket	2,000 Guineas Stakes	8f	£28,295 2s	9.0	L. Piggott	4/7	won
June 3	Epsom	Derby Stakes	12f	£62,311	9.0	L. Piggott	11/8	won

Date	Course	Race	Dist	Value	Weight	Jockey	Price	Place
June 27	Curragh	Irish Sweeps Derby	12f	£56,992 10s	9.0	L. Ward	4/11	won
July 25	Ascot	King George and Queen Elizabeth Stakes	12f	£31,993 10s	8.7	L. Piggott	40/85	won
Sept 12	Doncaster	St Leger Stakes	14f 127y	£37,082 3s	9.0	L. Piggott	2/7	won
Oct 4	Longchamp	Prix de l'Arc de Triomphe	12f	£103,744	8.10	L. Piggott	—	2nd
Oct 17	Newmarket	Champion Stakes	10f	£25,078 12s	8.7	L. Piggott	4/11	2nd

ROBERTO

Date	Course	Race	Dist	Value	Weight	Jockey	Price	Place
				1971 Season				
July 17	Curragh	Lagan Mdn Stakes	6f 63y	£847	9.0	J. Roe	Evens	won
Aug 28	Curragh	Anglesey Stakes	6f 63y	£1,806.25	8.7	J. Roe	2/5	won
Sept 11	Curragh	National Stakes	7f	£3,837.50	9.0	J. Roe	2/9	won
Oct 10	Longchamp	Grand Criterium	8f	£35,418.80	8.11	L. Piggott	—	4th
				1972 Season				
Apl 1	Phoenix Park	Vauxhall Trial Stakes	7f	£2,801.25	9.2	J. Roe	8/15	won
Apl 29	Newmarket	2,000 Guineas Stakes	8f	£27,538	9.0	W. Williamson	7/2	2nd
June 7	Epsom	Derby Stakes	12f	£63,735.75	9.0	L. Piggott	3/1	won
July 1	Curragh	Irish Sweeps Derby	12f	£58,905	9.0	J. Roe	15/8	unpl
Aug 15	York	Benson and Hedges Gold Cup	10½f	£30,955	8.10	B. Baeza	12/1	won
Sept 10	Longchamp	Prix Niel	11f	£9,166	9.4	B. Baeza	—	2nd
Oct 8	Longchamp	Prix de l'Arc de Triomphe	12f	£89,552	8.10	B. Baeza	—	unpl
				1973 Season				
May 7	Leopardstown	Nijinsky Stakes	10f	£5,812.50	10.3	L. Piggott	1/2	2nd
June 7	Epsom	Coronation Cup	12f	£11,571.20	9.0	L. Piggott	4/9	won
July 28	Ascot	King Geoerge and Queen Elizabeth Stakes	12f	£79,230	9.7	L. Piggott	3/1	unpl

THE MINSTREL

Date	Course	Race	Dist	Value	Weight	Jockey	Price	Place
				1976 Season				
Sept 8	Curragh	Moy Stakes	6f	£1,250.10	8.10	Thomas Murphy	4/9	won
Sept 25	Leopardstown	Larkspur Stakes	7f	£2,784	8.12	L. Piggott	4/11	won
Oct 15	Newmarket	William Hill Dewhurst Stakes	7f	£37,195.70	9.0	L. Piggott	6/5	won
				1977 Season				
Apl 2	Ascot	2,000 Guineas Trial	7f	£5,299	9.0	L. Piggott	4/5	won
Apl 27	Newmarket	2,000 Guineas Stakes	8f	£45,232.50	9.0	L. Piggott	6/5	3rd
May 14	Curragh	Irish 2,000 Guineas	8f	£39,855	9.0	L. Piggott	7/4	2nd
June 1	Epsom	Derby Stakes	12f	£107,530	9.0	L. Piggott	5/1	won

Date	Course	Race	Dist	Value	Weight	Jockey	Price	Place
June 25	Curragh	Irish Sweeps Derby	12f	£72,797.50	9.0	L. Piggott	11/10	won
July 23	Ascot	King George and Queen Elizabeth Diamond Stakes	12f	£88,355	8.8	L. Piggott	7/4	won

ALLEGED

Date	Course	Race	Dist	Value	Weight	Jockey	Price	Place
				1976 Season				
Nov 1	Curragh	Donnelly's Hollow Stakes	7f	£1,091.80	9.0	Thomas Murphy	7/4	won
				1977 Season				
Apl 20	Leopardstown	Ballydoyle Stakes	10f	£1,751	9.0	Thomas Murphy	1/3	won
May 13	Curragh	Royal Whip Stakes	12f	£3,751.50	8.6	P. Matthews	33/1	won
May 28	Curragh	Gallinule Stakes	12f	£5,624	9.0	L. Piggott	11/10	won
Aug 17	York	Gt Voltigeur Stakes	12f	£17,757.50	8.11	L. Piggott	5/2	won
Sept 10	Doncaster	St Leger Stakes	14f 127y	£52,867.50	9.0	L. Piggott	4/7	2nd
Oct 2	Longchamp	Prix de l'Arc de Triomphe	12f	£140,845.07	8.11	L. Piggott	—	won
				1978 Season				
May 12	Curragh	Royal Whip Stakes	12f	£3,306.30	9.10	L. Piggott	1/7	won
Sept 17	Longchamp	Prix du Prince d'Orange	10f	£13,333	9.0	L. Piggott	—	won
Oct 1	Longchamp	Prix de l'Arc de Triomph	12f	£133,333	9.4	L. Piggott	—	won

GOLDEN FLEECE

Date	Course	Race	Dist	Value	Weight	Jockey	Price	Place
				1981 Season				
Sept 19	Leopardstown	Oldbawn Mdn (Div 1)	8f	£1,242	9.0	P. Eddery	Evens	won
				1982 Season				
Apl 17	Curragh	Sean Graham Ballymoss Stakes	10f	£8,762.50	8.4	P. Eddery	4/5	won
May 8	Leopardstown	Nijinsky Stakes	10f	£8,856	8.2	P. Eddery	1/3	won
June 2	Epsom	Derby Stakes	12f	£146,720	9.0	P. Eddery	3/1	won

EL GRAN SENOR

Date	Course	Race	Dist	Value	Weight	Jockey	Price	Place
				1983 Season				
Aug 3	Phoenix Park	Collinstown Stud Maiden	7f	£3,452	9.0	P. Eddery	2/5	won
Aug 27	Curragh	P. J. Prendergast Railway Stakes	6f 63y	£8,212.85	8.10	P. Eddery	4/9	won

Sept 10	Curragh	B.B.A. (Ireland) Goffs National Stakes	7f	£36,760.30	9.0	P. Eddery	4/5	won
Oct 13	Newmarket	William Hill Dewhurst Stakes	7f	£44,219	9.0	P. Eddery	7/4	won

1984 Season

Apl 14	Curragh	Gladness Stakes	7f	£7,424	9.2	P. Eddery	1/3	won
May 5	Newmarket	Gen. Accident 2,000 Guineas Stakes	8f	£87,408	9.0	P. Eddery	15/8	won
June 6	Epsom	Ever Ready Derby Stakes	12f	£227,680	9.0	P. Eddery	8/11	2nd
June 30	Curragh	Joe McGrath Irish Sweeps Derby Stakes	12f	£134,241	9.0	P. Eddery	2/7	won

Index